MW00955123

Not Done

Not Done

Not Done

BURNT

By Gillian Clark

These are the events as I remember them. Those of you who witnessed these goings on, might have a different recollection of the events. I respect your truth. The names have been changed and there is a tiny bit of hyperbole around the edges. - GC

Copyright© 2020 by Gillian Clark
Not Done, Not Done, Not Done BURNT

ISBN 9781661117306
Independently Published
Brooklyn, NY

Gillian Clark (1963-

For my father, and the other heroes in my life.

Table of Contents

Prologue

SAUTÉ: French, from past participle of sauter to jump

I leaned on the rain-wet railing at the stern. I turned my head away from the exhaust bubbling up from the pipe at port. Storms had brought limbs down. And as the ship chugged along the Potomac, big water-logged limbs bobbed in the ship's wake. I made sure new my glasses were on good. They had been a bit of a splurge when the first busy weeks had us ringing in our first couple thousand at the new restaurant. These weren't just progressive lenses that hid my reading glasses in my regular near-sighted specs, but they also grew dark when the sun hit them—any light for that matter; so I usually didn't wear them under the hot lights of the restaurant kitchen, or when the cameras were on me. Wanting to be on deck more than in the tiny ship's galley, I had kept the sun sensors on.

That little galley kitchen was close and hot. Gabe, the sous chef, had hit me in the boob with his elbow one too many times. This last time while he was throwing dried rosemary over the wine-soaked chicken breasts in the steam table. I had to get out of there. With 45 guests mingling on the main deck and another ten upstairs at the bar watching the rain from the enclosed upper salon; there was no other place for me to go but the wet deck at the stern. The sleeves of my polyester chef coat soaked up the big drops from the railing. I leaned hard on the railing and tried to stretch the ache out of my back. It had only been four hours and I was already rolling my eyes. Gabe (who I later learned had been a cook at Buffalo Wings & Beer) was telling me how I needed to make my food look nice.

"Excuse me, Miss." He said. He held his hands out in front of him like two spatulas, his palms flat facing his chest. Then he rotated them round each other. I thought he was either going to start rapping or doing the Hustle. "Did you make the sauce for the carving station?"

"No, I didn't." I looked at him, now he was really talking crazy. "I asked you about it and you told me that you were going to get the powdered demi-glace and mix it with hot water and that you'd be right back." I hoped using his exact words would jar his memory. But when he'd come back empty handed, I knew that he had gone to the storeroom, maneuvered around the huge bins of linens and the staff members pinching cigarette butts from their lips, blowing smoke every direction. He had gotten to the containers of dried herbs (some of them two or three years old), rifled through them—a couple of them may have hit the floor—and there was no demi to re-hydrate.

So, with his Hustle Hands, Gabe left the ship and headed to the shore kitchen. He wandered around until his eyes lit on the big jug of red wine. He emptied it into the tilt skillet and brought it to a boil. He sprinkled rosemary and cornstarch into it. He watched it thicken and then cranked the lever so that the big stainless-steel box tipped the lumpy, thickened red wine into a shiny steel bain marie.

"Miss.... Miss." I'm not used to being called anything but Chef, so I didn't answer right away. "Here is your sauce." He handed me the bain marie of cloudy wine the still dry, yellow sticks of rosemary

3

meandering on the surface like a slow-moving log jam on a tiny red river. It was still warm from its quick boil in the big electric fired skillet. The hard-steamy stink of cheap red wine was making me nauseous. I put it next to the Apple-Horseradish sauce which contained no apple at all.

"Here, Miss." An hour ago, Gabe had handed me prepared horseradish and a tub of sour cream. "Just mix these two together."

"O…. kay."

By the time the tornado watch had been lifted and the boat chugged away from the pier, I wanted to disappear. I wanted to be anywhere but on this boat with these 55 people and a warmer full of terrible food. I was praying that nobody recognized me. "Weren't you just on the Food Network with that guy?", "We were rooting for you on CHOPPED." "Bobby Flay didn't stand a chance." I'd heard it walking in the street downtown, crossing in front of a stopped car in Baltimore, at Dulles airport watching my youngest daughter Sian go through the security on her way to visit Purdue. Please, please don't let me hear it on this boat with mismatched, dirty china, over cooked salmon, and ravioli pasted together with canned marinara. This was quickly turning into a panic attack. The skin was hot between my breasts and started itching like crazy. I stepped out onto the deck.

I was having that George Bailey moment. With two loans out requiring a key man life insurance policy, over half a million in checks would be written if the railing gave and the unforgiving Potomac sucked me down. The loans would be paid off and there'd be a little money to spare. Everyone close to me would be debt free and be able to start anew unshackled. And I wouldn't be there to make them stop the car so that I could look at another dilapidated building determined to turn it into a restaurant—quickly sign our lives away to a complete stranger who, once the ink was dry, would peel off his remarkably human looking mask and reveal Satan himself.

I gripped the railing hard and tried to put the image out of my mind: me pulling myself over the wet metal, my non-skid soles first to hit the murky cold, propeller roiling water. I thought about how cold and refreshing it would feel on my ankles and my hot, tired feet. The icy water would fill my heavy shoes and soak my socks. And as that poly-cotton black chef coat Gabe dug out of the storeroom for me that morning (the light had blown out months ago so he used his lighter to find an XL in the plastic wrapped piles that had slid to the floor) got soaked and heavy I would sink and shiver, bubbling my last breaths to the surface and maybe have that flash of regret.

"How did I get here?" I'd ask myself, my lungs on fire urging me to suck cold water in through my nose to put it out. My eyes open against the green water. But it was my first day. No one knew my name. Gabe was calling me "Miss". And Damien, the guy who'd hired me took me on a tour and stumbled when presenting me to the dishwasher, "Hugh," he called out as he opened his hand and sliced the air toward me as if I was what had been behind curtain number two. "This is..." He pressed his lips together, shaking his head to rattle my name down from his brain to his tongue. But it wasn't in there. There I would be at the bottom of the river and who would know? I hadn't told anybody after the restaurant had closed and the bank was getting ready to sell the stove and big round pot that co-starred with me on three different Food Network shows, that I had taken this job as a cook on a fancy party boat for a cruise company.

Sian, home for the summer from her freshman year, was the only one home; splitting her time between the gift shop at the Panda House and ringing up baseball jerseys at the new National's Stadium—the only one

6

who would scratch her head and wonder where I was. Magalee had left for Thailand. And Robin was in California, her mother recovering from surgery and her dad just starting to feel the effects of mesothelioma. There'd be no note. Believing my drowning to be a tragic accident would help them all get through this. Hundreds of thousands in life insurance would make it a much easier pill to swallow—all of the debt from my folly eliminated.

Now there was no use thinking or talking about all of the money that was gone; cash that I might as well have wrapped in a bundle and tossed into this river. Hundreds of thousands spent on restaurants closed and restaurants in my dreams that would never open. My big old brain full of concepts and ideas, full of all of the ways to make food look and taste good had brought me nothing but misery and cost me everything. The eggs in the basket that was snatched from me had been borrowed. I had no more eggs.

Court rooms have never been good places for me. So, I had a feeling when the landlord called us away from a busy lunchtime Wednesday to use the Montgomery County District Court in Rockville to get more rent, I knew it wouldn't go well. Years ago, things hadn't gone well in one of these wood-paneled room when Hakim, my-ex husband now living with his millionaire parents, wound up paying $50 a month child support which barely covered lunch money for his little girls in pre-K and 3rd grade. Years later, subsequent appearances had the judge taking his side. Not bothering to make the trip from his parent's house in New York didn't even disqualify him. I raised my voice and was threatened with contempt of court. "Do you have anything to prove, Mrs. Clark," she looked over her reading glasses at me, the stacks of papers spread out like a bridge hand, "that the non-custodial parent lived with you and with these children?" I had saved letters and phone bills. But still I wound up shouldering the costs of summer camp, prom dresses, and college tuition. Judges just don't like me, I thought. Or maybe I come off too strong and too confident. It's that other guy who's got trouble. The poor sap needs taking care of and has to save his spare cash for drugs and booze. Don't make him pay child support. And this guy here? Get her out of his building if she can't pay enough rent to cover all of his bad decisions.

So many decisions had morphed into bad moves that ended with me in a court room. We bought that boat—an 83-foot yacht built in 1919. It was like having a big wooden baby to save our marriage. "Let's restore it together," we declared to each other. But Hakim hadn't really stopped drinking and the old boat wound up listing in a country club marina that took us to court so they could remove her antique fixtures and set the rest of her on fire.

My marriage came to an end soon after that with him at the opposite side of the courtroom that may as well have had the Mason-Dixon Line drawn on the floor. He told the judge all about how he didn't have any money to pay child support. When the judge cracked the gavel down, I no longer had a husband and my children lost their father.

Since then I've been sued by restaurant staff, contractors demanding they be paid for the leaky roof and sputtering air conditioning they left behind, and landlords. I've been in small claims, federal bankruptcy, divorce, family…I've been in court more than anyone else I know that hasn't been to law school.

This time, this last time cost me. If my world were a game of Jenga, this last subpoena was that block at the bottom and that short hour in that courtroom poked it out from that snug spot in the foundation and my tower of hardwood blocks hit the floor. And here I was dumbing down my resume again so I could get a job, any job denying who I was to the bartender who thought she recognized me. "I have no idea what you're talking about." I said to her through clenched teeth. Maybe she'll think I'm crazy. I would tell her I was in a bad car accident if she pressed me, that I had no memory of anything. I got out of the hospital, grabbed a frying pan and made an omelet. I don't know how or why.

Here I am, pushing 50 and on the bottom looking up. My children about to start their lives as adults were watching their mother who tried so hard to be their role model, swirling down with the dirty dishwater, down into the grease interceptor. Why shouldn't I jump off this boat? I'd done all that I could. This summer had proved that my two greatest accomplishments an motivators were well equipped to carry on without me.

I pressed my palms into the cold, wet metal of the railing and curled my fingers around until my jagged nails dug into my palms. Like a gymnast addressing the pommel horse I pulled myself up against the rail until just the very tip of my steel toed shoes was on the deck. The rain spattered the brim of my baseball hat—I never wear a baseball hat, but the puffy toque would have been a dead giveaway. It had been my signature. I thought about it floating on top of the frigid and merciless Potomac River.

I was sorry I hadn't worn it today. I shut my eyes and pulled as much air through my nose as I could before flipping my legs up over the rail. I was sitting on the wet steel now and it rattled a bit under my weight. It was easy to slide off—I raised my hands above my head and stiffened my back. It was like the boat chugged out from under me. I brought my arms back in and looked down. Like a gaping mouth the water opened up and sucked me in. I felt my expensive glasses tear across my face and pull away from my ears. The baseball cap was gone, and the too big polyester chef coat had been yanked up by the force of my foot first dive. I raised my chin so the coat could spring free from around my neck. I plunged down until my feet hit what felt like an underwater rubber band and I could feel the pressure on my shoulders as I shot up like a half empty shampoo bottle pulled down then released in the bathtub.

I made it to the surface without kicking or flailing my arms. I could hear the rumbling of the boat in the distance. I opened my eyes to the darkness. But just as soon as I locked on the sliver of moon above me, an octopus of swirling river grabbed me around the ankles. The jolt brought me just under the surface and I stared up at the moon under a film of river water. The next jolt forced water up my nose. I kicked through the next pull and my heavy shoe circled up and around into my upper lip. I was suddenly very tired. My arms were too heavy to lift, and my legs were on fire. But my brain was tired—weary to be exact. Numbness came over me. What to do, what to do, now what? I had no answers and no instinct. Sleep on the muddy bottom seemed as good an idea as any.

I remember being this tired before I ever started cooking for a living. It was my first job. I was 15 and working in an insurance agency office filing and copying. When the receptionist quit just as school went out for the summer, they sat me at her desk. For three months the office got a full-time receptionist and all of that filing and copying for my underage hourly wage of $2.45 an hour. I had a half hour of training on the phone and a brief practice session on Angela's IBM Selectric. I was given a fresh pad of "While You Were Out". Then the switch board lit up. It looked easy when Angela did it, calmly putting callers on hold, chiming into someone's office and telling them about the call, putting the call through. Her long, flaming red nails never got in the way.

I fumbled, hung up, sent Donald's calls to Jerry and Jerry's calls to Dan. When Donald asked me to get him Mr. Goody on the phone I nervously thumbed through the rolodex until I found the handwritten number, pushed in the button for an open line, and dialed when the light under the button flashed a bright white.

"Mr. Goody, please."

"Who's calling?"

"Donald Shaffer's office," I said weakly with a clear of my throat.

"Hey Don," Mr. Goody was on and thinking I was Donald. What now?

"Sorry Mr. Goody. Could you hold for Mr. Shaffer?"

"In heaven's name, he can't dial me himself?"

This is how it went all morning. Me dialing for Donald and a bunch of businessmen obviously annoyed and irritated with me.

"Who the hell are you?" one asked me.

"Hold on for Mr. Shaffer." I responded.

"I'm answering my own phone; he can't dial his?"

"I'm sorry sir. Could you hold on for just a second?" My hands were shaking. I was a couple months shy of my 16th birthday. I hadn't sat in a chair behind a desk for eight hours before in my life. By 11:00 I was exhausted and praying that the phone would just stop ringing. When I got home that night, I was still hearing the fluttering bell that was the office ring tone. When our home phone let out its jangle I said, "Donald Shaffer Associates" into the receiver to my sister's boyfriend and my Aunt Ida.

"Angela," Donald's voice came on over the intercom, "get me Izzy Simon." I was on the verge of tears now. Isadore Simon was a thick business card stapled to a blank—the first one after the bright blue "S" tab.

"This is Izzy," he sounded like a chubby old guy. I could tell he grew up in Brooklyn in a Jewish family. His mother loved him, and he knew it.

"Mr. Simon, I have Mr. Shaffer on the line for..."

"Who are you?" it wasn't a mean question, just a question. I hesitated.

"I'm nobody. If you hold on a sec..."

"Honey," I could tell that Izzy had slid his feet off of his desk and was sitting up a little straighter in his chair high up in an office that looked over Manhattan. "Don't say that." He said. When he asked me my name, I started to tremble. I connected the call, grabbed the old wooden ruler that held the ladies room key with a paper clip. My shoulders were shaking when the bathroom door closed behind me. I locked myself in and sobbed with my head in my hands.

14

"What is wrong with Mr. Shaffer that he can't call me himself?" Mr. Levine wanted to know.

"I'm sorry, Mr. Levine..."

"This is inexcusable," he insisted. "Who does he think he is?"

"Mr. Levine," It was 3:00 and these old men just weren't bothering me anymore, "I thought you knew about Mr. Shaffer." I could tell he was the kind of guy that got a manicure.

"Yeah, what about him?"

"He caught a live grenade while serving in Korea."

"Oh...well...I..."

"Hang on let me put him through."

I remember being really tired when I went to the small den where Hakim and I and month-old Magalee were sleeping. It was Thanksgiving and we'd driven up to my in-law's house. Hakim had gotten so drunk that he had slid down the refrigerator door spilling a little of his beer on the linoleum. He sat there with his legs stretched out, giggling and sobbing. His parent's dinner guest made their excuses and left before finishing their wine. Before long Hakim was passed out on the sofa; his head heavy and hanging over the back pillows. His Adam's apple slid up and down in unison with the snorts of his shallow breathing.

"I'd feel better if I went to bed alone," I wearily dragged myself up the short flight of stairs in their split level, hoping they all got my gist: *please don't wake him up and send him up to that room so that I can smell his beer and whiskey spiked perspiration all night.* I woke Magalee to feed her and put the blankets back over her shoulders. When I came out of the bathroom with its underwater blue tiles and swordfish shower curtain, Hakim was sitting naked waiting for me. I closed the door behind me. I slid one of the cots that had been pushed against the other over to the fold-away crib where Magalee was sleeping.

"So, is that how it is?" he drawled at me. I could make out his head in the darkness, it seemed like it was just hanging by a thread now. He tried to look up at me, but he couldn't hold his head up long enough. I just wanted to close my eyes and forget any of this had happened.

"I just want to go to sleep, Hakim." I was pleading. But it was my annoyance and disgust that was slipping out. It got to him. He bolted up in the darkness and dragged me down to his cot by my hair. His knees were on my chest and he pulled my hair so hard that the crown of my head was

16

touching my shoulder. I punched at him in the dark, begging him to let go. I thought of the woman in a car that slid in a right turn through the red light while I walked out of the office with two work buddies years before. The woman in the passenger seat was telling the man behind the wheel that she was sick and tired. Through the open window we could hear the crack in her voice that meant tears were coming. The man responded by taking the curve one handed and clenching his free hand into a fist. He punched her. The crack of the blow made everyone in the crosswalk stop in their tracks and watch the little blue sedan screech around the corner and head up the hill.

Hakim tightened his grip, twisting the bunch of my hair around his hand. I tried everything to get him off of me. I flailed at him and rocked back and forth to get him to fall. He was talking quietly so they couldn't hear. His face was distorted with anger and hate. It was a face I'd never seen before. I couldn't protect myself from the truth and its shrapnel any longer. I had to let someone else in on this secret that I was tired of keeping to myself—buried deep somewhere in a closet full of folded diapers so I could pretend it wasn't true and everything was just fine. It was life or death now. I had to let it out even if it meant pulling the picket fence out

17

of the edge of the lawn and setting it on fire. With as much air as I could get in with his weight on me, I shouted—maybe just loud enough to get Magalee to start crying. The hallway light flooded the room in a long triangle that got bigger and brighter as the door pushed open and the weight on my chest was gone.

Tossed around by the pull of the Potomac there was no way to tell which way to the muddy bed of the river. It was pointless to struggle. The river was just bigger and stronger. I *was* nobody.

When Izzy had asked me my name years before a kernel popped in my head. It was the first of the popcorn kernels to explode like the quickened time-lapse image of blooming flower sizzling in the smoking hot oil. Soon after that, they erupted one after the other. I started walking with my shoulders back and my chin up. I came out of my shell. That shy girl suddenly became a believer.

I shook off the anxiety of the first weeks of freshman year at college and decided my grades weren't nearly as important as taking on every high-profile activity on campus. I decided I could be Classical Music Director of the radio station before the end of second semester. I was determined to be the features editor of the school paper when my sophomore year started. At the same time, I was the only freshman on the varsity fencing team. The only reason I didn't get into medical school is that I really didn't want to.

I graduated from college with a husband and enough extracurricular know how to make things happen. I didn't count on evil. How did I get to be 21 years old and not realize that people lie, cheat, and sometimes have very strange needs that can only be fulfilled by destroying the nearest person? There are parents who molest their children. There are people who would give their soul and their last shreds of human dignity and decency for one more drink or pill.

I had walked past all that when I was 21, never looking close enough to see and study its ugliness. But by the time I reached my 30th birthday, my face was turned in that direction and something held my eyes open so that the images were seared onto my brain. I stopped skipping. I forgot how. I watched girls in the neighborhood jump double Dutch and recalled with a tear burning my eye that a long time ago I also carelessly tilted my foot up at the ankle and jumped high enough to let two ropes skip around me.

I dipped the tip of my finger into the clarified butter—bright and warm as a urine sample. I brought the beaten yolks to the ribbon with the wire whisk over a pot of boiling water. But my fretting over them had turned the egg from bright yellow to a subdued chartreuse—not the shiny bright primary color in the food magazines. By the time I had whisked in the lukewarm butter drop by drop, the hollandaise was ice cold. It started to thicken as it chilled. The whisk stalled in the bowl.

It was my first hollandaise. And it was a disaster. I hesitated and doubted myself and I was paying for my lack of faith. But this was a year or two before I had gotten into the habit of leaping from the top of my personal skyscraper, confident that I could bounce off the awning below and land steadily—the soles of my shoes on the sidewalk. I had been the one that couldn't stand to walk by a window, although safely inside on the 10th floor. The dizzying height made me nauseous.

After eleven years, my marriage had failed. It didn't matter how much I protested. It didn't matter how much I cried and begged. Hakim loved Jim Beam more. And when the Wild Turkey wandered into his life, he held the bottle close. It strutted and scratched and glanced wickedly at me when Hakim covered its mouth with his. I didn't do it for him the way

20

the bourbon did. I was there during the tough times. I listened and cheered him on. I carried his children. But I wasn't any good at making the world go away. Turkey and Jim had me beat.

I convinced myself I could hang in there. I believed in the promises and proudly watched him slide the dirty dishes out of the way so he could splash the contents of yet another jug down the drain. But like dandelions at the edge of the lawn, more would pop up all of a sudden— more than I could count; bottles of amber liquid and tall cans of malt liquor. Then there was the behavior that followed that he couldn't keep at home. It spilled out of him just as he took his first wobbly steps out of the elevator. There were missed meetings, expensive mistakes. Before long, security was in his office to watch him clean out his desk, again.

There was no need for him to pretend anymore. Nobody was stupid enough to hire him now. Plus, hiding the booze only kept him from enjoying it fully. He sloshed around the house and blamed all of it on the first person to walk into the room. Was this the same guy that I had bounced through Nova Scotia in an old RV, the girls too little to remember the brown sand and rocky coast? The constantly clogging fuel pump stalled us several times along the way. For some reason, only I could knock the dew off of the windshield, and with my cheek resting on the steering wheel, coax the engine to turn over in the morning. This couldn't possibly be the man whose hand I squeezed until his knuckles blanched while we signed page after page of paper to become the new owners of that old red brick townhouse. We spent years soaking off yellowed wallpaper and scraping lead paint before the bank finally auctioned it off. No, this wasn't him. This drunk guy was an impostor.

But I had glimpses of him all along. I could not really claim to be blindsided. There was the night I put Magalee to bed and had to hold the banister as I carefully made my way downstairs. The unrelenting jarring had started in my uterus. I caught my breath on the sofa as Hakim stumbled around to find the keys. He tried to help me up, but his knees were too weak to support him, let alone me—heavy and pregnant with Sian. He was close enough now I could smell his breath. While I was reading to Magalee and tucking her in, he had been busy pouring the contents of one of those bottles down his throat. I knew the smell from my Aunt Melva's backyard parties that lasted too long into the night. Boozy breath was in the air above aunts, uncles and cousins as they stepped and swayed to the calypso music blaring from the speakers against the wooden fence. But this wasn't a party. I had gone into labor twice now this week. My bag and comfy shoes were by the door. The smell that was singeing my nostrils was out of context. I was confused—what is that smell?

The young, naïve me didn't recognize this smell when I was teaching at that private school and was called into a parent-teacher meeting. We sat in the room of oriental rugs and leather furniture with Martin's mom—English teacher (me), biology teacher, French teacher. His grades hadn't just slipped; they had fallen down the elevator shaft. When his mother started talking—making excuses and claiming ignorance—and the sharp, sweet smell of fermentation hit my nose, I didn't make the connection. I wondered about her choice in personal fragrances. It took days for me to figure it out.

Now that smell was blowing into my face again, as Hakim huffed and puffed and yanked on my arm to get me off the sofa and into the car.

Sian knew better than emerge from the safety of the womb that night. And the sounds of her father hurling the acidy liquor out of his stomach and into the toilet forced her to retreat for days. Now passed my due date, I had to be induced. He slept under the window of my hospital room, while I sweated and groaned, relieved that the unyielding pain had started and would finally be over and that I would never do this again.

The lies I told myself and everyone else had me feeling like I had put all of my chips on red and now the little white ball stopped bouncing to rest quietly on black. The window dressing was gone, and everyone could see that I was faking it. I was exposed, vulnerable and everyone could see it.

I opened a separate bank account and planned our escape. I concentrated on making a healthy world for my daughters and channeled all my energy on them and making cooking a career. If I concentrated on the fact that the person I promised my soul to years ago had drowned, I would unravel. Staring at a corner while the world bustled around me was not an option. As timid as my steps were, I had to keep moving.

I was afraid of everything. Nothing I believed in was true anymore. My "rock" turned out to be one of those spray-painted foam theatre props. There was no God. The earth wasn't round and that was why there was no way of knowing how many hours were in a day. Some dragged on for 28 or more; others lasted a quick 16. Money had a way of vanishing. My car needed a whole tank of gas to get to work and back.

The girls were being slipped foot growth hormone. And there was something in the dryer that ate socks, underwear, and little girl undershirts.

I lied, cheated, and begged my way out of that house we had lived all those years so the bill collectors couldn't find me. I worked two jobs in two restaurant kitchens to pay the rent and the babysitter at a big house in a better neighborhood. "Wow, Gillian," they'd say walking around the big back yard or admiring the way my parent's old furniture worked in front of the fireplace, "You're doing all right." With a freshly painted and newly carpeted outside to look at no one would suspect that things weren't anything but perfect. It was a miracle. I left my husband in favor of single motherhood and things went from bad to better. No one thought to ask, "Are you all really okay?" It certainly would have made our lower lips quiver and hot and heavy tears flow down. The three of us silently agreed to shake it off and move forward. Or maybe I insisted that we do it that way.

Hakim was there just enough to throw a monkey wrench into my plan; promising gifts and visits that never materialized. He kept the girls yearning and off balance. He could still grab a hold of Magalee on an odd year, but years later, when Sian was 12 or 13, he had no effect on her at all.

It took Magalee until her first year of college. Her letters were angry and challenging. His stopped coming completely. "You're an adult now, Mag." I told her. I had warned him that this would happen. "You're not that little girl just happy at the sight of him." She used her sleeves to mash the tears back in. "You'll judge him."

Meanwhile I was learning the meaning of nothing left to lose. While it wasn't sure footing by a long shot: for years I had at least the stability of an unstable partnership to hold on to. Now, I was alone in the world. It took me a few months, but I started to like it. My decisions were final—whether they made sense or not. For years, who I was and what I wanted never mattered. I suppressed my own personality to prop up my drunk husband while using my own body to dive on any evidence—a bottle, an unsteady walk just as my parents' car was pulling into the drive. Calling attention to myself and all that was going on was out of the question. I was even too cautious to laugh out loud. At a friend's stand up debut I snickered with my teeth clenched together. "You hated my show?" he asked me backstage.

I forgot all about not being "nobody." I was certain now that Izzy Simon was wrong, and I really was nobody. I was like the invisible man. Surely a nobody could go around undetected, do and say as she pleased. I could slip passed the Fates undetected. It was impossible for me to be caught or hurt. No one ever noticed a nobody. There was finally some comfort in it.

Despite my efforts, my marriage was over. I came to the conclusion that playing it safe had gotten me nowhere. I had to start taking chances. At first, I covered my eyes or ears when I threw caution to the wind. When disaster didn't follow, I put my head down and surged on. I started to laugh out loud. There was nothing to be afraid of. I was a nobody making a little noise, who'd notice?

I excelled in the small local cooking school. I received my certificate content to work in the back rooms behind a stove. There was comfort in the anonymity and being able to focus on a nicely browned softshell crab, a properly reduced sauce, and how they came together on a plate.

Two years after leaving cooking school, I was a running a kitchen. My footing was getting surer by the day. And I wasn't afraid of my own shadow anymore. I stuffed quail with scallops. I made pasta using corn flour. I covered lamb chops with shiitake mushrooms. And they loved it.

I climbed to the very top of the building. Then I jumped. Actually, I was pushed. Two jobs starting at 7 am and ending at midnight were killing me. One big job, with one big salary is what I needed—I pumped my resume with French words and more responsibility and applied to hotel restaurants, cigar clubs—any place that needed an executive chef. Becoming an executive chef was this single mother's financial and time management decision. I did not wake up one day and declare I was ready.

Airborne for most of my culinary career, I went through four restaurants in four years. I quit. I was fired—twice. I may have fretted at the time, but ultimately, it didn't matter. As I look back, the lows were temporary. I still had wings. The media and the dining public had already caught a glimpse of me. It didn't matter where I lighted. There were good reviews, my picture in the newspaper, people recognizing me at the DMV.

The attention made my humility disappear and I was as big an egotist as any other chef in town. I frequently committed hubris. It's hard not to when a kitchen full of people responded to my every bark and the results drew praise from complete strangers. I took the opportunity to reveal myself, to quit being nobody.

I was walking with my shoulders back, even after I was shown the door at Mrs. Simpson's. With my belongings in a milk crate—artwork by the girls, a few cooking magazines, and a collection of odd knives—I kept my hair appointment. There was still never a time for standing still. My dreadlocks twisted tight again and smelling of coconut, I headed to the government regulatory offices and then the SBA. When I got home, I called the number in the window of the storefront I had been staring at from the Laundromat across the street. Every Monday night as little jeans and chef pants were tossed around the gas-fired dryer, I recited the handwritten number to myself. This was going to be my restaurant.

I had learned a few things along the way. Create a menu I could do by myself, just in case the helping hand on the schedule falls off the wagon. Get through the first three months and get that first good review. Believe that the empty dining room will soon be too busy to handle. Establish my concept and stick with it. There are going to be people that come in and hate everything—from the soup to the color of the walls. I'm not going to repaint every time someone doesn't like something. The restaurant has to be an external, 3-D version of some part of me. There are going to be a whole bunch of people that are going to love it. Those are going to be my regular customers.

There was a small concession to the inner scaredy cat that was still hanging around. I picked a remote location for my restaurant. The storefront, the 1250 square foot with basement was nestled in a part of the city far removed from the traditional dining hot spots. Adventurous cooking in the nation's capital was found in the waterfront neighborhood of Georgetown. And there was bohemian Adams Morgan and clubby DuPont Circle. K Street was the steak and potatoes of the downtown. Colorado Kitchen was in the middle of nowhere. It had to be read about and driven to with GPS. Sure, there was no competition next door. But success also wouldn't be an accident. And who would notice if I failed? The red brick building in the neighborhood would simply go dark.

Dr. Schiff, the therapist I called in a last-ditch effort to save my marriage, had read the paper. He spent the evening in my dining room admiring the crowd around him. "You got free of that millstone." He smiled and took my hand. "Now you're soaring."

I had been on my feet behind a stove for so many years now, my body had transformed. I was no longer fitting into a size 9 shoe and had started buying the size 11 men's. I had become a big dog in what seemed like no time at all. For seven years, I reigned over the busiest brunch service in town. There were appearances on radio and TV. What couldn't I do? Another restaurant? Why not two? How about a barge churning over the Potomac with white tablecloths and a big band?

I was craving an empire. Why not? Everything I touched was working and working well. The girls were big enough to cook beside me or wait tables. Magalee was sending out college applications. Sian was at one of the city's finest high schools on a full scholarship. I rushed to school now to catch Magalee singing in the spring musical or Sian's clarinet solo. I didn't spend a great part of the day planning for their after-school care or worrying if they were doing their homework or if my being a chef was stunting their growth. There was room in my brain to entertain thoughts of different concepts. The kids were grown. It was time to have another baby.

Letters from developers and leasing agents fanned the flames. They wanted me to have that retail spot. Instantly giddy and greedy, I drove around with eyes bigger than my stomach.

Years ago, a friend suffering from anxiety was advised by her therapist to hang on to some—fear is a gift, she explained. But I was naïve. Even as I watched the new landlord at Colorado Kitchen tear down the old building to make way for condos (all that was left that day was the far wall of the women's bathroom, wallpapered with old magazine advertisements and recipes), I wasn't afraid.

I shook hands and signed leases. I grabbed at vacant commercial space in my sleep. My vision, my personal campaign to be the Mother Theresa of DC Dining—bring food to every untouched corner that other chefs couldn't be bothered with—were stalled by construction overruns and lawsuits.

As I stood inside a quiet, old building only part way to becoming a restaurant—idle drills and cold portable lights scattered around a dusty floor and against the mud-freckled drywall—I couldn't help but question my own motives. Why am I doing this again? Remind me.

"Is it true you've signed leases for two other retail spots, Ms. Clark?" the landlord's attorney held a copy of the newspaper in front of his reading glasses. He was sounding like a divorce lawyer. And I was sitting

32

in that chair beside the judge playing the part of the accused adulteress. This was bankruptcy court. This was serious.

I had barely survived the easy drone in that wood paneled room that ended my marriage. Since then I'd been taken to court by former staff, contractors, and creditors where amid the small claims I wondered if someone was trying to tell me something.

Any normal person would have quit but having built my personal renaissance on being a chef, there was no way I could survive without a restaurant to run. I would cease to grow as a person unless I opened more. I banked my soul on this business. I had long ago, when I first leapt, tied my self worth to the "oohing" and "aahing," the sound of fork on plate, and the line at the door. What would become of me if no one was eating my cooking? I'd be nobody—a nobody washing ashore just south of the docks.

Chapter 1

Just Call Me Chef

"And she calls herself 'chef.'"

"I know. Can you believe it?"

"How arrogant. Not Chef Gillian or Chef Clark."

"I know, CHEF, give me a break."

"Yes, that would make it a bit less oo la la wouldn't it?"

"Where does she get off calling herself CHEF?"

To be a chef, one independent of a chain and all of its formulas, requires one to walk to the beat of a different drummer. If we weren't different, we would see nothing wrong with opening the same box of chicken tenders that they're serving at the joint down the street. We want to be different. That's what gets us those good reviews that keep us in this business.

Any attempt to assimilate into the general population is futile. This has never really been studied but it could be that repeatedly burning our hands, cutting off fingertips, holding our pee does something to the brain. There could be a natural tendency that leads one to this industry, but then the continued exposure further creates an individual not quite fit for polite society. Sure, you've seen chefs work the dining room and behave like normal people when they leave the kitchen for the Food Network. But over time, they lose the knife callous—that hardened patch of skin at the base of their index finger. They are no longer at ease in the very kitchen where they caught everyone's attention, but still they might eat too fast and not use a fork or they might forget themselves in the produce section and slip lemons and garlic into their pants pocket as if they were in their own walk-in cooler with their hands too full to carry everything. I imagine these chefs are stuck in the middle. Maybe after years go by and the callous is completely gone, they can go out to eat and sit with their back to the open kitchen.

I buttoned up my first chef coat when Sian, my youngest daughter, was in training pants. By the time she started kindergarten, people at work were calling me chef. Success seemed to come easy and fast. There were great reviews, following good ones. I found myself running the kitchen at some pretty popular places. And as I left one kitchen for another I would settle into my new digs with less butterflies and the confidence that good press would be along any minute now. I was flying really high. Sian had started second grade when James Beard Award fantasies started to creep into my daydreams. And then I disappeared.

It wasn't drugs, alcohol, or a jail sentence. I was fired. Suddenly, I was feeling like I didn't belong in that stainless-steel room anymore. I certainly didn't deserve to be the one in charge. It was an inauspicious start to the new century. Survival meant getting a job, any job. I bumped myself down to line cook. I didn't have the time, energy, or mile high ego now to be vetted for a new chef job. I subsisted on the cooking stints I could get only by telling lies of omission on my resume. I wasn't the chef at Evening Star I was the kitchen manager. I was the breakfast cook at Broad Street Grille. Mrs. Simpson's? That bold line and paragraph just disappeared all together. If you called Mrs. Simpson's and asked about me, the manager would say in a wine soaked French accent that I was fired because I had let food spoil. I had learned the hard way on that one. The bad references that came after the owner fired me, kept me from the cushy hotel gig making pizza in a little kitchen I would have all to myself. The hotel chef read my doctored down resume and immediately inferred that I had no ambition other than to cook. I was over 30, a culinary school graduate, and I knew how to make hollandaise. As far as he was concerned, I was perfect. He showed me my locker and then my kitchen.

The hotel was phasing out the union staff. He pointed to a line of lockers where gristled women chewed on their gums and spat on the floor. They grumbled and complained about everything and took their sick days during the week the convention was in town. "You won't be one of them," he told me. But after checking my references, Human Resources decided I was going to wedge the walk-in door open with a brick before I clocked out at night. As much as he may have wanted to, the hotel chef could not call me in for the understaffed lunch shift—so that I could take over the pizza kitchen and free up his afternoons. I imagined he was taking it in the ass just one more time from the suits upstairs. I figured he probably really hated them as he stood over some youngster with a much cleaner slate and less objectionable past whisking lemon juice into a broken hollandaise.

This time there was no Mrs. Simpson's on my resume, and I landed the job squeezing sauces on to seafood clichés at a crazy $13 an hour. I was put where the girls go, dressing up the plates before the servers take them.

Less than a year later a conference center job that included uniforms came along so I took it. Most of the $40,000 a year I pulled in went to renovating the storefront building that would be my first restaurant as chef and owner. Colorado Kitchen was going to be my ticket out of this hell of job uncertainty and no one knowing who I was. Not that I had my heart set on becoming a household word. I wanted my pedigree to be reinstated. Somehow, the career moves seemed to go from endless highway in Finland in the winter to unmarked dead end road in West Virginia. Who I was and where I came from and the scraps in my scrapbook were being rewritten as fiction. I was ceasing to exist. I was that tree falling in the woods and no one was listening. What I had was wasting, if I still had it at all.

I held it in and acted stupid to go unnoticed—to not be challenged. I suppressed my inner chef at these jobs; resisting the urge to answer back when someone called the title out across the kitchen. I hoped that suppressing the instinct to fix the sauce or re-plate the entrée, would not lead to permanent damage. At one point I was sure that I had that combination of talent, vision, skill, imagination, toughness, work ethic, and fearlessness that makes a great chef. No one believed me. If anyone did believe me, they were convinced all of that stuff didn't matter. They tried like hell to convince me, too.

When the logo went up in the windows and the register was ringing at Colorado Kitchen. I breathed the first lung-filling breaths I had taken since college. It was a tin-ceilinged, leaky-windowed, 1200-square-foot spot with 48 red Naugahyde chairs on black and white vinyl tile, but it was all mine. Vintage appliances balanced on wall shelves and old recipes and advertisements papered the bathroom walls. Tom Sietsema, food critic at The Washington Post called me before writing his assessment of my cooking. He asked me what was different about the food here than from the other kitchens I had run. I told him that for the first time, I was cooking the food that I wanted to cook. Sian was about to start third grade and I finally had a place of my own.

I was right. I knew what I was doing. It did matter. The biscuits in the breadbasket were a hit. The burger offered twice a week was a well-timed and executed success of forced supply and demand. The roasted chicken made an entire city believe in simple food again. And the donuts at weekend brunch had everyone letting their guard down. I was in love with food again and too busy to notice that the staff had all started calling me "chef" and I was answering to it.

It started at Evening Star. I introduced myself to my first hire, Rosheana. She leaned in, positioned her ear close to my lips and held her breath. I repeated my name to her three times. She awkwardly attempted to repeat it after me, but she might as well have attempted that Southwestern African dialect punctuated with pops and clicks. For some reason, she just couldn't get it. When it came time during the day to ask me a question or tell me something, she would stop what she was doing and look at me, the skin above her eyebrows twitching.

"Uh...Uh...Guh, Gi, Gi." I'd say 'Gillian' for her, slowly. After a few more tries she got it out. But then an hour would go by and the phonics lesson was long forgotten. And I would get the brow wrinkle again. It didn't help that I had written remoulade on the white board: RAY MOO LOD so she could remember what to call that sauce she had to make every afternoon. I was convinced she would never be able to say my name and would resort to just shouting "HEY" across the tiny kitchen.

"Uh…. Uh…Guh, Gi Gi." I'd say it for her again. It took us a week of this and then a crew of Latinos before I asked that they just all call me Chef. They were relieved and it stuck. But it did nothing to keep the twenty-something wait staff from treating me like shit. They didn't care if those low lifes in the kitchen called me Grand PooBah. I still worked for them and I wasn't doing such a hot job. A well-done steak still took more than three minutes, and why oh why couldn't I just roast enough chicken that we didn't run out at 9pm. Surely by now I had to know that this operation was going to need to roast 40 or 50 chickens between 6 and 8 pm. If I knew what I was doing I would roast them all at 2 in the afternoon and not put anything into that oven all day long while those chickens were roasting. And when a customer asks for grated parmesan, by golly fill that six-ounce ramekin to the brim, damn it. It's $9 a pound but so what. They want to see generosity with ingredients. *You're too stupid to think about food costs. Don't be so stingy with those turned vegetables. Whenever a fussy baby comes in, I need you to heat up a good couple of handfuls of those carrots, turnips, potatoes, and Braeburn apples. These new age parents want their rug rats to eat well. Aren't you the dumb ass that insisted on not having a kid's menu, Chef?*

***

To a lot of folks, though, I still was a nobody; not worthy of any title. But to answer the question I heard while eavesdropping on a food blog, yes, my staff calls me "Chef." I didn't make it up. It is usually what happens in kitchens across town. Some cook is wanting to know if the soup he is making is any good, he is trying to get the attention of the person that is going to give him the thumbs up or down, he is probably shouting, "Chef?" In fact, there are a bunch of us in white coats and hats in a huge kitchen of a restaurant hosting a benefit and each of us has a staff member with us to help. There is going to come a time that this person needs a question answered. This person is going to say, "Hey, Chef?" and every coat and hat in that room is going to turn around and say, "Yeah, what is it?"

42

Did anyone else have to defend their right to the title? Why did I? I found the list of things I shouldn't be doing was growing the more I was in the paper or magazine or called on to join a panel on talk radio. Where did I get the notion that I could tell people the fact that we only had 45 seats prevented us from letting them sit wherever they wanted? And didn't I know that a crowded dining room during Sunday brunch was not conducive to crossword puzzle ciphering and slow coffee sipping? What made me think that I was so special that I didn't offer the burger every night? Who was I to put lobster on the menu and charge more than $20 for it? How dare I not let the paying customer substitute the mashed potatoes for the cole slaw? No kids' menu? My child only eats grilled cheese, hot dogs, and chicken nuggets.

Word swirled around town that I was a bitch. I hated children. I was arrogant and egotistical and cussed customers out regularly in the dining room. One person claimed that I had rolled a magazine into a snout slapping weapon and shouted at them as they took their seats. People were afraid of me. Even radio talk show hosts joked that they didn't want to tangle with the Angry Chef.

I led Colorado Kitchen, but no one really knew me. Worse…they were coloring me in with red crayon and sketching in horns. With my prohibition of take-out and bottles of hot sauce had an influential handful of people focusing on the "rules" and not the food. They marked me full of contempt and high-mindedness. They said that I thought I was better than the rest of them.

I had everything I wanted, finally. I was leading my own restaurant that served lunch only on Friday and did not serve toast. Popular items disappeared when out of season and we could not rearrange the dining room to accommodate parties greater than six. There was no need for a kid's menu when smaller versions of our most popular items were available. Sunday brunch was so busy there was often an hour wait. I wasn't doing anything unusual. But these were the things that had people shaking their fists at me, "What the hell is her problem?"

Then there is the busy Saturday brunch with an extraordinarily long line and orders coming over the kitchen printer in a never-ending roll like that doll that grows hair out of her scalp with a push of the belly button. My chef coat is stuck to my back and I'm "going down". The tickets are piling up and I'm thinking there is no way I'll be able to cook all of this food. This is when tempers flare and an angry customer would make her way over to me furious that there are no empty chairs and eating with us means standing in line. She's going to give me a piece of her mind. And you know what? I'm really not in the mood. Despite our testy exchange she gets back in line. I'm focused on the scrambled eggs and browning potatoes in front of me. I couldn't look her in the eye if I wanted to; I do hear her call me a bitch under her breath. Everyone else in line shifts uneasily from left foot to right. The rumbling of their stomachs becomes the pounding of sticks into the ground—someone is going to get their ass kicked. Angry and frustrated faces are turned toward me. "If she weren't so mean, we'd all be sitting right now and eating." They are all sick of waiting, yet none of them leave. "What is her problem?"

The line that often became a mob knew nothing of the anger and mean (remnants of the abusive, failed marriage; bitterness over losing the townhouse I restored over 10 years; resentment for the owners who fired me after I built or rebuilt their culinary programs) that I had to get passed to be here at this stove cooking for each and every one of them with as much care and love as if they were my own children.

This is a business of love. Did a loveless marriage drive me to this? I don't know. I just know that it was bursting out of me and I had to find a place for it. My husband didn't want it. It did nothing to quiet the internal chants of self-loathing and wasn't flexible enough cover his brain with a tube sock the way the liquor did. I ended my 11-year marriage with an affair. I was having a fling with the stove. I read cookbooks like romance novels. And when the instructor at culinary school put his fingers into the flesh of the veal leg separating muscle from bone and silver skin from muscle, I sunk low in my seat and squeezed my legs together like I was watching a skin flick.

We talked about love in the kitchens where I put to use the tools the years and cooking school gave me. In one of my first cooking jobs every cook on the line loved so hard that it came before everything. Each night we were tested and each night we were driven to take our bodies beyond what we perceived as its limits. The ladle is hot. Of course, it's hot. Otherwise the sauce would not be hot. But it is not too hot for you to stand it. Take that hot handle of that ladle between your thumb and index finger and hold on. I don't care if it's burning you hold it steady and tilt out just enough of the contents of that ladle to cover the potatoes and a corner of the roasted chicken breast. Hold it steady or you'll spill. That reduced chicken stock—that's all you've got, and it has got to last all night.

I cooked with Jeff, a sous chef who was big enough to play college football but still found his way to the kitchen. He checked my station one night when a menu item he had developed was making us all a nervous wreck. There was a squeeze bottle for the six different colors of sauce. He checked my squeeze bottle of parsley puree. And he looked to see if I had enough in the squeeze bottle of red pepper sauce. He held my squeeze bottle of carrot puree to the light and frowned but decided it would be enough after all.

"Jeff, I have it. I've got every one of the sauces, the squeeze bottles." At this point I just wanted Jeff to shut up. I did have to get the rest of the station ready: make mashed potatoes, finish grating parmesan cheese, and bake off the Potatoes Anna.

"Oh yeah?" he challenged folding his huge arms over his chest. "But do you have your squeeze bottle of love?"

"Yes," I grabbed my left breast and pinched it narrow. "As a matter of fact, I do." He turned as red as the red peppers and left the kitchen.

The love trumps everything. Certainly, we've complained about suffering at the hands of a chef that shouted and threw things. But I can't recall ever questioning a chef's capacity to love. I'd heard stories about the chefs who drove fancy cars earned from high-priced plates creating kitchens they couldn't stand to be in, leaving the heavy lifting to an uncertain staff they never saw or interacted with. It was easy to tell where there was love and where it wasn't. Love came easier for the chef that drove a 1992 Honda into the ground—giving the impression that greed and love can not coexist.

Love also can't thrive in the presence of fear. Restaurants don't open without fear. That first day brings nerves on its own. Add the terror-inducing notion of the chef/owner thinking about the loan to be paid back, the payroll to meet, and the landlord you can't stall another day. Love is hard to fake, and fear is impossible to hide. A chef can spend the weeks reluctant to open the mail, refusing to answer the phone, and looking forward to 5pm Friday; not only because a busy weekend can be distracting, but also because banks, law offices, and accounts receivables departments are closed for two straight days.

***

I was scared when I opened my first restaurant as chef. I had all of the love in the world but what if nobody turned the knob and pushed that door open to take it, let alone pay for it? At nine in the morning, I was certain there was plenty of time to get my long prep list done before opening. But the hands on the clock whirred around so fast, I was panting like a heavyweight boxer and nothing was done as far as I could tell at 4 pm. The stress filled me with a fear that came out in a short temper. I snapped like a mad dog at everybody that came near me. The word "love" was nowhere to be found. I started second guessing everything I was doing: the menu is too long, there are way too many things to prep, the food is too expensive, it's not priced high enough, we'll never be able to make this menu work, no one is coming, and no one is going to like it. What was I thinking?

And no matter how much success I've endured, the same fear grips me at every opening day or night. A couple of slow nights, long after that opening day goes off just short of disaster, that fear creeps up the spine again. "Is the bloom off of the rose?" I ask. Maybe this town is done with me and my food. What now?

Fear can come in both black and red ink. I've been swamped beyond what I believe is my capacity. "Going down," we call it—feeling like I left the bathroom without pulling up my pants and my hands are so busy, I don't have a second to simply bend down and hike them back up.

After more than 20 years and more than a million meals prepared, I have come to expect and appreciate the nature of this business. There are the lows that are comparable to floating on a trash can lid on the River Styx and highs that make you want the jet pack to slow down so you can enjoy the view. You can be paddling along on the River Styx at 5:00 and then completely turn it around by 8:30 and come to the end of the evening with condensed water vapor and ice crystals in your hair.

While you're up there, in the clouds, and maybe because you're up there; you'll be stunned to find a few folks with knotted brows and clenched buttocks hurling things up at you. One of them might have a rope, and with the confidence of Arizona Charlie Meadows, is fixing to get a loop around your foot and pull you down. Don't look down! The minute you look at them or start shouting down to them, "Hey quit that." You'll be lucky if all you suffer are grass burns on your ass. Maybe you're the chef that gets a taste of that thin air up there and you find your head swimming. You get too close to a bird of prey, or lose velocity trying some fancy mid-air somersault. You will quickly plummet back to earth. Oh, and there's no quickly dusting off your chef pants hoping no one caught that. There will be dozens of critics, bloggers, and amateur internet reviewers to document your personal catastrophe.

Better to stay down there on your trash can lid on the River Styx, pulling yourself along a little faster than the current with a swing of your big toe in the murky depths. Be sure to shoot a silencing glance at the nut that sees fit to champion you—make a big stink about you on some foodie web site. Suddenly the quiet of your drifting down the lazy river is broken by a spotlight and the fact that you didn't even bother to comb your hair will make it into the conversation along with every other way you suck. Great. Now you're the butt of a big joke for a couple of weeks until they forget all about you again.

It's not a normal life. I've seen chefs with promising careers laid out before them, with a great review as a starting square, walk away. I've also been tempted by that fork in the road.

When I first came to Washington, DC—where my career in food began, I bent the hood of my car back into my windshield after coming to a stop in the bumper of the Volvo in front of me. FOR LEASE in bold letters took my eyes off the road. Those signs still catch my eye, I just drive slower now.

I imagine the potential of the space and the fact that I've driven by half a dozen boil-in-bag joints with the same old chicken tenders and crab cakes, I can't help but feel called to take over the old dilapidated building on the corner and bring decent food to these long suffering people. Concepts, menus, kitchen layouts, interior design swirl around in my brain before I've even had a chance to see the inside of the place. I am Moses with a vision of something burning and two plates in my hands. Unfortunately, there still a good chance that there will be false idols and debauchery the minute my back is turned.

Things don't always go as planned. Projects are always over budget and under funded. There is always the potential that I'll have to turn in my chef coat and get fitted for that barrel and suspenders. And with liens on everything I own of value, there is little room for error.

52

There's no money in this business. For the amount of work involved, it feels like even less than that. Does any young cook think a fortune awaits? But there is always the opportunity to be at those heights where the air—thin and void of oxygen—is intoxicating. These moments are priceless. And when it is going good and I'm so far above that proverbial creek, I forget all about the burn scars, sputtering cash flow, and the holes in my chef pants.

Even from down there on my trash can lid paddling away or just drifting with the current, I can see a promising storefront. As low as I get sometimes, I still have hopes and dreams. I still want to take over the world. This is the fever of this business. I have to have more; I have to do more. This is my addiction. I have to be on the end of every fork in America...the world—chopstick, banana leaf, right hand, whatever utensil the culture dictates. Like it or not, I find my bliss in creating spaces where people experience food. And that's just it. There are days I like it. There are days I don't.

In 1993 Potocka, the Polish countess I sold high-priced, DC real estate with, warned me. I confessed to her that the business of selling houses wasn't for me. I had cash socked away to go to cooking school and I wanted to have a career in food.

"You love to cook, don't you?" she said, her deep voice tinged with the lilt and dip of Polish royalty, like she was asking a toddler if she liked to color.

"Yes, I do." I was waiting for the shoe she was holding over my head to come crashing down on my fantasy bubble: me in a chef coat and all kinds of wonderful things happening.

"You will grow to hate it," she predicted. Doing what you love for a living, she explained, saps all the joy out of it. When I'm into my 13th hour on my feet and the kitchen is a sweltering 110 degrees, I think of Potocka. "I told you, Gillian." She says, sagely. And I have to agree with her when a customer is demanding a refund on her $30 steak after having eaten half of it, but the hair she's found in the potatoes (which of course is her own over-processed hair that drifted onto her plate) is now rendering the plate of perfectly cooked rib-eye and mashed inedible. Or when the reviewer comes on my night off and an ambitious cook disposes of my crab cakes to debut his own—heavily spiced in old bay and in the natural state— none of the hard-to-find bits of shell removed.

It is a business that requires so much of you. Every day can be a battle. The food comes from a very personal place and has to keep coming several dozen times a day. There are also those occasions where that very personal expression is sneered at or publicly held up to ridicule. It is a daily exercise in physical and emotional exhaustion. The chef works too hard not to be burnt. I've had those days where I am slow to change into my street clothes because I've spent closing time with my head in my hands. I wonder if I am too burnt to continue on the path.

And there are also the days that Potocka, often merciless in her honesty, would certainly scrunch her lips together and ask, "Why do you do this to yourself?" The review is particularly harsh, a regular customer feels it's his duty to bring me the stack of complaints from his neighborhood listserv, and the purveyor hopes I won't notice that I'm being charged $98 for a box of trash can liners make me want to throw in the towel and drive a cab all day instead. Why would any sane person deliberately put themselves in this shooting gallery?

Sanity is relative. There is a degree of recklessness here that could best be equated to bungee jumping. I've admitted to myself at times that there is crazy in me. I hang on to the stretched thin fibers of sanity by coming to terms with all of these things that come with creating, developing, owning, and cheffing a restaurant.

I repeat to myself that I'm not superwoman. As much as I try to be—get it all done before opening, some days I can't. There are days I fail. As for the folks I hire to work for me, they have lives. Unlike me, the restaurant isn't why they get up each morning. It's a job to them. It's not their life. Sometimes it's a tug of war just to get a line cook to not over reduce the sauce to a cloying syrup or a server not to ramp up the food costs by giving in to crazy substitutions.

Even if I have a day where everyone in the building is on the same page, just the right customer can come in and scrawl black crayon all over it. There are times we give in and times we don't because no matter what we've all been taught, the customer isn't always right. Most of the time, he's wrong. A lot of the times he's just plain crazy.

Then there are those who dine out who revel in their allergies and food aversions. They're overjoyed to be allergic to red spices and avoiding soy products because the estrogen it produces in men kills the libido. They can't wait to tell you about it. And if they don't like onions, they'll be sure to make you pay for putting it in anything. There are customers who wear their food aversions like a badge of honor, awarded after countless sad frowns discussing the menu with that insensitive server who can eat anything put in front of him. Those who need to stay away from certain foods are special and unique.

It's been more than 20 years and there are still days I wonder. At 6 o'clock, facing five more hours of supervising a difficult crew and pleasing a difficult audience, I don't think I'm going to make it. Even though I felt this way last Friday and survived, I'm thinking tonight is my last and I'm going to be consumed, run into the street screaming or simply hide in the closet until New Year's Day.

And then I remember how shy I was growing up. I would go days without speaking a word. I never spoke in school. Teachers complained to my mother that I tapped them on the shoulder to get their attention. I was as significant as an emergency light in the hallway. But I couldn't stop the part of me that wanted to be noticed. I became a merciless practical joker. When I jammed my sandwich foil into the water fountain the stream would blast an unexpected drinker in the face and shoot 20 feet in the air. Even the biggest bully got laughed at and learned to approach the innocent but dangerous and ego-wilting water fountain with caution. Without speaking, I could have an impact.

There are few careers where every day I can touch people. I'm not changing lives or saving lives; but I think changing spirits counts for something. I am making the wonderful pancake that sticks with them. It is my roasted chicken that creates the food memory still talked about years later. That crab and corn chowder made that little girl want to go to culinary school. I still find it worth it to put it out there. There may be a small group that isn't happy with it, that relishes the thought of stepping on it. And that's okay.

I worried when I first had my picture taken for a food section that I would be standing there exposed and vulnerable. "Heh, what are they writing about her for? Her food isn't any good." Once I caught the public eye, I was in for it. I rediscovered the reason I spent my elementary school days annoying my teachers by tapping them on the shoulder. The nail that sticks out gets pounded down. And I've always just wanted to disappear into the woodwork. When one least expects it sometimes the spotlight will land on you. If you want to make anything of yourself in this business, you'll need it to. Yet, folks are either awed or offended.

We can't help it. There is no chef out there whose head doesn't pop into the air every once in a while. Some of us have just been up there while no one was looking. I've been on both sides of the issue. Toiling away unnoticed can have its charm. But once the light hits you as you're scalp and shoulder above the rest of the crowd, there's no going back. Well, at least not for a few months. At least until something bigger and better distracts the food "authorities".

But I don't think most chefs are guilty of arrogance. I don't think that is a superiority complex. Just as I wouldn't shove my plumber aside and grab his wrench, I believe that as a kitchen professional, I can tell there are people sitting down to restaurants and having horrible things to eat for dinner. I wouldn't be wearing this apron if I didn't believe that I was the one with the power to do something about it. That apron makes a fine cape if you cut the strings and let the wind swing it around behind you.

I itch to put a stop to all the bad cooking. I fantasize about opening right next door to that kitchen that doesn't care and shutting them down. He'll shake his fists at me as the line of my customers snakes along the sidewalk and blocks his front door. No one is going in there anyway. Who cares? Each new store takes at least a pint of blood. No matter how gracefully I appear to dive through that flaming hoop I've just lit, no one is as impressed with me as I am. It might be because there is still no children's menu of hot dogs and peanut butter and jelly. Vegetarian entrees have never been scarcer. I'm old. The burn scars mark my years behind the stove, the way annual rings reveal the age of the fallen oak. There is very little about me and how I feel about food that will change.

I hope it is only age, but there is no escaping the feeling that I'm done. The heat has gotten to me and I have to chip away the baked-on carbon just to put the key in the door. I'd rather it be age because the alternative is a chef who has grown tired of cooking for people. At the bottom of this river I would not have to answer that question. I choked on green water in a sob of self-pity. Let them figure it out

Chapter Two

Mise en Place

We never had to knock when we got to Nana's house. My mother would turn the knob, leaning her shoulder into the wood just below the window. "Ma Maaa?" she would call. Not Mama, but Ma Maaa; the accent on the last syllable and the "aaaa" trailing up the stairs to Nana's bedroom and down the stairs where she might be sewing.

There were plastic runners on the wine-colored carpet and all the way up the stairs to the living room, passed the fake fireplace—the black marble mantel was indiscernible under the school portraits of dozens of grandchildren and great grandchildren. We always made our way into Nana's kitchen and sat at the table under the 3D picture of fish underwater and the still life she pulled from the pile of trash when she helped us move into the amateur painter's house my parents bought (she refused to sell that painting, even after being offered $350).

When talk between Nana and my mother went places beyond me, I would wander around the house. There was the baby blue bathroom with the padded toilet seat. I'd let myself get swallowed up by the huge La-Z-Boy positioned in front of the TV in Nana's bedroom. In the hallway was a velvet picture of John F. Kennedy flanked by a statue of the Virgin Mary and years of palms from Sunday service.

Cautiously I'd make my way into Nana's formal dining room. During one visit I noticed a big leather-bound book—its contents overwhelming the binding. It was a find greater than the button that flipped the Lay Z Boy footrest into the back of my legs. I pulled out one of the huge oak chairs and sat down at the table with one of Nana's photo albums. There were pictures of my mother in a simple cotton dress that Nana had made—her elbows and knees her most prominent features. Sepia colored records of cousins and sisters standing for a photographer with serious faces and tight collars. There were dozens of candids from cruises and parties. Nana, young and ready to take on this new country, in a gown she had made. In one picture she held a cigarette holder in her gloved hand. She was surrounded by men; one more handsome than the next.

Separated from her husband and making her way on her own in a big new town and even bigger country, Nana left her daughters home with their grandmother and braced herself for what might be out there. Parties, dances, clubs—all of that living she missed getting married young and having three children. The nights were followed by long days in the garment district where, in big hot rooms, rows of machines whirred thread through endless bolts of fabric.

Frenetic nights in a beautiful dress surrounded by handsome men straining to catch her eye drove all the fear and desperation out of Nana's head. Maybe kissing one guy and dancing close with the next helped her forget all about the morning she found a nickel as she mopped the kitchen floor in the new walk up on 168th Street and Lennox Avenue. Certain there was more, she and her daughters tore up the linoleum until their fingers bled.

By the time I knew Nana, those days had faded away like some of the faces in the cellophane covered snap shots. But she could tap the face of a man in the picture and tell me his name and who he wound up marrying and what he did for a living. Most of her sewing went on in her basement now. Headless women with tape measure necklaces wore parts of suit coats and the bodices of wedding dresses. The reckless days left her no time to hone any traditional domestic skills. She cooked well enough to feed her family. But the real estate section held her interest way more than the articles detailing fancy ingredients and an easier way to bake off leftovers in a casserole. Nana spent her money on the house down the street, or the plot of land in New Mexico. She couldn't be less interested in set of knives or the copper core saucepan.

Meals at Nana's house weren't particularly memorable for what was on the plates. There were no adventurous attempts with lobster, or culinary flights of fancy with puff pastry. I remember the soup of yellow peas boiled into submission in a pot with beef bones and corn on the cob for it requiring both spoon and heat-braving fingers, but also for the warmth I felt around Nana's table and in her home. There was no shared ancestral cooking technique.

My grandmother's eat-in-kitchen, where I spent more time than any other place in her house, is my inspiration when I imagine how I want customers to feel when they walk into my restaurant. Nana was never too tired. She was never too busy. She didn't need a welcome mat. Nana was gracious and generous. All you needed to do was sit in one of the vinyl chairs around her kitchen table to feel that she had enough room in her heart for everybody.

The welcome had nothing to do with the quality of her cooking. Nonetheless, there are a great many folks who have enjoyed my cooking who wonder where else could I have learned to put butter and white wine together but from Nana. In my restaurant they are overwhelmed by feeling this connection to me. Even though it is imagined or perhaps from a story they read. They can't help but feel they watched me grow up and have firsthand knowledge of how I came to a professional kitchen.

"I have this fantasy that you learned to cook at your grandmother's knee on some huge porch in the Deep South," she pleads her hands clasped together so tightly her knuckles are white.

"Sorry," I have to disappoint her. "I am trying to duplicate the warmth I felt at my grandmothers house as a child in this restaurant, but my grandmother was all evening gown and cigarette holder," I can hear the sharp crackle of her bubble bursting, "not apron and skillet."

"Oh...." Her hands drop below her knees and she drags herself back to her seat.

I've become accustomed to that hopeful face. After a good meal of simple food—creamy mashed potatoes, buttery green beans with a crisp-skinned roasted chicken, a customer's mind can wander. A harmonica would breathe softly under a banjo strum and there I'd be: maybe ten years old and barefoot on the porch of wood house in desperate need of painting. There are woods behind us where Grandpa hunts possum and squirrel. I'm being raised by my grandparents, because like most black kids, I haven't seen my parents in years. After eating my food, they picture me the phenom. Home grown from nothing; I learned the way of the stove because I had to. There was no time for formal schooling. Gramma taught me to read and write by scrawling on the floorboards with the coals from the fire. She never got further than the third grade, so there wasn't much hope for me. But we were a determined lot. And I promised Gramma on her death bed that I would slaughter, skin, and can my way to the top.

I get it. It is easier to understand if the story is familiar. If it could read like the sequel to *Sounder* there would be nothing that required any thinking out of the box. If that black woman doesn't fit into this hole that

66

decades of stereotypes have dug, then everything we know about the world could unravel like a snagged knit sweater. And we'll be forced to walk the earth in a left ballet slipper and a right stiletto.

I can't help but not go along with the fiction and pull that stabilizing block of wood out of the tower. "No, I'm not from Georgia." I repeat to the woman who has money riding on it. "Actually, I grew up in New York," I say to the frowning man. There's no question that I take pleasure in telling folks the truth. I want them to accept the real me, not the chef they've created through the filter of required fifth grade reading assignments and bad television sitcoms.

This crosses all racial lines. There are the white folks that want it all to fit neatly into the box they've come to expect. It's safe. There are no surprises, and it makes their limited experience okay. For black people they can hang onto the comforting notion that only a black person can make food for black people. If the floor is staffed by a team of white servers, some black people crane their necks above heads at their own and other tables to get a glimpse of me before they decide to stay. "Oh good," they say to each other in hushed tones. "I heard this place was black owned. But then there are all of these white people up in here." But after

67

discovering that I hired that white server or I'm the one roasting the pork chops still pink inside and that there is no scrapple on the brunch menu, they come to realize that I may be the right color but I am not a member of the club.

Why not have the chocolate tart for dessert or the marble pound cake sundae? Instead they approach me without trepidation to suck in syrupy tales of my growing up in shot gun shack off a dirt road in a slow, sleepy town in the Deep South. Here I learned to make stone soup and preserves, not because I enjoyed it, but because my survival depended upon it. And it still does. It is the best and only lesson I took from that hard but happy life. Many of my black customers also find it much easier to swallow the stereotype than the kind-of-dull truth.

Not everyone comes for the story. The customers that count on it leave with the memory of a good meal supplanted by the bitter taste of the ho-hum truth. They are not a fan. I know it would be easier and I would be much more popular if I acted less sure of myself and more grateful for the miracle of me making it and having a place of my own—knowing that as the rain came and washed all the crops away that terrible summer in '72, it could do it again. The ones who come for the food leave happy. The few that come for the black-person-beating-the-odds salve for ancestral guilt leave disappointed.

The fact is I want them to love me...not that woman...that culinary blow up doll that is whoever they want her to be. So, I tell the truth.

I could fake it. I could go along and nod my head, agree that my grandmother taught me everything I know and that I didn't learn by watching a white man (Craig Claiborne) on TV. I could deny that I ever set foot in a cooking school with a French name and curriculum. But that just isn't in me. I don't want a false history to speak for me. And I want the evening-gown Nana to live on forever—that her need to get dressed to the nines and give everyone the impression that her life couldn't be better; was, for Daisy Barnes, one step closer to getting there. I want as many people as I can tell to know that she had ambition, dreams, and drive to make a little empire of her own out of nothing. Those dresses and cigarette holders were evidence that Daisy Barnes would not be domesticated.

Giving the atmosphere of Nana's kitchen table new life in my restaurant dining room, I thought I'd left nothing to interpretation. Most people who walked into the room got it. But many were left confused and

69

angry that it didn't all add up—that I wasn't who they thought I was. I was making the right food—food they had themselves growing up, or food they'd heard about or maybe saw the Walton's eating around that plain, happy table. The room stoked all of those memories, real or imagined. The problem was me. I was a phony, an actor. I was an impostor. Everything would lead one to believe that I had the natural talent of Grandma Walton. But the recipes hadn't been passed down from generations; they were concocted through the chef science of trial and error. I was committing a public fraud. The disconnect was unsettling and it made these loud few hate the place. Still, it was a curious distaste and they would wind up in that room, looking around until their eyes landed on something that made a part of their brain try and rise up against the gnaw of nerves in their stomach. If it weren't for the food, they told anyone who would listen, they'd never come back. But they had seen the roasted chicken in their dreams. They had kissed their wife that morning and tasted the catfish. So here they would wind up, sitting in my dining room, waiting for their food, with a sour expression on their face.

The division split families. Husbands rushed in after work and later explained to the missus as she warmed a jar of pasta sauce, that they'd

70

had a late lunch. A bunch of women lingered over a pitcher of mimosas at brunch because the Sunday three weeks ago was their husbands "last time he would set foot in that place ever again." After some pleading and maybe even more feeling left out, the reluctant dining companion often gave in and our little restaurant was granted another chance to disappoint and drive one more last nail into that coffin that would just not shut.

Not to say that there weren't just as many if not more who loved the place. They came three and four times a week. Some of the faithful had brunch and then came back for dinner on a Sunday. We were where people from surrounding neighborhoods would stop in when they just didn't feel like cooking, but also the place they would bring out of town guests or the in-laws. My little restaurant, this first restaurant of my own, held a special place for people. And knowing that gave me the strength to pull that Friday turnaround to Saturday double that melted into another turnaround double on Sunday.

But the dressing down at the hands of the angry in a crowded dining room can drown out everything else. Even on a busy night, a night where I feel all of DC is in the room and loving it; the one customer who has got to make it known it wasn't up to par can whip the rug right out from

71

under my Doc Martens. When the tickets start rolling in and after I've dropped the tongs, the spoons, burned myself and set a towel on fire, I eventually settle into a groove and I am in the zone. The zone can be an awesome productive place where a line cook becomes more machine than human. A glance at the ticket before I jam it into the rack, and it hangs where I can keep track and I'm off.

In less than ten minutes there need to be five roasted chickens, nine meatloaf, seven catch of the day while the soups and salads are carried out to the dining room. Dinner for eight tables is headed for the heat lamps and my brain stops speaking English to me. It is a noiseless hush that not even my own voice is allowed to disturb. Just the brain in quiet conference with my hands and even my feet and knees are in on the action—nudging the oven door closed or kicking the cooler drawer shut.

My ears have been conditioned to shut out all sounds except the sharper sizzle of the fat in the pan when the chicken is ready to be turned and go into the oven. The buzz of the kitchen printer—that sound is allowed in too. I don't hear the talking and the chime of fork hitting plate in the room. If my eyes shift upward and land on the face of a customer waving and smiling, it hits my retina and stops right there. I'd have to look twice—maybe three times—to see my own mother.

A glance at the hanging strips of paper and I take a quick count of what I've got and compare it to how many I actually have prepared to sell. This is the weak link in the chain. I have to interrupt, and the brain is way too busy with the hands to even hear me. I'm nudging. Earlier that day I blended all of the ground beef and ground turkey I had—the previous night's run on burgers had me about seven pounds short. Into the oven goes one full pan of four loaves. That means tonight we have 36 slices. That's only 18 orders. On a night like tonight with every table ordering at least one plate of meatloaf with mashed potatoes, red-eye gravy and green beans we are going to come up short. Wait, wait. Stop. I can't get a word in edgewise. I only have four left. Stop selling meatloaf and let me count. Nobody hears me.

That afternoon I didn't say anything out loud when I pulled the pan out of the oven, the four—now seemingly tiny—loaves of meat baked brown on the top and the juices puffing at the corners of the loaf pan. But word got out somehow. Meatloaf is in short supply, hurry. Get it now. Was there an article in the paper? Or is a server out there telling everyone he hands a menu to that it's his favorite? Could it be my brain has betrayed me and communicated telepathically with everyone sitting in the restaurant tonight with a napkin on his legs? I kept it to myself, I'm sure. The jinx is on if crisis is actually verbalized. And for that reason, I took the meatloaf out of the oven and thought to myself, "I hope four is enough tonight." I made sure not to sigh or wiggle a finger under the band of my chef hat to scratch my head, because surely someone would have asked, "What is it?" I would have to say aloud: "I don't think I have enough meatloaf for tonight." At that they would laugh and say, "Now you've done it. You definitely don't have enough NOW."

"Hey, the meatloaf is really good tonight and she's going to run out soon so order that, okay." Kitchen gremlins head out into the dining room spreading the news whispering into every ear they can squeeze into, "Tee hee," they giggle before they blow back into the kitchen and extinguish all of the pilot lights.

Have they messed with my ears, too? That's the only word I can catch from the open kitchen. "How's the meatloaf?" "Last time I was here I had the meatloaf." "I hear that meatloaf is the best." "I think I feel like meatloaf tonight." The declarations of love for meatloaf swirl around the

74

dining room until they pile up on each other and form a neat little stack so that the word is pronounced in unison by the entire dining room—it becomes a chant: MEATLOAF, MEATLOAF, MEATLOAF.

A big table making the most of their night out is ordering and when the seven-inch ticket grinds through the printer, I've got a good 15 seconds to catch my breath. I exhale and wait before I pull it and read it slowly this time and catch the order of three MEATLOAF for table ten. Now's my chance. "Three meatloaf?" Wait a minute, wait. Okay I have these three and that's it. Finally. I am rattled out of the zone and can put a stop to this meatloaf frenzy. "Eighty-six meatloaf!" I say as loud as I can. It echoes around the server station, even folks in the dining room reading the menu hear me. I watch them use their index finger to underline the meatloaf on the menu. They heard "eighty-six meatloaf" and just thought I was announcing how many I have and it sure sounds good to them. I see the server shake his head while the customer's mouth is still moving, telling him exactly how he wants that meatloaf.

"Make sure it is really, really hot. And I don't want that sauce..."

"Sir, sir...

"...okay put it on the side. And I want the green beans...

"But, sir…"

"I want the green beans, just steamed…

"Sir we're out of meatloaf…"

"…steamed, that's it, with no butter or salt or…what?"

"I said we're out of meatloaf."

"Wha…?"

"The chef just announced that we've run out of meatloaf. Do you need a few more minutes to make another selection?"

"I can't get the meatloaf?"

"No, sir, not tonight."

"But I want the meatloaf."

"Yes, I know that, sir. But we've run out." Almost a gesture to prove his point the server explains this while glancing around the dining room letting his eyes spotlight all the meatloaf leaving the kitchen—plates orbiting tables and plates in the process of being licked clean. This is always an action that the customer mimics. He, too, sees all the plates of meatloaf on the tables around him. But it brings him no closer to understanding what all that meatloaf currently being served on this unusually busy Tuesday night has to do with him. All he sees are happy meatloaf eating faces. He is watching a stranger make love to his wife.

He takes a deep inhale through his nose watching a less deserving man smear a sauce covered chunk around the plate to grab the last of the mashed potatoes. A little of the butter from the now gone green beans soak into that thirsty corner of potato before the forkful disappears into the guy's mouth. Now the customer longs for the meatloaf even more. He ponders his misfortune and questions whether the fates had come in to play here. Maybe he shouldn't have asked for the sauce on the side.

He'll ask one more time, "So…. there's no meatloaf left?"

"I'm afraid not, sir."

Eighteen customers leave happy. So do thirty that have had the roasted chicken and twenty-five diners who enjoyed the catch of the day. Eleven out of the twelve who had to settle for something other than meatloaf leave satisfied as well. But while the last of the desserts are going out, the dissatisfied one of the twelve stops by the open kitchen. The fury-wrinkled face in front of me washes my brain of all of the happy moments it witnessed. According to this face my restaurant is a failure. I'm a failure.

"What kind of chef runs out of meatloaf?"

I really don't know how to respond to this kind of anger. To me, it is only meatloaf. To this man it is so much more. Maybe I'm a lousy chef for not recognizing how important meatloaf can be. My night is ruined.

When I was a young chef, shy and still wet behind the ears, I had a hard time posing for the photographers and going out to the dining room because that table of ten was having such a good time they had to meet me. I learned to keep a clean chef coat hanging in the office. I memorized a few phrases to quickly explain things and get back to the kitchen, yet still appear humbled and gracious.

The anger was a different story. I am a little stunned that people are so quick to express the emotion that yesterday's newspaper shows can lead to violence and incarceration. I am a bit more reserved with my anger. It seeps out when the produce company wheels through the crowded dining room case after case of rotten lettuce an hour after I've opened for business or when no matter how much I plead, the new dish washer still empties a bottle of cheap cologne over his head before he gets on the bus to come to work, contaminating everything he touches with Eau De Doo Da Day.

Holiday anger has no rival. Because so many families celebrate the seasons by finding neutral territory (a restaurant dining room) to rehash all of the bitterness that's been brewing since childhood, many restaurants pass on the lucrative Thanksgiving service. But nothing beats the anger we endure on Mother's Day. The Colorado Kitchen dining room, at a mere 750 square feet, was too small to host the sibling rivalry and parent-induced bitterness that is stored up every year and released by adult children on Mother's Day. We had to close. The year we decided was our last saw daughters unhappy with their table waiting patiently to give me a piece of their mind and sons pouting with arms folded because their mother didn't like whatever I was putting in the pineapple-upside down cake. The whole day is ruined because now there is proof that Momma doesn't love them as much as Leroy and it is all my fault. The meal they envisioned having at the table that was more to Mother's liking would have fixed all of that.

"Why, you certainly are my favorite." Mother would say, "You took me to this great restaurant. Your sister would never have the good sense to bring me here." Or a simple, "Of course I love you more." But it never works out that way. After 30 or 40 years it's still hard to believe that your own mother hates everything you do and would rather be home in fuzzy slippers watching re-runs than be dragged to some noisy restaurant just because it's Mothers Day. And you hate me for it. You'll study the reviews and blogs and wind up at some other poor chef's place next year.

There have been scathing letters and emails, angry protests about the price of the donuts, the long line at brunch, and not letting guests in before the five o'clock opening time. Nothing drew more ire than the unexpected closings. The Friday lunch was canceled after a long Thursday night with the plumber. By 7 am the sewage was still coming up and out of the grease trap. It was later revealed, after over $4,000 in plumbing bills for a persistent clog that started week one, was easily solved now 6 years later. That first plumber left angry, shouting at us that he had lost the tip of his snake in our clog. He snatched the check from Robin and stormed out cursing as brunch customers took their seats. The new plumber snaked and "cameraed" for 12 hours with no answers. We'd been closed two nights, but the insurance adjuster could not help us with this man-made disaster. We broke through the cement out of pure frustration and continued digging a hole in the basement floor until we got to the problem pipe and found, not just the tip but 25 feet of snake left by that first

80

plumber—25 feet of snake coated with and catching debris—everything flushed and every seed and scrap of lettuce that went through the disposal.

Anyway, hours before taking matters into our own hands and digging the hole, we wearily watched the new plumber vibrate his snake down the drain at the back door. While the snake whirred out to 175 feet, (I'm sure it was going through the wash cycle in the Laundromat across the street), I went to talk to the confused and angry faces pressed up against the plate glass. There was banging on the door and fingers wagging and jabbing at the sign that read CLOSED.

"Sorry, we're closed." I tried to keep the door open just a crack. The smell of rotting grease, human waste, and black water was seeping out onto the sidewalk. Not only was he hungry, however, he was way bigger than I, and forced the door open so that he could squeeze in.

"How come every time I try and eat here, you're closed?"

"I'm sorry about that. But this is one of those times that even if I felt like feeding people with all of this going on..." there were greasy wrenches, buckets full of black water, and soiled rags on the dining room floor, "the health department would shut me down."

"I don't understand how you can operate a business like this and never open your doors." He raised his hands over his head and looked to the heavens. Either God was going to enlighten me and help me see the error of my ways or strike me dead. I preferred the latter. I was about to invite him in. Sit him at table 14—the one closest to the basement door— and make him wait in that stinking room a good 35 minutes for his well-done burger. But two women who had been waiting for the doors to open convinced the man that he could come back and that today he should just go somewhere else. They dragged him away as I shut the door on his shouting. He shook his fist at me—a nonverbal tongue lashing. He would not be silenced.

Diane Pitt was a regular who couldn't stand the place. She came at least three times a month and proudly wore her distaste for the décor, the menu, the staff, and the room temperature. We'd groan when she opened the front door, stepped in from the outdoors and took a good, long, nasty look around. When her food arrived, she'd send it back— "No sauce," she would swear she had instructed the server. "Medium-well not medium!"

was the order the week before. She'd shake her head in disgust and disappointment, "What's with you people." She dined alone. Always.

I gave up on trying to make Diane happy. The busy nights she came I really didn't have time to second guess her order, or double check. But breakfast was a different story. It was slow, quiet and I was alone. Breakfast was a one-man operation. Me in the dining room to greet and seat, and then I took the orders. I'd rush back to the stove. I'd put the finished plates in the window under the heat lamp and then run around the corner back to the dining room to pull them out of the heat and serve. I hated it. Nonetheless, I took it as an opportunity to make a community of the few people that showed up with any regularity. I learned their orders: how they liked their eggs, how they wanted their coffee. I pushed my shy inclination aside and tried to make small talk as I poured a refill or took a credit card.

"Bardot?" I said to the tall blonde handing me her Visa. She had been in once or twice before during one of my solo shifts. "You're not related to Bridgette, are you?"

"Yes, she's actually a second cousin or something," she replied, her eyes on her wallet. She was alone today. But she had been in Saturday with a tall guy holding his mass of dyed-black hair under a pork pie hat and his skinny white arms an exploded paint factory of tattoos. Sunday, she was with the girl that had our long-time server Randy slapping his knee at the dish station. "She told me she was a model," Randy guffawed. "That Uggo? A footwear model, maybe." I brought her card back in the black-padded folder and didn't say anything else.

When she came in again, I tried to guess her order, "Over easy with bacon, today?"

"No, scrambled soft, sausage." She slid the menu in my direction then pushed her knuckles into her red stained eyes. Her face was puffy and the skin under her eyes was gray. Her cropped blonde hair was smashed on one side from a pillow, maybe the carpeting, or even the sidewalk.

No one else came that day. I busied myself in the awkward distance in the room. She ate her food twenty feet away from me. But no matter how much noise I made—even the melodic "Colorado Kitchen" when I answered the phone, she kept her eyes on her eggs and I didn't exist. I imagined that somewhere in New York's Hall of Records, the ink on my birth certificate was gradually fading away. That helped me suppress any impulse I may have had to step around the counter and find out through

84

forced conversation what the hell was wrong with her. To find away to slip in one or two, "its not that bad," or "that can be fixed" or even, "if I were you...."

By the time we were in a position to have a server join me in the mornings, months had gone by and I figured that morning had been Bardot's last. But she returned. Another tattoo had settled into a bare spot on her shoulder. She and "Uggo" breezed in giggling and paranoid, looking over their shoulders and out the windows but laughing at the sound of the phone ringing or a woman across the street balancing laundry on her head.

My server Tyler waited patiently at their table. He grabbed his pen from behind his ear and poked the tip into the blank page of his pad. Six foot plus tall Tyler standing in front of them made them laugh even harder. Their faces turned red and they tilted and rolled sitting side by side in the padded bench by the window. Bardot took the menu in both hands to stop her hands from shaking after Uggo was able to compose herself enough to ask Tyler for an order of pancakes. I heated the pan. Bardot would get over easy or scrambled soft. I took a 7-inch non-stick from my stack and waited. "Scrambled soft," I read her lips. So, when the ticket came through, I was almost done cooking their breakfast.

The heat was low under the pan and when the butter had melted enough to pool, I poured in the broken eggs thinned with heavy cream. Scrambled eggs take all of my attention. When the eggs are in that pan swirling over the melted butter and curds are starting to form, I don't take my eyes off of them. I make the server wait for them, because the heat of the lamps will cook them even further. I called Tyler over to run the couple (melted together and giggling in each other's arms) their breakfast. I waited until his thumb and index finger were on the plate before I tumbled Bardot's scrambled soft onto the plate next to her sausage and hash browns. I watched Tyler place the plates in front of them. I admit that I wanted Bardot to say what so many who've eaten my eggs have said—they're perfect, the best in town, I can only get eggs cooked properly here. She'd eaten my eggs wordlessly dozens of times. Still, I watched her. Stoned or drunk, it didn't matter. She still went through her ritual. She rotated the plate a quarter turn. Unrolled her silverware from the napkin and placed the bright red cloth over her legs, just like her mother showed her. She moved her cup of coffee to her lips. After taking a cautious sip, she placed it just above the plate to her left. She took the saltshaker from its post on the white laced doily and pointed her index finger to the ceiling taking aim. But the shiny ceramic shaker was top heavy with salt and slipped. While Uggo was blowing pancake bits out of her mouth and slapping her knee, the entire shaker emptied onto the soft beautiful mound of gold before she could bring her index finger hammer down onto it.

Bardot wasn't laughing. She stared down at her plate and shoved it across the table. She thrust her long arm into the air and waved to Tyler. I had put another pan on the stove and started the process all over again. She was a regular and accidents happen. It's worth the price of a few eggs and a little heavy cream to make it all better. I was gently stirring a new batch of scrambled soft in a pan when Tyler brought the plate back to me.

"Uh, Chef…" he started.

"Yeah I know. I've already got a re-cook started."

"She says they're not right." Tyler missed the whole saltshaker incident.

"What!"

"She says they aren't right." He's insisting and losing his patience with me. Why am I making a big fuss when clearly, I screwed up?

87

"What do you mean they're not right?" Disbelief has turned to fury. "She ordered scrambled soft, didn't she?"

"Yeah…but she says they're not right," he's thinking all of that time and money spent on cooking school was a mistake when I can't even make a decent plate of soft scrambled. He shrugs and puts the plate down in front of me so I can get a closer look at these horrible eggs I tried to pass off as breakfast.

"She wants over easy instead."

"Fine," I manage through clenched teeth.

I made the over easy just as carefully and watched Tyler bring the food out to her. He bowed low and apologized. He was doing everything he could to make it up to her, a new cup of hot coffee, and a refill on her orange juice. She wouldn't look at him. She nodded her head impatiently. She shook salt and pepper furiously in the air over her plate, making enough dust that Tyler turned and walked away. Her fork and knife attacked the three yolks under their white blanket until they started to bleed. I didn't exist for Bardot. And now, she didn't for me either.

I thought for a minute that I had seen too much. Perhaps my view of Bardot during our sober mornings alone were more the real Bardot than any of her companions had seen. She rejected my attempts at being any more familiar than we were. She was hiding something. I had been witness to too much already. I knew that when she came in alone, she had left her apartment without looking in the mirror. Not because she was running late, but because she couldn't.

The toxic relationships, the bad romances love to eat out. They visit the restaurant nearby or the one with such a good reputation it is bound to distract them from their distaste of each other. "Will this perfectly cooked steak and full-bodied red let me forget for an hour or two that I'm stuck with you?" Even the best restaurant under these circumstances can't live up to its four stars. Still, they come back—this is the one thing they share, the one thing they agree upon. They say it together, "I hate this place."

When the break-up or divorce finally happens, they associate the innocent restaurant with the worst time in their life. They stay away from steak and switch to Vigonier. The breakup of the happy couple is also bad restaurant news. Who gets custody of their favorite spot, where they spoon fed each other a shared soup of the day and made hot crazy love to each other in the foyer the taste of foie gras and crab cakes still in their mouths?

We've seen the return of the now-single woman. Disheveled, tired, dragging herself in late after the stomach conquers the ego. She quietly orders two chocolate tarts and three glasses of red wine and calls it a night. The man waits the appropriate length of time before he brings in his younger new girlfriend. They giggle in each other's' faces and sit on the same side of the table. The romantic antics will include something idiotic like nose rubbing. He's wearing more jewelry, growing his hair long to cover his bald spot, and has abandoned the tailored khakis for low-rise jeans.

There are the couples in the middle of a separation that can't think of anywhere else to go. What happens after fifteen years of marriage that bring a man and a woman to the conclusion that they can't live together a minute longer? It's a table for two now for Joan and little Sarah on a quiet Tuesday night. But wait, are those three taking up a four-top waiting for someone? Why it's John, the always disheveled and estranged husband of Joan. His friends know he'll never survive without a woman to remind him that he wore that shirt yesterday, its time for a hair cut, or that his shoes need polishing. The familiar restaurant where John knows how to order and pronounce everything on the menu is the perfect spot for the first blind date. It's an awkward moment. We won't be seeing them for a year or so.

These chance meetings have been awkward at times and also devastating and hard to watch. A young woman is in early with an older work associate. They are about ready to order dessert and it's barely six o'clock. The server is telling them all about the lemon-coconut tart, when the younger of the two bolts out of her seat and heads to the far wall. She's terrified, shaking; in a second she's going to start screaming. She's the only one seeing something menacing and dangerous in the dining room. Everyone else is calm and acting as if nothing is happening, especially the older couple making their way to a pair of empty bar stools. Her eyes are fixed on the man—his pencil-drawn mustache and thinning hair. He and his wife are oblivious to what's going on. They talk over the menu but can't seem to agree on a wine—no bottle tonight, a glass or two will have to do. But the girl with her back pressed into the far wall, her fingernails digging into the plaster acts as if the man would rather be drinking her blood and she is too terrified to move and wishes the front door were closer. Meanwhile her companion has paid and is coaxing her friend along the 15-foot radius around the man. Fifteen feet is way too close. He might leap up, get her, and kill her this time. It is a nerve wracking seven minutes. But she manages to get her friend to the front door. She is crying, trembling, begging her friend not to leave her. Please don't let him get me. Please, don't scream. I've got you. You're okay. The companion thanks us as she leads the girl through the open door. She whispers to us, "That's the man that raped her."

For this young girl our little restaurant was one more threshold she'll never cross again. Her reasons are obvious. There are many former customers I can tell you with unwavering certainty; we won't ever see them again. For as many as I have figured out, there are twice as many that I don't have a clue how my little store rubbed them the wrong way.

What I do know is that a trusted restaurant becomes much more than a place to eat. It becomes a room of solace and that place that lulls, beckons, comforts, and does things to the psyche that can't be articulated. It's transcendental. It hits that spot in your brain that developed as you grew and saw, smelled, and tasted the world. It hurts when it's taken away or spoiled. It's hard to put a finger on it. But I know it has little to do with me as a person. Only that for fans, the spot on my brain and theirs must be very similar splatters of ink. Strangely, I don't think I can take all of the credit or all of the blame. The restaurant that found its way into that space after I signed the lease was really predetermined. The size and shape of the room required I put the kitchen there, the ice machine here, have the finished plates come up here. A restaurant design expert examined my first ever design attempt and insisted it wouldn't work. But after a weekend alone with the floor plan, even he couldn't think of a better way to do it.

Still, like any business that unlocks its doors and allows people to just walk in take a seat and ask for food and drink, we are subject to the whims of taste and temperament. To one person the food is too salty. Not salty enough to another guy. The music is too loud for one. It's strange they don't play any music, says another.

Intense dislike and unwavering devotion are closely related, I have found. I wasn't yet a teenager when I sat down with my father to watch one of his favorite movies. It was *The Vikings* starring Tony Curtis and Kirk Douglas. I was instructed to listen for the fortune teller who advised Tony, "Love and hate are horns on the same goat." Only then was I permitted to nod off, until I was nudged awake to see Kirk Douglas's "corpse" float away on a burning Viking ship.

It doesn't matter if Morgana (Janet Leigh) loves you or hates you, she was telling the young Viking. Both involve passion, isn't that what you're looking for? I can recall the intensity of the anger in the letters and feel with certainty the passion. The words and spit forced out through clenched teeth make me press my fingers into the flesh above the top buttons of my chef coat. They cut that deep.

I have hated, too, I confess. I hated Bardot when she lied about her scrambled eggs. I hated the woman and her daughter who ordered the last two bowls of shrimp bisque. After eating three spoonfuls, they called the waiter over. "It's too salty," they explained, unaware that I had overheard them confess to each other quietly they might be too full for dessert. I hated the man that came in to interrupt on a busy Saturday night to tell me that the milk shake he had three nights before wasn't thick enough and he wanted his money back. I despise the slob that comes in for the menu someone blogged about two years ago and leaves in a huff because its January two years later and we're not serving the crab cakes. I really don't care for the customer who sends back the strawberry shortcake because it comes on a warm and tender homemade biscuit and not the spongy yellow disk sold at the supermarket.

I don't really hate these people. I hate what they do to me. I hate that they give voice to that little goblin of insecurity that appears on my shoulder sometimes—the Little Person. She is quick to judge and frankly thinks I stink at everything I do. I'm just lucky my wardrobe of Emperor's new clothes has held up, she says. But when someone comes in and challenges my high-falutin notions of myself, the Little Person is quick to jump up with an index finger pointed to the sky, "Ah ha!" She declares, "Told you." All of my insecurities and self doubt have been given a clear, shrill voice. What feels like hate is really my, "Oh yeah...I'll show you." And I'm egged on to try even harder, to pursue perfection with even more tenacity. I am killing with kindness. Sure, in the haste to cook dinner for 15 people at once, I may let that medium rare tenderloin get a little too close to medium. But when the Little Person smirks at me, arms folded, the other 14 diners are going to have to wait.

How many detractors have I turned into fans? I don't know. But I feel like I've won when I pass the plate through the window and watch as it hits the table and I know that is going to be the best tenderloin they've ever eaten. I flick the Little Person off of my shoulder and forget why she ever emerged. My hate is fleeting and doesn't survive the evening. When that customer returns months later, "Bad feeling," I might think to myself. This time, I am certain that whatever they are feeling has nothing to do with me. There is no shrill chant of the little person, "I know you can't, I know you can't, I know you can't."

The sneering face looking at the menu can't shake my confidence tonight. I have seen that face in here before, so it has no power over me. I know why they've come back. I feel called. I know this is why I am here, and this is where my work does the most good. This unhappy person needs me. They are slowly becoming addicted to what I can do for them. They can be unhappy and mean-spirited and snarl at the server and leave a lousy tip. But they avert their eyes from me. They don't want to ruin it. They want to be able to come back if they need to. And they will need to. They are going to need the solace of those green beans. They are going to crave the mouthful of security blanket that is the mashed potatoes. The chicken breast is their mother's breast and it is everything they can do to not press it to their cheek and weep.

I may become a repository for their bitterness, and I turn the other cheek. I don't get angry and give them the silent treatment. I cook for them. There are days that these unhappy faces test me. Even though I know there is something making them bitter and it certainly isn't me, I can't help but get angry. Of course, I've thrown a plate or tossed a ladle with a clatter into the wash tub of the sink. It is because I don't understand. I don't know why a person can't just come into a restaurant and stay if they like what they see or leave if they don't. I bristle at the notion that there is an unhappy segment of the population that acts as if they are repulsed by what I've created. And I am stunned by the ones that play it as if they are unaffected.

That was Bardot. Until she got sober. I hadn't seen much of her after she over salted her own plate of eggs; maybe because I stopped looking for her. It did become clearly obvious that she was gone. In the seven years, the countless hours; I had forgotten about her. Then there was that Saturday Bardot came back. She was pounding on the door at 4:55.

"Should I let them in?" Randy looked at me he was walking toward the door and I was getting ready to say no and to stop him. And then I recognized her, at that point I was going to shout at Randy and yell "NO!", but the door was open, and Bardot looked me in the eye for the first time. She had gained some weight was showing a lot less skin. She was smiling. This was something I really had never seen. Bardot was smiling at me. She rushed over to me and took my hand.

"I moved to Seattle," she explained. Her hair was combed, and she had color in her cheeks. "But I never forgot about you and this place." She could tell I was stunned and not getting any of this. She told me that she had hit rock bottom. The men and women she was sleeping with, the drugs she was taking, her life was becoming an unseemly blur. Some days she woke up not knowing where she was and not knowing the person in the bed or on the floor next to her. But she would stumble into Colorado Kitchen and know that I would be there, and the food reminded her of her mother. Breakfast at Colorado Kitchen was the only sane and real thing in her life. And as it spun wickedly out of control, she lost her job, she lost her apartment, she had little money left; she had come to count on that simple plate of eggs.

Lonely, sweaty days in rehab she would dream of the soft scrambled and the delicate biscuit. It gave her the strength to go on. Life was worth it. She was worth it. There were still good things in the world. And she could have them.

Bardot was crying and then laughing and then crying. I just watched. I couldn't get a word in edgewise. I don't think she wanted me to. She wrapped her long arms around me and squeezed. My feet left the floor.

Bardot's companion had been seated in the meantime at a two top in the back. She had jaw length brown hair and was wearing an oxford shirt and jeans. She looked like the type of person that had a normal job. This woman got up at 6 to be at work at 8 and didn't put up with any bullshit. Just what Bardot needed. Before she sat Bardot turned and waved at me—the only part of that reckless past she cared to remember.

We would be closing Colorado Kitchen in a week. Bardot had good timing. If she had made the trip from Seattle and found only the recipe papered wall of the women's bathroom left standing like so many did who waited until mid-July to visit, she'd have been heartbroken. I was glad that she had made it. I had that feeling about a lot of familiar faces that had become customer and then friend. We'd kept it a secret, that our days were numbered. We wanted to go out quietly, just as we had appeared. The lease was up, and some idiot thought that the space where we served over 500 people a week in 45 seats would make a better condo than restaurant. They'd knock our 100-year-old building down and build a new brick, 5-story monolith on the spot.

Word seeped out about the auction (we put the equipment and furniture on the block) and the town was abuzz. There was chatter on the blogs and headlines on the food sites the last service was imminent. Our air conditioning was on the fritz. At this 11th hour it didn't make any sense to call the repairman. The last days were warm and sticky. Part of me felt guilty for not telling anyone. But we knew that it would be worse than the day of the review. That wicked crazy Sunday the entire staff—front and back of the house—felt like we were drowning. And the phone rang angrily all day. It was better to keep it a secret. Those that kept up, followed the restaurant news would know. It was a small enough population that we could handle it. Still, it relieved my guilt to see a favorite customer come in and have what was secretly their last meal at Colorado Kitchen.

The air was getting heavy on this warm night in July. I watched Lydia pause before digging into today's catch. She covered her face with her napkin. I still saw she was crying. Lydia worked at the Army Medical Center. She'd come in for lunch or an early dinner with a soldier—one young man had the latest in prosthetic arms. More often it is a guy with the long stainless-steel rod of a leg. Her shoulders were shaking, and I was sure it was terrible news. Did one of these young men not make it? I've heard of infections and the increasing suicide rate. I swallowed hard. I was going to have to step up to this one and do what I could to help her through this.

"Lydia," I asked quietly. I didn't want the crowded dining room to turn and gawk at her. "Are you okay?" She looked up at me, her face red and streaked with tears. She got up and came toward me. She was shaking and making it over to me wasn't easy.

"I'm going to miss you guys," she hiccupped and collapsed into my arms. I don't know how my little restaurant came to mean so much to her. But it helped me silence the vocal minority that claimed they saw this coming. And that it was a day that they looked forward to—these were the people that were going to dance on my grave. No matter how much I declared it, they would never believe me. I come in peace. I'm bringing food. I'm full of love. Pish posh, they'd answer back. You can't run a restaurant like that and expect to survive. After seven long years they got to grab a hold of my Little Person and carry her around on their shoulders. Hip Hip…or Ding Dong…I never liked that long line at brunch. Grilled Cheese for the kids, is that really too much to ask? It's just plain ridiculous that I can't get ranch dressing. I thought this place was black owned, harrumph. No reservations. No carry-out. No private party rooms. Why doesn't she smile more back there? I had given up trying to please everybody. And for seven years, the place was a success that changed a neighborhood, brought people out of their homes to dine out again, and made brunch a service that restaurants that wanted to compete in this town had to take seriously again...and not leave to second string cooks and hotels with huge buffet equipment.

I turned to my Little Person and said, "Mission accomplished." She looked at me.

"You think so?" She shoved that sliver of doubt under my fingernail. She knew like I did that as much as Colorado Kitchen made me; who and what I was, was still up for interpretation. *What good did it do to try to speak? I was being tossed about by the current. "Stop. Wait. This is who I am." My protests only filled my mouth with murky water. It was too late now to object whatever definition of me was swirling around. Or if it was safer being a nobody or that perhaps I really was still a nobody—faceless, nameless, and free to be sketched in and painted by whoever had the pen. The truth would be at the bottom of the river with*

me.

Chapter Three

The Mother Sauce

The sixth-grade curriculum at John F. Kennedy Elementary School was interrupted for one week. A long, yellow school bus rumbled to Ashokan Camp in Upstate New York. For $42 our parents could ship us off on the school sponsored trip for a week of reacquainting with nature. The place was a sprawling wilderness with a huge wooden great room where we took our meals and met in the morning and in the evening to hash out the day's events with the staff of hippies—warless hippies fighting for the rights of squirrels and rabbits and not in Vietnam.

On this day I traveled with a quiet counselor named Maria on a nature hike. She was born deaf and talked quietly with wet and rounded syllables that made hearing people stop what they were doing and lean closer to her. When Maria and her group of ten sixth graders made it to the swamp—all of us wearing the rubber boots (number twenty on the list, right under Kleenex and before extra socks) we were instructed to bring— we stopped. We were ready to turn around and call it a day when Maria's face bloomed with a big smile. She suggested we do what she loved to do when she took this walk and wound up at the swamp.

"Let's go hummocking!" she said, cheerfully.

"Wha…?"

"See those tufts of grass?" She pointed to the humps of swamp grass that dotted the stream of mud. Some of them were sixth grade foot sized dry mounds with thick muddy water swirling around them, others supported a scrawny tree, thick enough to clench at the elbow to keep from falling in. She demonstrated for us. We watched as she gracefully hopped from the dry safety of the grassy field to a mud surrounded tuft of grass. From there she wrapped her arm at the elbow around one of those scrawny trees and landed on the next "hummock." She waved her hand to us, her silver thumb ring shining. One by one we followed her bouncing along on the hummocks, squealing as we did our best to keep out of the mud and away from the frogs. Until the wet grass of a hummock slicked the bottom of Glen's bright red rain boot. He grabbed the tree with both hands, but it was too late. Both of his feet slid off of the hummock and he was ankle deep in the mud of the swamp. As he settled into the brown slowly swirling around him, frogs leapt out of his path, girls around him squealed and some of the boys splattered with the spraying mud held their sides and laughed until one by one they slid into the mud around him. Before long, twenty bright red, yellow and basic black boots were sliding off of hummocks and kerplunking into the mud, and then back onto mud covered hummocks. It was a cacophony of shouting, squealing, laughing, groaning of tree limbs, and the cries of birds diving down to snatch up the frogs leaping out of our way.

On the other side of the swamp, stood Maria. She was screaming, too. But there was no look of unbridled glee on her face. Instead she flailed her arms at us and there were tears in her eyes. As we stomped and smashed our way closer to her one by one, we stopped stomping and squealing. The only sounds now were the birds shrieking with hungry delight and Maria in her deaf-person-tongue-folded speak begging us to stop.

"Look," she grabbed us by the shoulders and made us turn around and see what we had done. "Look," she was sobbing. Her voice was strangled by the sobs bursting through her lungs and into her throat. The orderly swirls of the swamp were gone. The scrawny trees were bent over. Hummocks were stained with mud. Water of the swamp pooled in deep, ugly boot prints while two or three birds tore at the homeless frog they'd gotten a hold of.

"You have single handedly destroyed an ecosystem." She turned her back on us and walked back toward camp. She didn't speak to any one of us again for the rest of the week. And for our part we avoided her. But at the end of the week she was there to wave goodbye to our bus like the rest of the hippie counselors. She took each one of us in her arms and apologized. "I'm sorry," she said as she gathered us around her, "I should never have taken you to the swamp." We were all just about to turn 12, not one of us had grown very much pubic hair and she had expected us to favor preserving a fragile ecosystem over playing in the mud. Our bus pulled away and I waved and smiled at the twenty-year-old deaf girl that hoped she had reached us. Rain had started to come down before we made it to the highway. I knew that the rush of water would carve new rivulets through the mud and our boot prints would disappear and frogs would find their way under the hummocks to tongue at flies out of the view of those mad predatory birds that had come to appreciate us.

Maria had taught me something. Some things are lost on some people. Hummocking holds no fascination for a group of kids that just wants to play in the mud.

Sometimes it is not the message, it is the audience. A menu item can play great in one restaurant and fall flat at another. A restaurant's and a chef's failure can mean only that he was fiddling blue grass to folks who were looking to waltz. Or maybe they came to see a classic Hamlet, not the leather and biker rendition. Some of my best efforts have been pushed to the edge of the plate—that "I'm not going to eat that" no man's land of stuff not to be touched. I've seen servers scrape into the trash the rim of pork fat that sweetens the chop, the traditional slab of foie gras that garnishes the seared breast of duck, and even the Riesling jello meant to cut the creaminess of the monkfish sauce. Pearls before swine? That's one way of looking at it. Sometimes it seems like a language barrier. I might as well have just uttered, "Not the soap, the radio." No one is at fault here, really.

A chef is a messenger. We all have something to say. We're noisy people. Words have never been enough. We have spent our lives looking, spying, eating, and listening. These images have all found a way into our brains and they can not be removed. In our kitchens we need the world to hear and feel what happened to us when we had that first bite of foie gras or brioche right out of the oven. Whatever food history we have, the lessons in the kitchens do nothing to deter these. We are imprinted with the first pots and pans that thrilled us. We are the chefs that we are. Take us or leave us. But there are also more factors than food. Were we indulged? Were our parents terrible cooks? Were we potty trained too soon?

I remember the day before I was part of the wild band of sixth graders that destroyed the swamp. I joined the crew that set off with cornmeal and a cast iron skillet to cook in the wilderness. I remember the big black pan getting hot over the fire and the sizzle of the crumbly, yellow batter tumbling into the hot fat about ready to smoke over the glowing bits of hickory. After it baked slowly over the coals, we all descended upon that hot pan of corn bread and devoured it without honey or butter. The edges were crisp, and the cake crumbled hot and moist in our fingers. I had had cornbread before. But I had never had this.

Before we even realize it's happening, moments like this make us the chefs we are today. At the hands of hippies in Vermont I had my first perfect pancake. It was a Stowe Bed and Breakfast run by a sister and brother (he had let his straight brown hair twist itself into dreadlocks) and their flannel-wearing friend—a lanky guy with a big coarse beard who would take the orders then rush back to the kitchen to pull the turnovers out of the oven. They manned the kitchen in overalls and t-shirts. It was mid-June so most of the beds were empty, but people came from all over to crowd the log building for breakfast.

The wild blueberries in the pancakes had been harvested from the fields behind the barn. The berries were tiny but addictively sharp and sweet; they had to be cut with the milder ones from the farmers market before they were tucked into the bran flour dough of the turnovers. But in the pancakes, they studded the light crepe-like batter with bleeding blue excitement. I was about to turn 14 and I had been introduced to a pancake standard that has never been met and one that I still try to meet. The pancake was light and so soft teeth were optional. But the edges, where batter had crept away from the circle and baked wafer crisp, brown, and curly were the best part. The edges shattered under the fork and exploded like malty Pop Rocks against tongue and palette. These were the best pancakes I have ever had. More than 30 years later I can describe them as if I had them every day of my life. Next to "pancake" in my mental dictionary, is that crispy-edged wonder.

As a line cook, you cook what you're told to cook. You bring to life another person's food vision. It's kind of like being the voice of a book on tape but not the author. You can get really good at making that grilled New York Strip with Onion Jalapeno Jam. As a line cook, you might even feel that you own it. It's yours. But it's not. You can make it your own, but only quietly. Chef does not want you to show in his food. When a customer makes up his face over the onion jam, the line cook just shrugs; whatever. No skin off your nose. You're just doing as you're told. Chef wants onion-jalapeno jam. What do you want from me? I'm just following orders.

I played in the high school orchestra. We were busy with Beethoven, Liszt, and Brahms for months at a time until Mr. Thompson unveiled his Symphony. We filed into our places on the rehearsal stage and found his neat, hand scrawled notes on our stands. It was long, slow vibrations from the fattest strings slurring together for the cello and bass sections. Staccato squeals came from the violins. And there were mournful outbursts from the brass. The bassoon sobbed quietly in the corner. The room fell silent after we squawked out the last, harsh note. The half hour piece we sight read through, brought the entire room to the same sad place. We forgot about the A on the paper or that we had made the baseball team.

"So, I'm pretty much standing here naked in front of all of you," Mr. Thompson said to us with an awkward chuckle. No one said a word. The bell rang and we wordlessly packed our instruments and fled the room for our next class.

We were silent because we didn't want to say the wrong thing, hurt Mr. Thompson's feelings, or give him any indication that we understood that he was telling the world how rotten things were going for him. It was awkward. I wonder how Mr. Thompson's piece would have been received by a critic sitting in the balcony at Carnegie Hall. His orchestra smiled polite smiles and chalked it up to our own musical inexperience and maybe our familiarity with the composer—it was a side of him we were uncomfortable seeing. Maybe a paying audience would love to hear Mr. Thompson's pain and heartache. To a group of strangers, being introduced to his life's horrors through brass and strings would have been enlightening, cathartic. I imagine they would have leapt to their feet with tears in their eyes as that last note blared through the hall.

Putting ingredients together is a similar, but far less emotional expression of self. Still, it's personal. Who we are generally determines how we cook. And our first kitchens leave an indelible mark. We love our approach to food. That's why we are wearing that silly outfit. I personally had a brief love affair with posole and thought it would be pretty damn close to brilliant next to a pork chop and slow roasted tomatoes. A regular although often grumpy customer didn't agree. He instructed the server to, "Tell the chef the posole was a bad idea."

My food receives a great deal of praise. But there has been the occasion where what leaves on the plate from my kitchen disappoints. Warranted or not (a customer publicly questioned my serving foie gras hot) I usually hear about it. If you're disappointed in my foie gras and posole it can feel like rejection. Ouch, if you feel compelled to tell me about it. It's a sucker punch if you go behind my back and tell everyone you know. It can best be described as protracted speed dating. You come into my restaurant and try me out to see if I will make it on to your list or will I be rejected. It hurts like hell that you can't wait to get on your computer to tell everyone how you didn't like me. Could it be that we are just not compatible? There was no fast food in my hometown. Maybe we're just different people. We were not meant to be together like that. I can accept that this time it's just not a good match, if you can. "No," you say in a crowded room, "it's not me, it's you."

Then there are those that fall head over heels for me or maybe just the idea of me. He was a big fan from the beginning. He loved the décor and that he could see what was going on in the kitchen. He was one of those customers that were waiting at the door for us to open. He would ask for his steak as well as I could make it. No appetizer or anything to drink but a glass of water with no ice, he didn't mind waiting 20 minutes for the oven to tan his steak. He would give me a nod and a thumbs up when his steak arrived. I couldn't help but watch with train-wreck fascination as his server brought him an extra plate. He'd carefully remove the steak from anything I put with it—sauce, starch, vegetables. On the clean plate he'd use his butter knife to scrape of any remaining sauce, salt, or pepper. His steak was now completely naked.

"The gentleman at table four sends his compliments," the server would tell me heading back to the guy's table with a fresh bottle of ketchup.

"His what?" I had nothing to do with that steak. As far as I was concerned, he was pleasuring himself while looking at a picture of a strange, unattractive woman and calling her my name.

I know, I know. Once that food leaves my kitchen it's not mine anymore. I get that. I really do. But it is almost impossible for me to reciprocate any feelings when you don't trust me (sauce on the side) or if you tell me you dig me, but you'd like me even more if I changed (substitution).

It's hard to accept the rejection when so many times it's been good. I've seen the colored lights in the clean plates, the sounds of longing from a spoon scraping an empty bowl, and the customers moved to vainly search for recipes on the internet for something that sprung from my imagination.

The steak guy would be the one to eulogize me when my body finally emerged from these murky depths. He would tell the crowd gathered at some make-shift memorial about how I grew up in the low country where food was scarce. But once I got a hold of some, they could tell I was gifted. I made magic happen.

115

Chapter Four

Beat to the Ribbon

The murk of the Potomac was in my eyes, but I could suddenly see everything very clearly. "Is this the answer?" I asked myself. I gulped down a mouthful choking on a sob growing in my chest. It was a voice in my head that wasn't mine answering back. The voice was low and rumbling. I felt it more than I heard it. The words were more like a sigh— not really fatigue more just sick of repeating himself. I nodded my head as the voice told me again and again that nothing matters or really makes a difference. The bitterness and grudges were gone. All of my hurts were erased.

"She doesn't want to work for someone so dark." Marta whispered to me. She pursed her lips and raised her chin in Fabiola's direction. Still I shook my head, more to rattle the words out of my brain than to express disbelief. I was having trouble accepting what I was hearing. But earlier I had seen Fabiola run her finger over my white sous chef's arm. "I like you," she said. Then she glared at me before plunging her hands into the hot dish water pulling out the pans, I had dirtied, "O Diiioooossss miiiiiio!"

I had heard that there are some Latin American immigrants in DC that do not like black people. And that in many cases the feeling is mutual. There are black folks who complain that Latinos take all of the jobs, steal what they can't earn, live five people to one a bedroom apartment, and then buy a store and a house with all of the cash they've socked away. As far as some Latinos are concerned, blacks are mean and lazy and don't want to work. Too good for low wage jobs, they're poor and uppity all at the same time.

However, in the commercial kitchen where book learning, speaking English, and high school grades are not nearly as important as knife skills, the stove is the great equalizer. Blacks and Latinos are forced to work together. And work together as a team.

From what I've seen, these relationships transcend ethnicity. In restaurants across the city, friendships and bonds are formed comparable to the battle-tested camaraderie of war buddies.

I could handle Fabiola's irrational dislike of me. I pretended I didn't know. Her being Latina didn't bother me one bit. I hated that she was a drunk. I secretly wanted her to get so sick of my black ass that she walked out. When I caught her in my office twisting the cap on a brown-bagged bottle of Johnny Walker Red, licking the residue from her lips before she applied a new, thick coat of fire engine red, I *really* couldn't stand her. My ex-husband's inability to control himself around the stuff (his brand was Wild Turkey) cost me my house and cushy lifestyle. When my first child, Magalee, was born he was consumed with hiding his addictions. Bottles tumbled off of closet shelves, hidden behind stacks of diapers. When Sian came along, why bother. He was sloppy drunk all day and night and still in bed when I took the kids to school.

She hated that I was really cooking in that kitchen, unlike the white chef who had just been fired. The stacks of dirty pans clattered sharply on

118

the soiled dish table. Chicken breast and beef tenderloin were seared over high heat, staining the pans with fat, collagen, and blood. So, Fabiola was working hard. Her old boss heated boil-in-bags of sauce and roasted meat on precious nonstick pans. The mashed potatoes never stuck to a pot and masher; they were a powder mixed in their toss-away can with hot water from the coffee machine. Before I got there, Fabiola had plenty of time to sit on the green milk crate bent and snapped in places from her weight.

I'm black, and I had her. She was a drunk and she needed this job. She cursed under her breath when the calm of 6:00 turned into the searing heat of 8:30. Dirty plates and hot dirtier pans obstructed our view, but we could hear Fabiola cursing. In the middle of it all she'd disappear, and I knew she was in my office moving the stack of books and receipt tape to get to her bottle of JW. She had the cap off and was covering the threaded top of the bottle with her bright red lips.

One night when the dust had cleared and the plates and pans were cleaned and put away, Fabiola pulled her sweater off of her plump belly so I could see how wet she had gotten. She was pissed. "I can't work like dis!" Jacques, the manager, appeared with the plastic apron he had ordered. Apparently, Fabiola had gotten soaked at the dish station before. And here was Jacques with the promised waterproof apron. "I can't wear dat!" She was livid. I knew she needed a drink, and this wasn't going to get any better until she could get to the Johnny Walker 100 feet away. Instead it escalated with Jacques snatching the apron and shouting back at Fabiola, his long arm extended, and his finger pointed at the door. Fabiola bit down on her lip that was starting to quiver. She brushed passed Jacques, grabbed her coat and the brown bag out of my office and was gone.

I was sorry to see Fabiola go. I knew that it would come to this eventually, but secretly I enjoyed being her boss. I enjoyed being the black one that she complained about on the bus ride home. I liked being the black woman in her nightmares and whose face she wanted to wash out of her head when she put that bottle to her mouth. And, although I suspected that she was the reason I ran out of Turkey mid-way through Thanksgiving dinner service and letting her carve was a bad idea, I held on to the notion that I could make her pay for her hate, slowly but surely.

Simmering under the surface, the irrational hate can't help but slip out. I worked in-between chef gigs at a big seafood house. Long past its prime and with a staff that had long stopped caring; this place was surviving on reputation alone. I worked the daytime hot appetizer station with another single mother. Jennifer had emigrated with her husband from Jamaica fifteen years before. A week before her second daughter was born, her husband disappeared. He hated the states and couldn't tell her. She got a long-distance call from his mother that he had come back home. Jennifer, although often toiling away at her list of chores on her own, seemed to get along with everyone on the mostly Hispanic staff. But she was a favorite with the small core of Chinese immigrants. She was glad to have me work with her a couple days a week. Finally, there was someone she could relate to on a level she'd never had in her fifteen years at this job. I got her jokes. I'm the daughter of Panamanian immigrants. I also studied Spanish all the way through my junior year of college. So, whether I wanted to or not, I got everyone's jokes.

The locker room on the top floor was roach and rat infested. I was coming to work completely in uniform with two knives wrapped in a towel. I was down in the kitchen before the rest of the crew when Jennifer joined me, and we loaded the steam table with the hot menu items. While we worked, Jennifer prattled on about the price of yams and the trouble she was having buying this house she had been renting. Maria arrived and was at the cold station. Her big mass of wavy hair barely fit under her hat.

Three colors of eye shadow faded from blue to gray up to a tight arc of eyebrow and her lips were outlined in black, then brown, and then filled in with mauve. I was glad she worked the cold station. She had way too much paint and fingernail for the hot side. It took me a good 15 seconds to take it all in. She smiled at me and got busy.

Jennifer emerged from the cooler, "*Hola, Maria, mi amiga.*" She said in the little Spanish she could faithfully recite each morning.

"*Hola, cabrona.*" Maria replied without even looking up from her unwrapping lettuce and setting bottles of dressing. I don't remember making a noise, but I may have sharply sucked in a shock of air, or I blurted out a staccato "AH!" The sound that came out of me made Maria turn fast and look at me. She put the bowl of crab meat down and studied my face, not sure if I understood.

"Jennifer?" my eyes still locked on Maria's whose hat needed straightening after realizing the *negrita nueva entiende*.

"Hmmm?" She was busy with her squeeze bottles of sauces.

"Do you know what *cabrona* means?" I had heard the word outside of classroom study. Probably when I first started cooking for a living. The loose translation is a hulking, uncivilized beast of a person.

122

White folks have "white trash," black people fall under the word "nigger", Spanish speaking people say, "*cabrona*."

"Not exactly," she was still digging in the cooler for the last of her bottled sauces, "It means something like *amiga*, right...friend or something?" I didn't answer.

"Does she call you that every morning?"

"Yes, for 15 years. As long as I've worked here." Jennifer stood up straight, pulling her chef coat taut with her hands on her hips. Her station was set and ready. She waved and smiled at her *amiga*, Maria. Maria glanced at me and squinted out a smile, shaking her gloved hand in Jennifer's direction.

Language can be a weapon. I've used it. I never found it necessary in a stress-free kitchen like the one in the old seafood house. That's the kind of place where if things go well or not...what the hell? Tomorrow is another day. But as a chef and as an owner, the small things, the minutes, the forks, carry more weight than staff can recognize. At Colorado Kitchen we often went through a bad workforce pattern. It would roll in like a cold front pushed south by the jet stream and there we were; no dishwasher, not enough servers for Saturday night or Sunday brunch and these were the days that the equipment joined in—the ice machine, usually, would drop one glass full of ice all day long.

The worst part of these days was new staff training. Robin handled the servers. I had to bend the dish washer into shape. It sounds like an easy job, but it isn't. It takes organizational skills and stamina to not get overwhelmed and start to unravel. I've had dish washers whistling and relaxed. Then as if from nowhere pans pile up and the bus boys would bring in tub after tub of dirty plates. The calm dish washer was now running around the dish room not knowing where to begin.

Part of the training is always a lesson in organization and keeping one's cool. But the job had to be done without sacrificing the health code. Wash, rinse, sanitize and dry. The temptation to wipe the plates and plastic containers with the towel slung over the apron you'd been wearing to peel shrimp was great. But it violated the health code. "*Seco para aire*," I repeated four or five times in an hour when I saw the towel going over my plates. I'd take the stack back and put it in the pile of dirties again. "*Seco para aire*," I'd say again, this time after getting a stack of wet plates.

"Yes, I know," said Roberto. Sergio had sent him to us. Sergio is the employment director at the Latino Social Center. New to the country, down on their luck, recovering from addiction, they came to Sergio for a hand up. He'd dust them off and straighten their collars and send them to us when we called. It often took four or five phone calls before we had a match. Roberto was phone call number two, and I knew before the night was over, I would be calling Sergio a third time.

"*Que haces?*" Roberto spoke perfect English. I knew that. He had a Maryland accent. I knew that he had grown up here. "*Seco para aire, por favor,*" I repeated. I refused to speak to him in English.

"Okay."

It was Saturday night and I had very little time to repeat myself to a dish washer who knew perfectly well what I was talking about. I explained to him about the germs on the towel that are transferred to the plates and then into people stomachs. I explained that wet plates stacked and trapping water also become breeding grounds for colonies of bacteria.

"*Comprende?*" I asked him, fixing his eyes with mine.

"Yes, I understand." He was irritated. Because I wasn't speaking to him in English or because he didn't want to be working as a dish washer; I didn't know or care. But I was a camel and the straws were mounting. I had a dining room full of hungry people and instead of cooking I was

125

soaking my chef coat bringing stacks of wet plates back to an obviously intelligent, physically capable, English speaking dish washer. His willful disobedience was going to break one of us. I had few weapons at my disposal; language would have to do. I could eliminate his American upbringing, his high school diploma from a local school, and put him on a sugar cane truck back in El Salvador by refusing to speak to him in English.

"*Eres tonto o pendejo?*" I asked him. My voice had progressed to a growl.

"No, I'm not stupid and I'm not an asshole," he answered too calmly for my liking.

"*Entonces por que no lo haces el camino le pregunte?*" I was throwing the plates at him now. Roberto was showing incredible restraint. Like me, he was ready to explode. But instead of punching me in the mouth, he shrugged. I had gotten close enough to see his eyes had grown red and watery from bottling in his anger. I was getting under his skin just as much as he was getting under mine.

"I'm done with you, man," I walked away from him and back to the line, "*Vaya te!*"

* * *

"I'm sorry to say it, Gillian." Kenneth said, mopping at the sweat gathering in his eyebrows. "But I am sick of these black guys."

"I'm sick of them, too." I took the last five-dollar bill, all the cash I had until pay day and stuffed it deep in my pants pocket. If anyone of the crew saw that bill they were going to try and weasel it out of me. I had heard all of the sob stories now. Milk, rent, phone bill, bookie—the truth was as I was slow to learn, all that money was being spent at the corner liquor store. It is a place that black, white, Hispanic staff all had in common.

But this time we were all feeling taken. Even the liquor store's best customers had parted with booze money thanks to the latest dish washer now AWOL. Howard had come in big, strapping, handsome and simple as a field hand. His smiling, "aw shucks" had all of us fooled. "I came up from Nor' Cahlina with my uncle." He explained. "E'ry year he come up nort' selling melon. This time I decided to say up here. Try my hand at city life." We all smiled at him and nodded along. He thanked us for everything: a job, family meal, a glass of ice water—a dozen thank yous each time he was handed something. "I'm stayin' at the YMCA. It sure is good to have a shower with water that's all yourn."

His second day he asked me if I noticed he was wearing the same jeans he'd had on the day before. I admitted that I hadn't noticed. "I'd like to buy me a couple new pairs of jeans." He smiled and told me about a sale at the Sears down the road. "They got 'em for $15 a pair." He fished in his pockets and pulled out a few buttons, a metro bus token, and four nickels. It was as if he was wearing someone else's pants and was sure that the treasure in his pockets was going to get him jeans and a new car. Finding only buttons and nickels his lips closed quickly over his bright white teeth and his chin touched his chest. I thought he was going to cry. "And its two weeks 'til payday id' n' it?" His drooping lower lip brought his big, square shoulders down. He was shrinking down to my height right before my eyes. "You don't think you could lend me enough for a couple a pair 'til pay day, could ya Chef?" I took two twenties and a five out of my wallet and placed them in his big hand. "You sho' are the nicest folk." He raised his shoulder to wipe the corner of his eye with his shirt sleeve, his hands now elbow deep in soap suds.

Howard was in a good mood those three days he worked the morning shift washing pans and dishes—he'd sing along to the radio and get the words wrong on hymns out by the trash. He watched me clean the

15 pounds of squid that I was showing him how to prep. "I just don't get how you peel that skin offah thar." His eyes bright with wonder.

Then Friday came. I unlocked the door and was a little surprised he hadn't come in right behind me. Before long it was three in the afternoon and my chef coat was wet and hot from washing dishes and then running back to the stove to sear a burger. We had to say it out loud to believe it. The employee who had become our favorite was gone.

"Guess, I ain't gettin' my $10 back," said Rosheana, grabbing a handful of ladles for the salad station.

"Wait…" Stephanie was putting the pieces together, "You lent him $10?" Rosheana nodded. "I gave him $50 so he could get his things shipped up from North Carolina."

"I gave him $30 so he could buy groceries." Kenneth confessed. He had started to polish a glass but stopped and realizing he had been snookered, put the spotty glass on the shelf.

"I gave him my last $5 and about $40 in food stamps," Ronald admitted, reluctantly.

"Add my $45 to that." I said. Stephanie did the math after polling the rest of the staff. Our simple country boy had taken us for about $300.

"I'm sure he's back on that melon truck and headed back home by now," Stephanie broke the bad news to us. We all quietly vowed to be less trusting and more suspicious than we had been. I decided that in the morning I would stop at the beggar's toll booth off of the bridge and invite one of the cardboard-sign-carrying men down on their luck to get into my old Subaru and make an honest wage.

I rolled down my window and a man lowered his cardboard and held out his hand.

"Get in. I need a dish washer." He looked at me with suddenly wide eyes. Was he scratching his beard to ponder the possibilities—a real job, maybe a bed to sleep in? Or did he just itch? "I'll give you $50." He turned his back to me and headed for the open window of the car beside me to collect the quarter held out to him. Okay, maybe he didn't understand me.

"*Venga!*" I shouted to him. His dirty blonde hair matted into white-guy dreadlocks under the ski cap gave him away. The light turned green before I knew it. I lingered for a bit until the traffic behind me urged me to get passed it with anxious horn blaring.

But when I got to the restaurant, Kenneth was showing a slight man in ill-fitting clothes how the three-compartment sink went from *lavar, aguilar,* to *disinfectar.* "He doesn't speak a word of English." Kenneth explained with a big smile on his face. "You'll see," He assured me. "Hispanics are just better workers. No more black guys."

Humberto was a little slow. The daytime crew was frustrated when dirty pans weren't coming back clean when they needed them. They would wind up with nothing to sear a tenderloin or toss pasta in sauce. The stack that sat on the burner had dwindled to the one white hot one that was used to quickly reduce a sauce in an emergency. They left the line to go over to the sink and scrub them out themselves. Humberto would step back and watch Richard or Best scour five or ten hot pans and then splash them in the rinse sink. When they were done and back at the stove, he'd take the sponge in his hand and go back to rubbing soap on the pan he'd already been working on for the past five minutes.

An unexpectedly slow lunch had us scratching our heads the next day. Humberto spent the first two hours filling the sinks and arranging his sponges. The rest of us pulled equipment away from the walls scraped the grease-dirt-food glue that the exterminator wanted us to get at, pulled out all of the fish and covered it with ice, re-wrapped the pork chops, and set chickens on to roast. We didn't see Humberto fall. But when we heard him cry out, Richard turned around.

"What wrong wit you, man?"

"*Dolor...dolor...!*" Humberto was on the floor. He managed to take off his apron. After Richard helped him to his feet, he clutched both kidneys and stumbled through the dining room and out the front door.

"What was that all about?"

"I think he wants the rest of the day off," Ronald concluded. "Chef, you gonna tell Kenneth what happened to the beaner?"

Kenneth came into the kitchen his face red and his baseball cap damp on the brim from perspiration, "Don't call him that. He works harder than all of you combined." He got really close to Ronald. Their hats were close to touching before Ronald stepped back.

We forgot all about Humberto, until the next morning. He had come back, in all of my years in the kitchen this happens only when there's a paycheck to be collected. But here he was in the same clothes he'd been wearing all week and standing upright and it was another week until pay day. Kenneth rushed to the door. Humberto backed away and held a pastel green piece of paper out to Kenneth.

"Sign." He said. We'd never heard him speak English. Kenneth kept his distance but tilted his head slightly and said, "*Como?*"

"Sign," Humberto repeated in the same bland, emotionless tone, unaffected that our angry manager had stepped even closer to him. Kenneth grabbed the paper from him. His eyes darted back and forth, and his breathing came fast in sharp drags through his mouth. He turned the paper and held it in the middle with both hands. He was shouting something I couldn't understand and was throwing the jagged bright green pieces in Humberto's face.

Tearing up the paper did no good. Kenneth still had to show up at the hearing at the county offices and explain that Humberto did not hurt his back the day he screamed and ran off. There was no basis for his Worker's Compensation claim.

But it was Shorty who did more for black and Latino relations than all of the town sponsored festivals meant to build community. He stood on a milk crate at the dish machine and worked with an unwavering scowl. He could clean a stack of hot pans and then jump back on the crate and clean the entire dining room worth of plates and glasses. He worked wordlessly but kept a wooden spoon in his pocket to unclog the disposal but also to slap any hand that attempted to take a sponge or snatch a towel. Shorty feared no one. His spoon came down on some pretty big hands. *Hang on Sloopy* would come on the radio and Shorty would sing along in Spanish.

"What you singin', Shorty?" Ronald laughed, "That ain't how that song go."

Shorty interrupted himself just to curse at Ronald in Spanish then went right back to singing. The entire kitchen erupted in laughter and started singing right along with him in English, Spanish, or whatever came to them.

At a little more than four and a half feet tall, Shorty had the temper of a much bigger man. "I had a table say something about it," Chrissy explained. "You're making a little too much noise back here with those plates."

"*Ay, puta*." Is all he said before throwing his arms in the air, his apron to the floor and tossing the wooden spoon from his pocket into the stainless-steel door of the dish machine before storming through the crowded dining room and out the front door.

"What did you do?" Kenneth shouted at her. "You'd better go after him." The all black line stared at Chrissy. Pans were over heating, nothing was dropped into the fryer, tongs and ladles were motionless. Chrissy was starting to grasp the magnitude of what she'd done correcting Shorty. Her arms folded over her chest her lower jaw moved slightly from left to right and she shifted her weight as if her shoes were too tight.

"Well?" Kenneth asked.

"Hmmph, I'll go get him," Rosheana glared at Chrissy. Her narrowed eyes moved up and down over the owner's small frame as if she were looking for a soft spot to jab the paring knife. "She's liable to say somthin' stupid and make things worser." She grabbed Shorty's apron off of the floor and made her way through the crowded dining room. "Damn, she gotta big mouth…Shorty gone…. she done fuck up a wet dream." She cursed Chrissy as she made her way across the black and white tiled floor and out into the street. Through the plate glass window, we could see her lips moving spit and swear words flying out onto the sidewalk.

135

***

It had been three years now and we had settled into a comfortable groove at Colorado Kitchen. Much of that was spurred by a purging of dysfunctional staff. The server who was stealing out of the register was long gone. The one-armed dishwasher found a new job. The neighborhood kids so anxious to prove themselves at our store as bus boys couldn't make it through the slow summer. They dozed in the dining room and couldn't stand to see their friends through the plate glass window with rolled beach towels under their arms. Robin and mine were the only familiar faces by the time winter came.

Good reviews brought positive attention and folks who really wanted to work for a living. The more experienced staff quickly got the rhythm of each day. It seemed we could absorb the crazy busy of a Saturday night and keep our stride. I had even gotten the kitchen to work like a well-oiled machine. We ran out of food, rarely now. Menu items came together without confusion and panic. I had more moments where I could exhale and look around the room. Customers could see I was relaxed, and it was safe to approach me. They'd ask for recipes or advice about

136

roasting chicken and baking rolls. Some would offer suggestions or congratulations.

And then there were the comments that made me stop what I was doing completely and bite my tongue. A black man about my age came up to me as the full dining room began to clear out. The kitchen was closed, and the last desserts were in the pickup window. "I appreciate what you're doing, building a restaurant in this neighborhood," he turned his head toward the front door. Superman (the damaged Vietnam vet from the drug rehab half-way house around the corner who wore the superman t-shirt under a brown, pinstripe suit jacket) was making his twenty-first lap around the block. "It's a shame you couldn't hire more of these young African-Americans to work here."

"I guess it is just me and Edward, now," I answered making sure he could see the temperamental and always perspiring gay man bringing coffee to table 10. "Honestly, it's not like we didn't try." Not sure he would have cared to hear it. But he left before I could tell him how hard we tried and that it seemed that our young African-American staff was determined to ruin us. Robin and I silently agreed that race would not be an issue when we hired people. It would not appeal to some of our

137

neighbors or community leaders, but it meant survival. There was black, white, and Latino staff that thought nothing of setting the law on us.

* * *

By the time we got passed the metal detectors it was already ten minutes after nine. We counted on a long list of cases that Friday morning and hoped we wouldn't miss our name being called and have to see the judge or pay a penalty or worse have the clerk shout out "COLORADO KITCHEN" a bunch of times. I was hoping for discretion, slipping in and out unnoticed. I wanted to do nothing to call attention to myself or this ridiculous situation we found ourselves in.

The courtroom was crowded. We could be here all day. We had decided to close for lunch, but now I worried that there wouldn't be enough time to get ready to open for dinner. It all depended on the efficiency of these slow-moving wheels. A heavy sigh and my shoulders drooped.

There's an awkwardness when walking into a courtroom that no matter how many times I've found myself in this predicament it overwhelms me. I marvel at the ease with which those men and women in suits carrying fat brief cases stride around these rooms where they make their living. I suppose they would say the same looking into a restaurant kitchen. Plaintiff? Defendant? Good? Evil? Where to sit? We made our way through the center aisle and headed left. I had gotten to the middle of the pew, sliding along on my ass in one of the few pair of pants that aren't chef's hounds' tooth. Gray hair and thick, smudged glasses emerged from the black and white curtain of newspaper behind me. "Have you checked in with the clerk?" He asked, his ill-fitting partial snapped down over his words. We slid back out of our seats and stood in the line near the witness stand. When it was my turn, I did what everyone else had done. I handed the clerk the form letter printed through carbon that had come in the mail last month ordering us to appear in DC Superior Court Civil Actions Branch. Broome vs. Colorado Kitchen.

"Are you Colorado Kitchen?" she asked not raising her eyes from the list. "Have a seat." Sliding back into the seat I was about to whisper, "He's not here," into Robin's ear. But just then she pointed with her chin to a tight, wrinkled, beige suit a couple of rows ahead of us. "He probably wore that to graduation." She muttered.

"I don't think so."

"That's right. He dropped out, didn't he?"

Barton Broome didn't look good. His hair was wilder than usual and his calm, surfer-dude chill was gone. He was wide eyed and jittery as if the ill-fitting suit was lined with angel hair. It was hard now to recall the day he walked into the storefront that was on its way to becoming Colorado Kitchen. He was handsome and anxious to learn. He seemed to want to put his bad boy days behind him. He had quit school, engaged in petty crime, and started a rap group. Lately, there was more petty crime in his Friday and Saturday nights than parties and rapping. A job at Colorado Kitchen just might be the way to get out of this mess.

I liked him immediately. He was a likable guy. He got the joke and had an easy smile. Customers thought he was charming. A woman dining alone would find herself listening to Barton tell her all about the car he was planning on buying. And after 15 minutes of listening to tales of fuzzy dice and chrome rims she'd suddenly remember that she came to get something to eat and that she was hungry. But what the hell, watching this handsome young man talk, his hands tracing the shape of the fender, licking his lips as he talked about racing stripes and flaming skull decals was much more interesting than eating. The meatloaf could wait. Sometimes I'd have to interrupt from the open kitchen, just to get the plate of meatloaf from under the killing heat of the pickup window.

Having no work experience, he was a clean palette and more trainable than the kids who had worked at KFC and thought the same rules applied and whose food knowledge was limited to two-piece dark or two-piece white. In no time at all Blanton had become one of our best servers. Not that we had a stellar professional crew. There were nights I hid my face in my hands or threw a plate across the room. Behind the line, my eye would catch a blunder in the dining room more often than not. Sunday brunch refills of orange juice from the frost covered plastic jug. "Don't mind if I do," to the customer offering a bite of her apple crisp. Blueberries being scraped off of a slice of cheesecake because the server forgot the order was berries on the side. Barton took correction in stride, though.

"Hey, Barton. Do you think the blue stains on that cheesecake will give it away?"

"I suppose it might, Chef." The scraping spoon gradually slowed down to a halt.

I couldn't help but get him another piece and then forget all about it. He didn't argue with me. He didn't get defensive. He looked at the piece of cheesecake in his hands. His best effort of making good on forgetting the SOS would not get past a 5-year-old. And he knew it. That's what made me like Barton.

I had 13 years in this business and still there were servers that would have taken that blueberry covered cheesecake to a customer and waited to be called back over.

"I'm terribly sorry, Ma'am." He'd briskly remove the plate from the offended customer. "The kitchen is just not on today," he'd add with a "we're-in-this-hand-basket-together" smirk.

I was stunned and hurt that I had to leave the kitchen during a busy Sunday brunch and help Robin pry Barton's fingers off the door jam and throw him out. I was the one that pressed the panic button that called the cops when he came back with his uniform rolled into a medicine ball and threw it into Robin's face.

Both his cousin and best friend had only been able to manage to work a couple of days. Cousin Alvin left in the middle of his shift. Snuck out the back door, hopped a fence and ran home. Jason washed dishes in the morning and walked out after I yelled at him for writing on the piano. Somewhere in the back of my brain, I knew Barton wouldn't last. Those two crabs in the bottom of the crab pot would pull at him and tell him he's a fool for working—working for those two women who didn't appreciate him. Why not just take the money, buy the car…yeah, have them work for you? But I never expected to get the letter in the mail from the DC Superior Court informing me that Barton was suing his former employer for "unlawfully dismissing him and costing him $14,000 in potential wages."

"It's an auspicious day, yo' Honor," he pronounced carefully, with a broad smile.

But his smile had somehow gone from being able to illicit thoughts like "how did I wind up naked oh never mind come here you" to "can I run faster if I take these shoes off?"

"I've forgotten what Friday morning was like in this courtroom," the judge said, looking at Barton, his eyes moving up and down over the slivers of his reading glasses. The room erupted with laughter.

When Barton started to tell his story, I stopped worrying that the judge would somehow see his side…poor kid against the two big bad business owners.

"You do understand, young man that this is Civil Action," the judge told him his arms folded over his chest and the humor gone from the corners of his mouth. "And you representing yourself here for a pretty large sum of money. I'm going to treat you like I'd treat any of the other attorneys in this room." There was a hush and grumble in the room as the ones in gray and pinstripe acknowledge their own wounds met at the hands of this judge. "Why don't I do us all a favor and dismiss this Civil Action and let you re-file in small claims."

Barton's day in court wasn't turning out like he'd imagined. The car wasn't going to be a solid gold Cadillac and Colorado Kitchen wasn't going to turn over all of its assets to his recording company. Still, this was one of those experiences that can spoil your palette with your own bile.

It's probably one of the most difficult things to swallow as a chef and business owner. One day the person you hired, the one you trusted to do a job because the science of cloning just isn't there yet; will turn on you. I've had a lot of people work for me. I've been lucky that only one has taken me to court. For the most part, most of my relationships with staff and former staff have been positive.

This is the industry that attracts and sustains people that are barely hanging on. There's a great deal of cash every night if you're a server. There are plenty of mindless tasks back in the kitchen—washing dishes,

144

peeling potatoes—you can do well enough burnt or still stoned. Folks compromised by addiction, psychosis, even itchy fingers try to become part of society—get a job pay the bills, come home at night. But they can't. They try really hard—or as hard as they are able. And the old friend from the neighborhood, the fuck buddy from back in the day, a gift bottle of cheap vodka can tip the little choo choo that is so easily derailed.

But I've also hired the one that knows who he is and likes it. He loves his addiction and wouldn't leave it for the world. This guy is just faking it. He smiles sweetly, gets the door, cooks the recipe just as he should, fixes the problem—is the perfect employee, that is, until its time. Then he's gone. And if he's the itchy finger kind, so is all of the tenderloin you ordered for the weekend or the entire tip jar from Saturday night.

These are the ones that stick with you. The ones that ended in or limped along to disaster stay with you and keep you from hiring a guy with the same kind of turn of the lip, or a gal that shares a previous employees delay in returning calls, or something as silly and simple as he has the same name as the one stealing you blind. The years have taught me how to tell a drunk. I've also learned that they come in all shapes and sizes, income levels, education, race, and gender. Some chefs are strong enough to fire on the spot. I admit I've given in. I've allowed the third and fourth one more chance. I've bought the story—a father's funeral turned out to be the fifth or sixth time the old man has been buried, there is no child to get sick, or mother to fall down the stairs and need looking after.

Now I take a quick survey when the checks come back with the bank statement: who's cashing their check at the liquor store, who has a bank account, who's using the check cashing place that gouges them for 25%? I keep an eye on the staff that bank at the liquor store. The fast talker telling me how great a dish washer he is but needs his pay that same day in cash so he can catch a cab home gets the heave ho as soon as I can get a word in edgewise.

A few years ago, I would have let this guy get passed his first day. I would have given him enough cash to get home and bit my nails hoping he came in the next day. I would be so relieved to see him; I couldn't possibly give him the negative reinforcement of an old-fashioned shouting at. The finally exhaling smile I give him as he apologizes for being an hour late could well have been me collapsing into his arms and batting my eyelashes as if he just yanked me off of the tracks. Maybe if I let him stay, he'll blow all of his pay on heroin or crack so that he won't be able to come up with the $60 he needs to pay for his room. He'll take that green plastic trash bag and carry a box of pork chops or a nine-pound tenderloin out with the trash—hide it somewhere he can grab before he hops on the bus. "Can I put you down for an order of the clear trash bags, Chef?"

A restaurant kitchen is a busy place. My left eye twitches with anxiety over the rotten box of lettuce the produce guy tried to leave here. I'm also wringing my hands over the inventory…too little ground beef and too much red snapper. The floor under my feet widens with cracks. Things can easily not get done, go missing, or disappear. Finding a staff person that jumps right in and takes over with confidence and competence is like a gift box wrapped in ribbon falling out of the sky. It hurts when it's this person, someone you've come to rely on that you've got to cut the rope on. He's the Sherpa that got you up the mountain, he's eaten more than his share of the rations and that's okay. But now he's fallen from up there hammering a spike into the rock, dangling and swinging—if you don't rub the edge of your knife across that groaning rope right now, you're all going to go down.

I remember pushing the kitchen doors open every morning to find the stove lit and every burner occupied, the steam table puffing away, mise

147

en place brimming from all of the squares in the cooler and Castro in his chef coat with his apron tied tight under his round belly.

"Mornin' Chef," he'd say, way too cheerfully for 9 am.

"Hey, Castro." buttoning the top of my chef coat, I'd peer into the pots he had going on. "You need the consommé to get started or the potatoes ready to boil?"

"Got it all done, Chef." He answered wiping his red, pudgy hands on a towel. Then he'd lift the lids off of the bains in the steam table and show me the leek-studded mashed potatoes, white and creamy filling their 2-gallon container. Then he'd show me the consommé—steaming hot, clear and smelling of roasted chicken.

"How long have you been here?"

"Been here since 7, Chef." He shifted his watch so that the face rotated to the edge of his hairy wrist bone and he could see that it was just about 9:30. "There's a lot to get done before that lunch crowd gets here."

He was adding an extra 10 hours a week to the payroll. I didn't care. It was 20 things I didn't have to worry about every morning. I needed Castro. I was at that point where I could not imagine my life without him in it. Maybe it was showing. I would look for the veal bones in the walk-in and they'd be gone. Castro had them already in the 40-quart spigot pot simmering gently with onion scraps and carrot ends. The salmon was already cleaned and portioned. It wasn't until I noticed that my usual 25 pounds wasn't lasting the week, did I notice something was wrong. I started counting and weighing every day, still I ended the day with a phone call, "Liam, I'm going to need another 10 pounds of salmon."

Then the worst started to happen, and the honeymoon was over. I pushed the kitchen doors open and the stove was cold. The steam table was full of ice water. There weren't even any potatoes peeled. I was out of shape and caught off guard. It had been months since I had done the set up. Where the hell was Castro? I ran around that kitchen, to the stove, in the walk-in, back to the stove, grabbed a knife. I looked like a rookie, breathing heavy and cutting off the tip of my finger. I was obviously distracted—should I be worried or irritated? It's 10:00 am, do you know where your morning sauté cook is?

The next morning, I came in my shoulders sagging under the weight of my chef coat seams. Still no Castro. I rushed around again that morning. Ahmed came in behind me and took his position at a prep table.

He pulled the apron strings from behind his back and tied the bow above his belt.

"Castro is out there, Chef," he said quietly. "He wants to see you. I think he's crying." I went into the hallway and saw Castro sitting with his head in his hands at his locker. He was still wearing his prize denim jacket, the one he kept in his car so the smells and grease in the air wouldn't get to it.

"I'm really sorry, Chef," he hiccupped. "My wife, she got that utero cancer and I don't know what I'm going to do if she dies." I gave him the day off and let him come back. He promised to beat me in the next morning. Just as he said, Castro beat me in the next day. Steam wafted over the pots simmering on the stove and he was mashing cream and leeks into a big bowl of potatoes. It was a happy sight. Things were looking like they were getting back to normal. I left the kitchen to Castro and went into the walk-in. Yesterday's delivery of salmon was gone.

I stood there for a minute staring at the ice bin. There was fish in there last night. Now poking out of the half-melted shards was a couple of pounds of jumbo lump crabmeat, and 5 pounds of squid tubes and tentacles. The ten-pound flat plastic fish box had just a few cut and cleaned fillets. It didn't do any good to look around. The walk-in was neatly organized. Butter and eggs on one shelf. Produce on the opposite side. Fish was waist high above the tenderloin sealed in skin-tight plastic.

I must have been in there a while. When I came out the rest of the morning crew had filed in. Ahmed had the blender going, pureeing his mock lobster bisque that oddly required corn flakes. Sotera was busy filling squares of puff pastry with caramelized onion for the Caramelized Onion-Gorgonzola Turnovers. But Castro wasn't in front of the stove.

"Castro?" Ahmed shouted, he must have noticed me standing there, staring at the cold pots, my hands on my hips and my breath coming in short and fast. "He said he had to go get a lottery ticket." I could hear someone shouting. But by the time I noticed they had been shouting my name, I had my old Volvo in reverse, and I was starting a sharp, squealing three-point turn out of the parking lot and after Castro's old red Firebird. I made a left turn at the light and came around the corner north of the hardware store. I caught up to him at the bar that I could tell from the outside needed a visit from the health department. I'd never been inside. But the windows were tinged yellow from airborne grease. There was enough gap at the bottom of the door for rats to squeeze in from the cold.

Castro worked there during football season when they needed an extra hand to drop fries and toss wings in hot sauce. There he was leaning back a little as he laughed. His hand stretched above his head as he guided the trunk of his car open. As I pulled up beside him, I recognized the guy that owned the place. He wasn't laughing. He squinted his sleepy looking eyes to focus on Castro. He grabbed the cigarette from his lips and blew smoke out behind it. He was shaking his head "no" and dismissing the contents of Castro's trunk with a soft wave of his hand.

I walked over to them without bothering to slam my door shut. But I guess they heard me breathing. Castro turned around sharply and fumbled to get his hands out of his denim jacket pocket to slam the trunk shut. The bar owner just pushed his heavy eyebrows up at me and tossed the cigarette onto the pavement.

"Castro, is that my salmon you've got in there?" I was wishing I had brought a baseball bat or something. I was out hundreds in salmon and here was this shiny red Firebird. My salmon was paying for the wax he rubbed all over it. I wanted to smash the windshield. No one was saying anything. With the flick of his lighter, the bar owner lit another cigarette and did his best to be heard over my heavy breathing.

152

"You know, Chef," he took a second to pull air through his Camel and the end crackled and glowed red. "He's been bringing me this shit about three times a week. Listen, I don't know who he's selling it to. I don't want it." My eyes were fixed on Castro. He was looking down and wishing I would let go of his trunk so he could slam it shut and pretend it was just old rags and tire irons in there. "He's a jerk for stealing from you and I've told him I don't want any part of it." The cigarette hit the pavement and he left Castro and me out there to pick up the pieces or just kick them out into the street to be run over by the traffic racing over Leesburg Pike. Castro tried to sob his way out of this one...his father's death, his wife's cancer (she died two weeks later). He needed money, he told me. While he sobbed, I carried the salmon like a wounded child into my trunk. I slammed my door shut, shifted into first and left Castro in that parking lot. In my mirror I could see him kicking the bits of crap that littered the pavement out from under the fat tires of his Firebird. "Son of a bitch," I shouted at his reflection.

Castro taught me to look the gift horse in the mouth like I am the gift horse's dentist. But nothing prepared me for Raul. Raul was the kind of worker you could set your watch by. He came in 15 minutes before his

153

start time and got ready for work. He did everything exactly as I showed him; from mopping the floor to cutting onions rings. He limped around on a bum leg tirelessly, carrying full bus buckets and racks of glasses hot and wet from the dish machine. He never whimpered under the constant flow of dirties during Sunday brunch. And when Raul's shift was over, he left the kitchen immaculate. Two years into my time with Raul there came that Saturday he didn't come in. We washed and cleaned in his absence, hoping he'd be in the next day with a sling on his arm or a black eye. He didn't come in Sunday. We washed and waited all the next week until we had to say it out loud to ourselves. Raul was gone. His size 8s were big shoes to fill and we did it after four or five tries. We had stopped missing him when he stumbled in months later. He wanted his job back, but he would take his check if that was all we were able to do. His eyes were red, but glistening and giddy. He reeked of marijuana. I noticed the woman—short and big-breasted waiting for him outside.

I'd hire Raul again, taking the risk that he wouldn't let a pair of tits drag him off of the wagon. Some of my best workers have had some addiction or another. Mike was a tall and handsome server who, on his first shift, glided around the dining room like he designed it. If someone

154

ordered the monkfish by mistake, he'd sell it to another table before it had a chance to die in the window.

"Oh sorry, I didn't mean to order Monkfish, I need a steak,"

"Damn it, Eddie."

"Sold it," Mike would be leaving a table and heading for the POS to punch in the order. I found it hard to believe that someone needing a certain level of intoxicant in his body just to keep his sail from luffing and his keel in the water was always so aware of the chaos around him. And, still have the wherewithal to put out the fire. But on a Friday or Saturday night, Mike would fill the glass a bit too full, drain it and fill it again. At two in the afternoon he still couldn't hold his pants steady to get his foot through the pant leg that was avoiding his big toe like a roach discovered under the edge of a throw rug. I would fantasize about how great it would be to have a dining room full of tall handsome Mikes: tall enough to reach all of the plates in the pickup window, smart enough to know how to sell ice cream in December, but without his addictions.

His wagon was hitched to wild horses. They were going a pretty good clip when he fell off and he too disappeared. How many restaurants can you charm your way into, be the best server for nights on end and then suddenly be a no show then call an hour after you should have been there to say you can't find your wallet or you're lost in Gaithersburg? With a little bit more than 40,000 new restaurants opening each year, Mike can pretty much live like this until his liver fails.

In my years running kitchens I knew what I was searching for, although it was impossible to articulate until now. I was looking for that reliable, knowledgeable, trustworthy staff member. Capable of almost reading my mind, this person was almost a clone but could also function as the eyes in the back of my head. Yet this cook could also have the ability to help me focus without the distractions of my own ego. I was searching for a well-seasoned pan.

I was wrestling with my young staff. No one would work on Sunday nights. I found myself in an empty kitchen once the brunch crew cleared out. Some brunch shifts were staffed only after I begged and cajoled and promised a $1 more an hour.

"Soccer," offered Chip, the bartender on step 11 of his 12-step program.

"Not church?"

"You're kidding, right?" He laughed at me. "Church, that's a good one."

I was feeling defeated and tired working the line and being chef all at the same time. I had no time to make those food cost saving soups and specials with scraps and leftovers. Food costs shot up to 36%. Turning around after a hectic Saturday night, made me dread Sundays all the more.

I was too busy and too tired by Wednesday. As lunch sputtered to an end late in the afternoon, I ignored the server when she came through the swinging doors to tell me there was a cook at the bar waiting to see me about a job. I knew how this was going to go. There had been as steady stream of friends of my current cooking line and soccer squad. He was going to tell me how great and fast he was and how he could work three days a week and not at all on Sunday.

Kathy came in again and I had to turn off the pepper grinder to hear her. There was no way she could shout over the peppercorns flying away from the blade; smoking and the occasional crack pipe had taken much of her lung capacity.

"Chef, you should talk to this guy." I looked up at her over my glasses, still not convinced I should even budge. I turned the grinder back on. But she was still standing there. She said waiting for me to turn the grinder off again. "He's old. He's not one of those kids."

I washed my hands and went out there. She was right, he was old. Not quite a grandfather but getting there. He had ten years on me easily. But when I came close to the table he sprung up from his chair and took my hand with a slight bow. He quickly pulled out a chair for me and slid it close behind my legs. He jetted back to his seat and had his butt in the cushion before I could bend my standing-all-day-stiff knees and sit down. He started talking immediately. "Chef?" his accent was sing-song Bolivian, dotted with Mid-Atlantic clichés. I wasn't really listening about his running the kitchen at the Irish Pub across the street and his cooking stints in London. I was already fitting him in on the schedule, starting this Sunday.

Carlos and I worked the Sunday double like two old cooks that had been at it together for years. As I smoked oil in the aluminum pans to gloss them to a non-stick finish, he'd chuckle to himself as the smoke was sucked outside by the exhaust fan.

"Chef, you send de smoke. They know we are open now...hee hee hee." As tired and worried or stressed as I was on a Sunday morning,

158

Carlos always got me to laugh and let go of it. He remembered all of the times I snapped at a server.

"Hey, Hey, here comes cheese boy." He laughed. "You remember, Chef? Zaki came in and ordered the AHM AH LETT?" He was holding his sides, the yellowing chef coat tight around him. "He said he wanted cheddar, provolone, mozzarella, Muenster, pepper jack, parmesan, American." No matter how many times he reminded me and Zaki about the incident it still brought tears to his eyes and he could barely get it out. "And you said, okay, okay cheese boy." Carlos never let me forget a flash of temper. More than that, he made me laugh at them. He was constantly reminding me and whoever cared to listen, that I was human.

We were the oldest in the kitchen and sometimes it showed. We had the savvy to anticipate what might go wrong. I could count on Carlos to snuff a fire before it got out of control and even before it started. He knew how to stall if someone had ordered a soup of the day we didn't quite have—that is until hot water from the steam table and a heat-resistant rubber spatula could resurrect the remnants stuck to the sides of the soup well.

159

There were many reasons for me to love and appreciate Carlos. He held down the fort on Saturday until I could get the kids to the babysitter and rush in to get things together for the busiest night of the week. On one particular Saturday, Tommy one of the owners, planned to debut his rendition of the Sheraton's Prime Rib. The recipe made the little hotel restaurant a sensation in One-Stoplight, Virginia.

I came in to find a rarer than edible roast resting under the heat lamp, covered with oddly shaped hunks of celery and dried herbs. Whatever was on the top shelf in dry storage was now on the floor in front the walk-in cooler. Tommy, in an apron, was red-faced and cursing.

"He wanted the beef base, Chef." Carlos explained, he was pouting, his chin to his chest.

"Carlos, we don't have beef base."

"I know," he was holding his sides now, trying not to laugh. Tommy would definitely kill him. I added up the evidence and surmised that Tommy had torn up the dry storage looking for this tub of chemicals that made gravy taste like you'd put some time and effort into it. Carlos could not contain himself, "I told him it was on the shelf."

160

Carlos didn't care if Tommy was angry. If I were upset, that was a different story. The few times I lost my temper with Carlos; he sulked for hours and didn't leave at the end of his shift until he'd made it up to me. The rest of the folks in the building didn't matter.

This became a problem after I handed in my resignation and left that restaurant without saying goodbye to my crew. The new chef came in and took my place beside Carlos. She turned the heat down as he tried to burn oil in the pans to "send smoke" to the customers before brunch started. She set about changing everything on the menu except for the leek-studded mashed potatoes. And for Carlos, she worked too closely to him—checking, spying, bossing, grabbing, interfering, correcting. He shoved her.

"Watch out!" she shouted at him.

"No!" he held his hands out to her to shove again, "You watch out!"

Carlos was called to the office and cried with Matt the other owner. The new chef was bold and charming, but she could not get the food out the way I had. The 45 seats at the bar had to be cut off from the kitchen. Sixty-five seats in the dining room were already more than the kitchen

161

could handle. The place was slipping from every body's grasp. The course had been set and there was no going back.

I was at Mrs. Simpson's, my dream job. I had visions of James Beard Awards and my picture in glossy magazines when I heard of the troubles at my former employer, The Broad Street Grille. Carlos called me. He had to leave. The new chef was making him miserable. She wasn't me.

It was reassuring in Mrs. Simpsons kitchen that was still new and strange to me to have Carlos giggling and chuckling at everything again. And I always had two or three fewer things to worry about. "I've done the soup, today," he'd announce. Or "How do you want me to cut this fish?" When he volunteered, "I will make salmon tartar from what I can scrape from the skin and bones for a special tonight." I was so glad Carlos was with me again.

I was certain this story would have a happy ending until I got the phone call at home. It was 9 o'clock at night and I had put the girls to bed when the phone rang. It was Mr. Bloomer, the owner. He was one of those guys with a great deal of money and no experience in the restaurant business. Someone had convinced him it would be a good investment to

162

own this old dinosaur of a restaurant. Mrs. Simpson's had been around when I was fresh out of college and teaching English at a local private school. By the time I had a real chef coat and not just one I wore around the house, the original owner's drug addiction had taken its toll. Not even the 6 pm to 8pm happy hour could save the place. An attorney friend talked fellow Mrs. Simpson's regular Bloomer into paying off the tax debt and taking the title.

But Bloomer had had enough of me and my chutneys and gastriques. When I refused to meet him there in the dark cold dining room on Monday night, he insisted I come first thing Tuesday. There was a check for $600 and a milk crate already packed. I ran into Carlos when I got to my car. He took the crate for me so I could open the trunk.

"Fuck him," the sing song Bolivian accent took the sting out of the phrase. "We are all leaving. I'm right behind you, Chef."

"No, Carlos." I looked at him seriously, trying to penetrate his brain through his eyes with my own. "You stay. Make this work. Mrs. Simpson's needs you." I pushed the button to make my window go up so there would be no words and no arguing.

Colorado Kitchen opened and I forgot all about the milk crate and Carlos breathing heavy and angry. I heard through the restaurant grape vine that Mrs. Simpson's was gone. Bloomer had given up. He had sold the place and it was now an Italian restaurant with a bright red awning and new furniture. We were busy and I had worries of my own—staffing, training, and paying bills for two households. I thought about the old crew and if Bloomer had told them or let them get off the bus or up from the Metro and find the doors locked.

Carlos called me not long after I had heard the rumors. Indeed, the doors were locked one morning, and when folks were allowed in to get things out of their lockers they made off with butter and pork chops. Emi, the young African chef who had replaced me, could not bring himself to quit his night shift room service chef job at the Hyatt. He prepped and made eggs until 8 am, and then he hustled over to the kitchen at Mrs. Simpson's. He caught up on sleep behind the stove on the oil resistant, anti-fatigue mat.

"Mr. Bloomer caught him one night," Carlos giggled. "He kicked him." He covered his mouth with his fingers. "Hee hee." Carlos watched old Mr. Bloomer get older before his eyes. He stopped keeping his hair appointments and the grey hair was taking over. One night as Carlos locked the walk-in, he heard heavy sighs coming from the office. Emi had left early, snuck out actually. No one knew he had gone. Tomorrow was Friday and the walk-in was empty like a Sunday night. Bloomer was in the office. Carlos was certain he was crying. "Mr. Bloomer?" He put his hand on the old man's shoulder. The navy wool gabardine of his suit jacket felt good under Carlos's hand, but still, a suit and tie at 10 o'clock at night? "I could not," he confessed.

"Mr. Bloomer call her. Call Gillian, she'll know what to do." He said Bloomer looked at him, sad and weary. He looked like he was dying.

"I can't, Carlos."

A year had flown by since Carlos put down the milk crate and gently closed my trunk. He was waking up Emi to tell him what to order. Making sure the Challah was in for Friday delivery for the French toast on Sunday Brunch. When Emi was rested, he was great, Carlos told me. They had fun behind the line talking about women and old times when cooks they knew horsed around and spilled hot oil all over themselves. And even then, Carlos felt needed and important. He was making things and the

165

dining room was digging it. He was making a dent and helping Mr. Bloomer save this place. He was doing what I would do.

"I asked him," Carlos told me, "Mr. Bloomer, it's been a year. Can I take my vacation? My daughter is living in Argentina and her baby is coming."

"Can you wait a month or two Carlos?" Bloomer knew he could count on him, the way I had. "We need to get through this busy spring."

"But she will have had the baby," he was sad, but sad for Bloomer, too. "Okay. I will wait."

It really hurt when Carlos—putting off his vacation time again and again, hoping to see the little grandson he hadn't met—got off of the bus and no matter how hard he pulled, the staff door to Mrs. Simpson's wouldn't open. He and Marta hung around for an hour, something must have happened. Mr. Bloomer was sick. Jacques the manager was in the hospital. They weren't thinking the worst until they came back the next day to find Mr. Bloomer at the door. "Just get your things as quickly as you can," he looked at them like he was angry, Carlos recalled. "And then get out."

"Who would tell Emi?"

I hired Carlos immediately. As we got ready for service, I watched him. His chef coat was yellower, and he wore his glasses all of the time now. There was more gray in his hair. He pulled the pictures of his grandson out of his wallet. The little boy was riding a tricycle and his little sister was in a wagon. He still hadn't seen them. "I will make the soup, Chef," he announced. "I will make potato-leek." I smiled cautiously. Carlos seemed different. He left bruises and flecks of skin on the potatoes plunking them into tepid water. He chopped the leeks carelessly—too much green even for the Broad Street Grille. Instead of lifting them out of the silty water he poured them sending grit into the soup before I could stop him. He quickly changed the subject, "Chef, where is the gar leek?" Garlic, what's that for? I got him a head from dry storage and watched as he chopped it finely and added it to the soup as he finished it with cream. His cell phone rang, and he answered it as the door was unlocked and customers took their seats.

"Excuse me, Chef." Carlos giggled. "I have to take this phone call." He chuckled all the way to the men's room and slammed the door shut. Orders started coming through on the kitchen printer. I had three tickets hanging and two salads up in the window when Carlos came back.

167

He used his towel to wipe the smile off his face and looked at me tightening his brows. "Okay, Chef." He pulled his apron strings tighter, the buttons on his chef coat groaned a little. "Let us go." Then his phone went off again. He didn't leave the line this time. Instead he had phone sex in Spanglish with a woman on the other end. I could hear her switch from sultry to cackle. Carlos cooed back at her promising her things and swearing not to do other things. Confident he had plans for later, he hung up.

A server came into the kitchen and ladled a dab of Carlos's potato-leek soup into four sake cups. This was our amuse bouche at Colorado Kitchen—a sample of the soup. It helped sell some of our obscure renditions—cauliflower with red onion, yellow squash with spicy almonds. But it also reconnected diners with classics they hadn't had in ages; like potato-leek. "I don't know about the soup, Chef." Randy said, as he prepared samples for table 12. "People aren't even finishing the sample, let alone ordering any."

"Hum?" Carlos looked up from tossing a salad. "Is there something with the soup?" I touched the surface with the back of my pinky and dabbed the velvety liquid of leek and potato onto my tongue. It shriveled under the intensity of searing raw garlic. I spit into the trash can.

"Carlos, why so much garlic?"

"It is how we make the potato-leek, Chef."

"How *who* makes it?" I held a spoon of it in front of his lips. "I don't think you've ever seen me put garlic."

He snapped onto the spoon and swallowed its contents like a lizard. "It is perfect!" The line was silent the rest of the night, except for Carlos and his girlfriend on the phone.

In the old days, Carlos would have tried to make amends for his short temper. He'd make me leave the kitchen and finish cleaning up himself. I smiled at him, "Chef," he said handing me the broom, "will you be ordering the strawberries?" It was January. There was no way I was ordering any strawberries. Carlos had told me all about his little victories at Mrs. Simpson's. He loved telling the one about the strawberry dressing he made with all of the canned preserves discovered in dry storage. "The sa LAD," Carlos would say, "I used the mesclun, fresh strawberries, and I used the jelly in the dressing. hee hee." He would tell this one as he tossed my much less interesting salad of mixed greens and sherry vinaigrette.

"They loved it, Chef. And Mr. Bloomer was very, very happy." He told me how Bloomer patted his back and had Carlos make one big strawberry salad for him. With Bloomer happy, Emi was safe for one more night. Carlos did everything in his power to keep Bloomer happy.

"Emi needed me." Carlos would say seriously, explaining why he would let Emi sleep while he jumped around behind the line working the grill and then pulling the calves' liver off of the fire at the sauté station before Emi let it burn.

Carlos and I were a week into our reunion, and I wasn't happy. "This is how we did it," telling me about the vegetable soup they made every day with V8 and two bags of frozen mixed vegetables. "They loved it, Chef. And Mr. Bloomer was very happy." I was officially sick of Carlos before week two even started. I was starting to snidely answer back to his tales of happy Mr. Bloomer. "Oh yeah," I'd say with a smile that would certainly belie the sarcasm for a native English speaker. "Bloomer was so happy; he had to sell the place. I'd love to be that happy." It took just ten days, and I was planning Carlos's murder.

"Emi, I would like to leave early tonight."

"Emi, I will make the soup today, no?"

"Emi—I mean, Chef shall I make the meal for the FAM IL LEE?"

I didn't exist for Carlos anymore. He was calling me Emi.

The worst thing you can do to a well-seasoned cast iron skillet is to let the dish washer get a hold of it. He'll toss it smoking hot into his dirty sink brimming with soapy water. Then he'll take a stainless-steel sponge and rake all of the oil, garlic, sugar, salt that coats the surface. It's a priceless non-stick finish that not only sheds sauce and entrée like rain on a waxed Ferrari, it imparts a sweet and smokey taste to whatever touches it. My seasoned pan was as clean as the day I acquired it.

Carlos came in for his Tuesday shift half an hour late. He was in his street clothes and not the tight, yellowing chef coat that he wore his chest full of air as if the Cordon Bleu crest were on the breast pocket. He had on sunglasses and the bomber jacket that he had bought for $15 at the thrift store.

"Chef," he said to me with his chin pressed into his chest. "I was looking at the top of his baseball hat that he was now wearing all of the time since his hair started thinning. "It is Emi."

"I knew it would be," I said, now I was running around the kitchen preparing to work the shift myself not really interested in Carlos' explanation.

"He has the big hotel job now and..." the rest was mumbles followed by giggles and he was gone. I was relieved to have the kitchen to myself. But how could I not feel like the betrayed wife; and a little pissed at Emi, the home wrecker? He only came back to me for the two or three paychecks he would earn until Emi called him. We didn't have a future together and he knew it all along. That was never part of his plan. I pushed a heavy sigh through my nose, and I got to work.

I got a lesson in bitterness from Jacques, the Frenchman who was the tall and handsome manager in many of DC's finest restaurants. He was a weary drunk by time I got to work with him at Mrs. Simpsons. He'd come into Broad Street Grille and was greeted with applause and admiration. There was plenty of respect to go around, but Matt stopped shy of offering him a job and took advantage of Jacques' offers to "help out". We ran low on shrimp at a benefit. Jacques appeared with over two pounds of black tiger and rolled up his French cuffs to peel and devein. This only got him an enthusiastic thank you. His reputation had preceded him. But he was no longer keeping up with it. The old, stale French places were changing, while Jacques was sticking to old and stale. The wine-soaked Maître d' wasn't charming anymore. The rest of the industry viewed him as a fossil. But when Bloomer bought Mrs. Simpsons from the brothers who spent the restaurant's money on cocaine rather than paying its bills, it was the stale and old that he counted on making vogue again. He called them the old flavors and he counted on me to cook them and Jacques to hand folks a menu full of them. Bloomer found Jacques running the cafeteria at the Conservative Think Tank. The daily lunch and the occasional event didn't require much, and he could be a little tipsy all day. But at Mrs. Simpsons there was wine everywhere and Jacques was tipsy by noon, giggling by four, hot tempered by seven. He stayed at tables a couple of beats too long and he grabbed at the overcoat-plush backs of occupied chairs, clenching menus in his other hand as he wobbly sat a table of four.

"If I leave the keys in my car out front," the woman asked as she stood in the foyer shaking water out of her umbrella, "somebody will take it, right?"

"Yes, madam," said Jacques, his accent a little heavier with the wine behind it, "Someone will definitely take it."

By the time our worlds collided at Mrs. Simpsons, Jacques and I were at opposite ends of career enthusiasm. He spent his days stifling yawns. While I couldn't wait to get out of bed and get to the restaurant by 8 am to meet the fire inspector. His contempt for the customers was spinach stuck in his teeth—it was obvious if you looked closely. There was a blunt instrument hidden behind his icy charm. A couple of folks caught on and left irritated and insulted. I was horrified and swore whatever was going on in Jacques would never happen to me.

Jacques was sober enough one evening to see me wince when he tossed a thinly veiled insult to a large woman as he held the menu out to her, delicately unfolded a napkin and placed it on the broad thigh meat that made up her lap, "I'm sure you'll find something to devour in this selection of delights."

He followed me into the kitchen mumbling about answering stupid questions to a clientele that would never get it. And when the phone rang, he could well have been a slave just caught stealing, only he was talking so loudly it was hard to take him seriously, "Well of course doctor," he was

174

scribbling on the reservation book. "There is no problem for tonight at 8pm. If we have to, we will pull the fire alarm so that you have a table." He walked a very thin line between "just joking" and "I can't stand you".

Jacques had become so bitter that there might as well have been a lemon rind tucked between his cheek and gum. He had been the handsome king of so many of DC's top dining rooms and here he was with an old son of a baker (now turned millionaire) bossing him around a has-been restaurant. He had long started to hate himself and found the bitter taste in his mouth went away with enough wine.

I imagined why Jacques had become so bitter. He'd spent his professional life as a well-dressed ass kisser. And where had it gotten him? Perhaps when he came to America the thought occurred to him that he would work his way up using his good manners and good looks to one day have a place of his own. The cash and accolades would be rolling in. But he stayed too long at the place where he'd felt comfortable—that old French Inn with the faded wallpaper and carpeting worn in spots. New places opened all around and the clientele that had brought the place from obscurity were all in assisted living. He'd tried to move on but there was no hiding—even with his good looks and fluid French—that he was just not a decent person and that he wasn't very smart. He was rude to the young girls that came in to work the dining room. He'd had enough when the new chef corrected his pronunciation. With his little savings he joined a couple of disgruntled workers to open a place. But it was too much like the old French Inn—that was all they knew. The critics weren't kind, and the place closed in less than a year. One of his old partners found his way to the booming dining scene in Las Vegas and Jacques followed. But by now he was way too old for the fast pace and even faster money. He came back to DC his tail between his legs and hid out in his Chevy Chase house; the one thing he had been able to hang on to. He was relieved that he hadn't sold it. He'd rented it to a grad student; with the thought in the back of his mind that Vegas would not work and that he'd be back.

His suits were at the dry cleaner going on four months and he hadn't shaved when the phone rang. It was Manuel from the French Inn. He was now the kitchen manager at a huge cafeteria in an office building downtown. It was a posh dining room for the Washington think tank PhD's and their guests. All Jacques had to do was pretend he was back at the Inn: stand tall and slender in his suit and tie and kiss ass like in the old days. He'd remember a name, offer a well-timed joke about the wife, and step in to pour another glass of wine. He could do this job in his sleep and with a blood alcohol content of twice the legal limit.

He was often recognized by the men and women in the cafeteria. They had been dragged to the French Inn as children on Mother's Day or Thanksgiving. When one would call out his name and wave a napkin at him, he'd get hot behind the ears and his neck would turn red. They'd grab his sleeve and insist that he remember them or listen to stories about their now dead mom or bedridden dad. Sometimes they wouldn't even wait until they'd chewed and swallowed. Jacques would cover his brow with his hand in a gesture that might imply embarrassment or a flash of recognition that touched him. But he was really just smoothing away perspiration and hiding that underneath his hand his eyeballs had shot up to the heavens and were rolling back down again very slowly counterclockwise bringing the lids down with them.

One evening at a cancer benefit it was Mr. Bloomer who waved a fork at him—his lips opening and closing around a mouthful of egg salad he'd ask the kitchen to prepare for him. "Jack!" he shouted. "Boy, am I glad to see you." It had been years. Bloomer had been in the French Inn with a girl he was trying to impress. They had just celebrated their 40th wedding anniversary.

He didn't fully understand what Bloomer was telling him—but he caught restaurant, job, and need you. For Jacques it was a lifeline. He'd be running a dining room and there'd be no one watching. He could make every customer who came in pay for all of the wrongs he'd suffered with quick jabs of sarcasm. He could make it his own and usher in a brand-new form of ass kissing: pursed lips that quickly turned into a size 11 boot. Jacques did not count on me. He had been hired alongside an equally bitter French chef who stirred dried tarragon into Hellman's and called it Béarnaise and had cooked himself weary with Jacques at the French Inn.

The French chef and Bloomer hated each other. There was never enough food to get through a Tuesday night and he had hired his friends and declared them salaried to the bookkeeper. Even the dishwasher, Fabiola, was salaried. Stealing me from Broad Street Grille was Jacques' way of saving his own skin. He really had no idea that I would come in determined to put Mrs. Simpson's back on the map. He had been overwhelmed by 50 customers in the 100-seat dining room. I prepared to fill the place during the week and turn the tables twice on Friday and Saturday nights, and again on Sunday Brunch.

I made a splash at Evening Star, disappeared into obscurity at Broad Street Grille, and suddenly I emerged at one of DC's most loved fine-dining spots. The cult had been temporarily disbanded and now was back to drink whatever flavored Kool-Aid I'd be churning out of this kitchen. We had one solid review and the word was out. The phone was ringing off the hook and the dining room was full. An hour wait for a table stretched out to the foyer.

Bitter Jacques' head was spinning. He was starting to miss the sleeve tugging grown children at the Institute. I had to go. But not before I worked the chef's least favorite part of the year—the last quarter. Thanksgiving, Christmas, and New Years are a quick succession of tests of purchasing savvy, organizational ability, and allocation of manpower. Thanksgiving with the one tiny oven was a real challenge. I started roasting Turkeys at midnight, came back at 4 am and roasted all day until service started at noon. Christmas dinner's limited menu offering either Sea Bass or Tenderloin made sure that things could happen without overnight cooking. New Year's Eve I was stunned that the big seller was the $19 mushroom stuffed zucchini squash. But the leftover poached lobster was a big part of an incredibly busy New Year's Day Brunch, so nothing went to waste and food costs was a surprising 27%. Despite the surge in business, I was fired before Valentine's Day.

To say being fired was a shock would be an understatement. I sobbed driving the new babysitter home thinking that I had been the team player who was spending my spare time at the batting cages. And I could slip into the cheerleader skirt on the sidelines and throw my body into the air to get everyone as excited about Mrs. Simpson's as I was. I was willing to stay where I wasn't welcome. But the door was locked. If I pressed my face against the window, I would see them in there dozing and serving bottled dressing.

I was a casualty of Jacques' bitterness. He had long lost the itch that makes us all stay in this business. He put on his suit and tie and walked into the restaurant to spend the day reading the paper. With me gone, the phone was ringing a lot less. I wasn't there doing everything I had been trained to do to get all 100 seats full every night. He could once again drink his bottle of wine in the cozy quiet of an empty restaurant.

I thought of Hakim. I had finally accepted that I wasn't chef at Mrs. Simpsons any longer. "Old age and treachery will always overcome youth and skill," Hakim liked to remind me on the nights I came home from my Director of Marketing job at an association and drank from my bottle of antacid. I would slip off my patent leather pumps and stand on the cold bathroom tile fitting the little blue cap back on the bottle. I would wipe the white stain of antacid off of my upper lip and fix my gaze on my own sad and defeated eyes in the mirror of the medicine cabinet. I was young. I would always be young and a victim.

Years later I can look back and not feel sorry for myself. With callouses and gray hair and the knowledge that a drunk's happy endings are short lived, I know that getting rid of me didn't make it all better for Hakim who wanted nothing more than to be left alone with his bottles of bourbon. The girls and I were just in the way of his favorite pastime. And Jacques? He soon lost his cushy job watching over a slow dining room while consuming two or three bottles of the house's finest Cotes du Rhone.

It is funny and sad to think of Jacques, Bloomer, Carlos, Emi, Fabiola—quite simply the ones that made me miserable and taught me everything I needed to know to sink to the bottom of a river. They are going to outlive me. Now how sad is that. For a minute it made me want to kick my way back up to the surface and suck in the warm damp air of post-thunderstorm Washington, DC. But this was so much easier. And why shouldn't I? I worked so hard, so hard. Can I do the easy thing just this once?

Chapter Five

A Crouton is Toast with No Moisture

I had my own place now. I was hoping that the lean years would soon pay off and that I would finally be able to cash my checks, have health insurance, and cook food that I felt good about and not fear being fired.

I was tired when I opened my first restaurant, tired and depressed and in an anemic fog when I opened the second. The first was special. I was full of excitement and anticipation on what doing things my way would mean. I had worked like a dog for non-chef coat wearing owners who thought nothing of my standing in that hot room from 9am to midnight. In fact, nothing I did was enough. As my own boss, I'd set the pace and have no one to blame or thank but little old me. I was glad to have the final decision be mine. We would close on Thanksgiving. And why not open for brunch as soon as the New Year began at 12:01? Not every idea was a good one, but they were mine. But all of it was mine. The bills were mine; the responsibility was mine; the buck was mine and stopped right on top of my cutting board as soon as the doors opened, and anybody could just walk right in.

Having a restaurant is very much like having a baby—a test tube baby. You have some control on the color and the theme. But then the regulatory agency has a say on things and other factors—budget, architecture, neighborhood—all ultimately have an impact on the end result. No matter how she turns out, it is hard not to love your baby. But the baby's feet get bigger, she tries to cross the street by herself, she is unsteady on her new tricycle. It's a bundle of joy and a source of anxiety all at the same time. I worried about everything: the cost of soap and toilet paper, being robbed, and the nightmare of fire. The architect, building inspector, and everyone that had a say in whether I opened this place; worked tirelessly to keep us all safe on paper. But there is nothing in those big rolls of sharp lines and elevations to protect us from the people that walk in the door.

184

It is one of those things you have to have, says the engineer. And now it comes standard on the kitchen exhaust package in a screened box that blows on the neck of anyone at the stove. While tons of hot air and air borne grease is sucked out of the tight hot space of the kitchen, air from outside—the make-up air—is brought in. On those days where the temperature dipped below freezing, I wore a thermal shirt under my chef coat. The three H's kind of weather: hazy, hot, and humid; the suffocating make-up air meant a frozen towel around the neck and semi-frozen red Gatorade in the big bottle. When the wind was blowing in just the right direction the powerful fan sucked in whatever was in the air. Trash ablaze in the Chiminea ® next door, an old car burning oil at the stop sign on the corner, and whatever was coming out of the back-bathroom vent.

I rarely thought about make-up air. But on the days, it made me miserable it is all I thought about. On the moderately cool September mornings when I worked breakfast alone—serving and running back to the stove to cook—I didn't mind it at all. That is until the red jaguar pulled up at the curb and a curly headed man in jeans and wire-rimmed glasses emerged from the driver side, yanked the front door open and ran past me straight to the back bathroom. It didn't take long before the aroma from his efforts was pulled out of the bathroom through the vent fan and into the still air above the building. The wind took it to the mouth of the intake fan and then right into my face. I left the kitchen and stood at the register behind the counter, ready to take his order and pour him a coffee. But he ran out just as quickly as he came in and before I could say, "Welcome to Colorado Kitchen" the red jaguar was gone.

I saw that car again: first thing Tuesday Mr. Jaguar Poops came in; he breezed past me again a week later. He never looked around to admire my dining room. He didn't once stop to read the menu. It never occurred to him to slow down and smell the bacon in the oven. He came into Colorado Kitchen for one thing and one thing only: to get rid of whatever he'd consumed at some other restaurant hours before and use my water and toilet paper to do it. This guy was costing me at least thirty cents every time he came in—soap, paper towels, and by now a roll or two of toilet paper. It was adding up. Seeing him pull up in that jaguar each time did nothing but make me resent him more and more. We still weren't making enough money for me to cash a paycheck. And whatever tips came my way—and there weren't many for breakfast—these went straight into the cash register. Mr. J. Poops didn't even have the decency to wish me good morning or slap a quarter on the counter. Nothing deterred him from coming into my empty restaurant every morning and run past the uncomfortable silence between us. I was determined to put a stop to it.

It was a Thursday morning and the youth ministers were in. I had made Rick his hash browns without onions and served Tyrone (the ex-football player) his three eggs over easy, French toast, side of grits, and two sides of sausage when the Jaguar came to a rough stop at the curb. I figured Mr. Poops would be more apt to listen to me on his way out, so I let him race past me as I cleared plates and took a credit card. After his usual five minutes of bowel moving, he emerged and was rushing for the door when I stopped him.

"Sir," I said it loudly as he got close to me and I forced him to look me in the eye instead of breezing past me like I didn't exist as he had dozens of times before. "You can't keep doing this."

He smiled nervously and chuckled, "Doing what?"

"You can't keep racing in here and taking a big, stinky dump in my bathroom without having the decency to be a customer." Tyrone and Rick quit planning the basketball tournament and looked at us.

"I haven't been doing...."

187

"Yes, you have. You've been coming in here three or four times a month and you've been doing number two in my bathroom and you've got to stop."

He started to deny it again, but I raised my hand. I pointed to the complicated air handler above the stove. "I can smell it." I kept my eyes on his. The red started at his neck and moved quickly up to his forehead, right under where the light brown-flecked with gray mop of curly hair started.

"Well, uh…I," he started to deny it, make an excuse. I don't know. But I fixed my eyes on his, refusing to allow the awkward conversation to force me to look away, to relent. "I…. I'm sorry," he said finally, rushing out faster than I'd ever seen him go. I remembered Tyrone and Rick. They had witnessed my little victory, but quickly looked down at their calendar and brackets for their one-on-one matchups set for the church gymnasium. I never saw J. Poops again. But it wasn't the end of the make-up air battles.

Smoking isn't allowed in restaurants in DC and hasn't been for years. And as a non-smoker I'm glad about it. But there are people who enjoy a smoke after eating and many of my staff smoke also and we'd see them—sometimes together, staff and customers, a clique—mixing their smoke in a cloud above their heads just outside the front doors of the restaurant. Even when short days and cold air descended on us, they'd tighten their scarves and head out for a puff or two in between courses. Thanks to the make-up air, I discovered that not everyone was taking their cigarettes out of the building. I'd rush to the bathroom as soon as I could. The butt would be floating in the toilet, or in the trash nestled among the paper towels—the end no longer lit, but still hot. "It's against the law," I said, when the server shrugged at my irritation. "It's also a fire hazard." I was determined to catch this crazy smoker, this addict that cared nothing about my restaurant or the 50 souls in the dining room. Addicts don't care about anybody!

Dotty usually came in on Friday. She always ordered the fish with several slices of lemon on the side. No matter what the menu read, she'd spend about a minute before she dug in squeezing the juice out of ten or eleven lemon wedges onto her plate...even if the night's fish special was Seared Salmon with Meyer Lemon Beurre Blanc. One Friday night right after she paid the check, Dotty came to my window. She tugged her black felt beret to a slant over her right ear and tightened the knot at her neck to adjust the hang of her black and jade pashmina scarf. "Your cooking reminds me of my mother's," she told me. "I'm going to bring her in next time; she's going to love the place." Dotty looked to be a woman in her early 50's, so I imagined her mother to be a matronly woman in her 70s who never went out. She probably needed to be reminded to take her apron off before she struggled to get into the tiny car her daughter drove now in an effort to reduce her carbon footprint.

I met Dotty's mother a few weeks later. She had on a dark green beret and a turtleneck sweater. She'd left her pashmina scarf on the chair. And I don't think she owned an apron. I imagined she cooked with a wooden spoon in one hand and a cigarette in a holder in the other. "Dotty's told me so much about the place." She patted my hand; burned tobacco was in the air around her. She smiled at me her lips unevenly smeared with metallic purple lipstick and headed for the bathroom.

I had turned back to the stove and had already forgotten about the mother-daughter dining companions at table seven. But then I smelled smoke. Someone was smoking in the bathroom again. I looked around the dining room. It was just starting to fill up. People were coming in and slipping out of their coats. It was that time of the evening where 30 or 40 people come in and tables fill up and no one leaves the building for another hour or two—the characteristic start of a busy night. My eyes landed on Dotty, sitting alone at table seven. She smiled at me and waved as her 70 something year old mom shuffled back to her seat.

"Couldn't be," I told myself. But as soon as there was a break in the action, I headed for the bathroom. In the trash, buried by dozens of wadded up paper towels was the snuffed-out butt. The cotton end was ringed with a kiss of metallic purple.

Dotty's mother eluded me. I was on the war path to catch her red handed—coming out of the bathroom exhaling her last puff into my face and I'd grab her still hot butt out of the trash and kindly ask her to never come back. But I'd always just miss her. I'd smell the smoke and head to the bathroom, just as a non-smoking woman was stepping in. Or I'd be on my way out of the kitchen when a customer would stop me, "I love that roasted chicken, Chef." I could see smoke coming out of the crack at the base of the door. "How do you make it?" Then I'd catch a glimpse of the old lady stepping onto the sidewalk, the front door closing behind her.

She was coming in with Dotty, or with a group of ladies her age that all cackled in unison when the handsome server left their table after pouring the wine. The old woman had become a regular. My restaurant was now a part of her life. It had become her place. Nonetheless, when she came in with two of her cackling friends and an older man I'd never seen before I declared, "today is the day". We'd just opened the doors and the popular four top in the window was free. I had little to distract me tonight. But it was too difficult to focus on her. It was Saturday night and we all got caught up in making sure we didn't have a crisis later. Prep can go on all night on a Saturday amid the filling of orders. When I had a minute to look at the four top in the window the old lady was gone. The old folks still at the table scraped the last bits of chocolate tart off of their plates or looked at themselves in the side of a knife, dotting lipstick on their puckering mouths. I tilted my head up to the steady breeze of the make-up air and sure enough fresh cigarette smoke poured over my cheeks and my eyelids. I put down whatever I was working on and headed for the bathroom. She was making her way quickly to her table while I retrieved the butt stained with her lipstick from the trash. She sat quickly and clutched her purse to her chest when she noticed me standing beside her. I held the butt out to her the lipstick smear visible as I pinched it with my thumb and forefinger.

"I think this is yours," I said to her.

192

"Why I don't know what you mean." Her watery eyes looked up at me. Up close I could see just how old she was. Her face was a New York subway map of wrinkles and the Broadway local gathered at Penn Station on her upper lip—the close tight wrinkles of a long-time smoker.

"Listen lady." I was trying hard to control my anger. "You've got to stop smoking in my bathroom." I hadn't counted on her companions. They shouted all of them, all at once. Accusing me of insulting their friend for no good reason, swearing that they never heard such a thing, and demanding I apologize immediately.

"Susan does not smoke." One of her friends insisted.

"She quit years ago." The man looked at me, his eyes on fire he was so angry. His voice was trembling. He waved his finger at me. Yes, they were all old and I had a glimmer of my inner child (afraid of folks way older than I), but I pushed her back down in there. I ignored her companions and kept my eyes locked on Dotty's mother.

"I'm going to have to ask you to not come back to my restaurant." I told her sternly, "You cannot smoke in here."

The old man stood up and moved closer to me. If I had given ground, he would have stood in between me and his friend. But I didn't budge. He had to be content to yell at me from beside her. I still didn't look at him. "Listen, young lady," He was practically growling at me. "She does not smoke. Go ahead and search her bag." The two other women seated in the bench at the window agreed, "Yes search her bag. Go ahead. Search it." The old woman's watery eyes popped open wide and she clutched her bag even tighter, pressing it closed against her chest.

She finally spoke, talking above the shouting of her companions, "Let's just go." She slipped her coat on, still holding the bag tight against her chest. "This is not worth the humiliation." I never saw the old woman, again. And it would be a long time before Dotty came back. I had no way of knowing if her mother told her about our conversation. There were subsequent nights I watched her squeeze lemon all over her monkfish with a Riesling Vin Blanc and tried to meet her gaze to nod hello as I did other regulars, but her eyes never drifted to the open kitchen.

Old Lady Smokey and Mr. Poops forced me to come out of my insulation and fight for my business. There was too much at stake for me to bury my head in a stock pot. Once that door is unlocked, anybody can just walk in. And as the owner, I had to be prepared to fix it. And be prepared to defend it.

"Can I help you?" I growled. I had learned to reach for the biggest bottle of Cuvee when someone stumbled into the dining room after we had just put our dishes from staff meal into the bus bucket of dirties. Excuses and white lies would spill out of booze-sticky lips and then they'd see my weapon. My fingers wrapped around the metal paper holding the twisted wire against the glass of the bottle as I prepared to shatter the big bell of the bottom against the counter and point the jagged end at the space between their eyes. Raising the bottle slightly usually cleared the room and I never did have to break one.

But we were in a neighborhood that politicians, white kids explaining away their parent's fears, real estate agents, called "transitioning." Graffiti on the two-story brick wall of the warehouse across the street, a drug deal on the corner, brown bag wrapped open containers were part of the scenery. From day one we knew we were in a "colorful" neighborhood. The street's know-it-all crack head had cornered me one morning as I put my key in the lock to the wobbly old front door. We had removed the security cage that made the 1200 square foot storefront look like a liquor locker or a prison so that a six-foot cooler with double shelf could make it through.

"You gonna serve neck bones?" The question scratched its way out of Donna's throat. It sounded like a tumble weed made of razor wire, like it hurt coming out. She was about a foot shorter than I and eyed me with the tilt of her head standing a little too close. I assumed that was because she needed to put her one working eye forward, the other was clouded over and milky. "Well, you gonna serve neck bones?" I hesitated, I knew the answer was no, but the question was more of a challenge. My mouth-gaped-open silence was all the answer she needed, and she couldn't hide her disappointment and disgust, "How you gonna name a place 'kitchen' and not serve neck bones?" She drew saliva through her teeth and slapped the air beside her with an open palm. She strode off with a limp, muttering to herself.

Soon the rest of the neighborhood knew. The super at the apartment next door who had sole custody of his five children while his wife did hard time, the old man who collected old Dodge Rams and spent his days sitting on a milk crate in front of the graffiti of the warehouse sipping from brown bagged bottles, the impaired Vietnam vet who walked the blocks around our building his suit jacket open so the big S of his superman shirt earned him the nickname—we weren't going to be their place. We were the beginning of the end. Soon "nice" stuff was coming and Paula—the skeeza (a $5 a blow job drug addict—a staple in the DC sex worker trade) who never went to the hospital to repair her broken neck and had to hold her head up with a fist planted firmly into her chin and her elbow pegged into her hip—would need a new street to do business.

Not all of them were against things getting better and "nice" stuff coming. We co-existed peacefully on that small commercial block in an up and coming residential neighborhood, just two blocks east of a city landmark (the Carter-Baron amphitheater that hosted free Shakespeare and an international tennis tournament.) The folks on the street were our neighbors, and we treated them like that. We bought liquor at the corner liquor store, empanadas and curtido at the Latino mini mart, we washed napkins alongside them as they washed socks and boxers at the laundromat across the street. We rubbed elbows.

While none of them ever set foot into our store, they watched, and I'd like to think admired, what we were building. Superman occasionally came in and announced in a hoarse high-pitched bark that he wanted a milk shake. One day he poured a filthy dollar and change into Robin's hand and got one.

197

There was an unspoken agreement of mutual leave me alone. It meant we let things go and simple drug use or public drinking never had us calling the cops. Until one day a line was crossed. A homey returned to the neighborhood from a long bid at Lorton Penitentiary. Donna welcomed the ex-con and he invited her to share a rock of crack against my storefront. He didn't know, but Donna clearly should have steered him to the alley. I didn't need to call the cops. I just opened the door and reminded Donna that this place wasn't vacant anymore. She apologized and led her friend and his burning rock of crack out of sight.

Then a stranger, someone obviously testing the block would wander in. Unfamiliar with the treaty, he'd begin to beg customers, servers and have to be physically removed or shouted out. A rarely seen Latino drunk came in right as we unlocked the doors on a bright Saturday evening. He stumbled to the two top at table 8 and put his head down. We knew that there were things you don't wait for the cops to fix. If we didn't get rid of this guy, he was going to sleep it off at that table until he was ready to go. Not on a Saturday night he wasn't. We needed the table and we needed all of the bums, ne'er do wells, skeezas and beggars to know Colorado Kitchen was not the place. He sat there while Robin and I discussed the best way to extract him. We began by moving the chair away from the table and when his big arms fell loose, we each grabbed one and slid him backwards as the chair fell out from under him and by the time he thought about kicking his feet, Robin had the door open. We had just enough strength and the leverage of him falling back to toss him onto the sidewalk.

Another young man wearing a shearling coat and over-sized, loose laced Timberlands came in after a recent mention in the food section. The Friday lunch crowd was uncharacteristically large. He sat at the counter and I could tell the way his eyes darted back and forth that he was losing his patience. He bared his teeth for a minute, and I could see they were covered with metal. Lunch was busy enough that I had one server. A strapping guy about my age who, while great at his job, sweat a lot and was easily flustered. He had a full dining room and the door kept opening. We should have planned this better and had more help today, but I knew it would soon be over. The dining room was full, but just about everyone was already eating. The young man with gold teeth at the counter spun around in his counter stool and watched two women come in, Kenneth grabbled two menus and started to seat them, but the table glistened with condensation rings and crumbs. They sat but held their menus to their chests as Kenneth went and got a rag. The man with the teeth watched his every move, I could hear the air coming hard out of his nose in short, angry puffs. Kenneth, his brow seeming to melt, his gray polo darker gray at the small of his back, told the guy, "I'll be right with you to take your order."

Was this the wrong answer? The man slid off of the bar stool and put his hand into the chest high opening of his coat. It was a move I'd seen only on television. Kenneth was wiping down the table while the two-woman smiled and talked, scooting their chairs across the vinyl tile getting closer to the damp but clean table. I had to do something—was he about to shoot the place up or get lunch at gunpoint.

"What do you want?" I shouted to him above the dining room din of idle chatter and fork on plate. There were old women, local politicians, a regular who came almost every Friday with the nanny and her baby in a highchair. I had to steer this in the right direction. He turned to look at me. His hand still in his coat. "What can I make for you, sir." I added. "You won't have to wait; I'll make it right now." I tried to sound as calm and natural as I could. He put his hand back on the counter and was about to sit back down and then he narrowed his eyes at me.

"Wait a minute. I know you!" he shouted, the dining room still noisy, but some heads turned and noticed him for the first time. Kenneth was at the damp table his pen moving across his pad crumpled from being jammed in a sweaty pocket of his black jeans. My picture had been in the paper a lot lately and recently I sat in the window looking out as the photographer snapped a shot of me as he stood on the sidewalk. "You was in that magazine yesterday!" he said this even louder. I put my index finger to my lips. Bold move to show calm, I was going to be motherly and quiet him down.

"How about a burger?"

"YES!" he was all smiles now.

"Bacon, cheese, well-done?"

"YES!" he sat down with his coat still on, a celebrity was making his lunch. And no one at Colorado Kitchen was going to be shot that day. Kenneth came back and poured him an iced tea and placed the rolled red bandana with knife and fork in front of him.

Then there was the unexplainable way we weaved our way into the mysterious fabric of people's lives. One morning, before the sun had risen high enough to make it not look like midnight outside, a man got out of a cab and yanked at the door. I was 10 minutes from opening but I handed him a menu when he sat down at the counter. I waited on him and a few others during that slow morning and didn't think of him again until he returned with his wife just a few days later. He had discovered a place and he wanted to share it—these were the kinds of customers who thrilled me.

"Don't you have scrapple?" she said, twisting her face and bringing her lips into a pucker like she was tasting something incredibly sour.

"No…. I don't…. applewood bacon and really nice sausage."

"Hmmmm." She answered. They talked about grits and eggs and then got up to leave. "We didn't wear our dentures." She confessed. I swallowed a chuckle and wished them a good day. In three or four months they returned. I was happy to see them, and I wanted to make sure they knew I remembered them. I dropped the check at their table.

"I'm so glad you remembered to bring your teeth this time," I said quietly. Their eyes got big and they stared at me. I had taken their soiled plates from the table—sausage and bacon had been eaten. My ears got hot, had I offended them?

"You remember us?" She blinked at me. I looked at the elderly pair who had spent so much time together they pretty much dressed alike, down to the denture wearing. I adjusted my glasses. The woman put her hand over her mouth and giggled. Then we were all laughing.

In an effort to get more people to come during our first few months we tried everything. Flyers, promotions—everything we could do without spending a lot of money. I thought about the turkey burger that had been such a hit at Breadline when I slipped it on to the menu while the owner was out of town. People went crazy over it. Maybe this little American restaurant should be doing a burger? We could do it cheaply, once or twice a week (creating artificial supply and demand). It also gave potential customers an easy, inexpensive way to come in and try us out. Despite my years in the business I still didn't have a name yet in this town—a name that created a following any way. I was close at Evening Star, but my abrupt departure from over work and nervous breakdown, followed by a run of career instability at short-lived chef posts meant I was still not drawing crowds on name alone.

But the burger: a thoughtful combination of ground chuck, roasted garlic, and minced red onion served on a curated brioche bun was getting a reputation of its own. In fact it was main topic of the review that turned our fortunes at Colorado Kitchen and had ravenous customers insisting I do burger night more than just twice a week (the large cast iron skillet covering two burners made working the line on burger nights a challenge—two nights was all I could sanely manage.)

Lunch time the burger had an odd fan that came every Friday. He'd order it rare pouring half a bottle of ketchup under the bun and all over the onion rings. He was a tall older man always wearing a suit and the telltale lanyard of a government contractor. He'd order the burger and a coke, paying for it all in cash before his food came. In three bites the burger and onion rings were gone. His fast and furious burger consumption often resulted in a hunk of onion ring in his hair or a blob of Heinz on his nose or forehead. It earned him the nickname, Mr. Hamburger Dude. We didn't think we'd see him again once Colorado Kitchen closed.

About a year later and five miles away Hamburger Dude has discovered The General Store. He is 50 pounds lighter—perhaps feeling the effects of an end to the Friday burger lunch. Apparently, we've opened in his neighborhood. We've never seen him with a woman, this older lady eyeing the place above her reading glasses has got to be his wife. I catch him looking at Robin and then looking at me. He turns white, then disappears around the corner. The woman wants to know everything: "How much butter is in that?" "Do the greens have a lot of salt?" She notes her husband has heart trouble and needs to be careful about what he eats. The Friday hamburger "dine and dash" is now making sense. She orders carefully and they take their order to go.

After a couple more awkward orders he soon realizes that we're not going to blow his cover. Now she trusts him enough to come to The General Store (famous for fried chicken and mac & cheese) by himself. Of course, he has to make several calls to the wife to see if she agrees to the selection. With every order he manages to order a "forbidden" item and, with the same intensity as his burger lunch, snarfs it down in no time flat. He is out the door with his approved meal, sporting some sort of sauce on his face. Usually if we see him leave with a tell-tale sign on his face, he's lost his privileges and again he is accompanied by his wife on the next visit.

He came in one night and made several calls home. His wife approved the teriyaki salmon club, BUT the wasabi mayo had to be on the side. He asked for two sides. After a few minutes he returned to the counter. He wanted one of the sides now. I'm thinking, "no way." After he left, I went looking. Sure enough, there was the plastic container completely tongue-swiped clean.

The time at Colorado Kitchen helped me learn a lot of things about people, about human behavior. Perhaps I hadn't learned enough about myself. It wasn't long before I was at it again. I traveled down a horrific road to opening another place. The General Store showed me what I hadn't learned. I hadn't learned when to give up.

Chapter Six

Golden Brown & Delicious

Why doesn't she ever smile? I said it to myself. The water was cold, and I couldn't move my lips. I blubbered out air or water. I'm not sure. But now I couldn't force my cheeks to budge. I wanted them to find me that way—smiling. So, I kept trying.

There's a lot of my college freshman year that I don't remember; mostly because it was over 30 years ago. But I remember the first week. For the first time in years I was going from room to room to spend seemingly endless periods of time with people who didn't know me. It was like having the first day of school in a new school 24/7. There was no retreat to familiar folk who knew what made you laugh and what made you cry. There were days of lonely awkwardness, insecurity, and fear. My father, as my parents were about to leave me there alone after having spent the weekend in Baltimore, could see it in my eyes. "Oh, no you don't," he was one step closer to an empty nest and I wasn't about to spoil it for him. "But, Daddy," I pleaded. I was about to tell him I'm scared. I caught myself. How could I tell this man who joined the army and went from peaceful and poor Panama to the Korean War just so he could become an American that I was scared?

My mother wasn't paying attention. She was searching in her bag for a twenty. When she looked up at us and saw my father and me—he glaring, me pleading—and not bothering with that bill, she immediately knew what was going on. "Gillian. You'll be fine." Thinking the best cure was a fast exit, she grabbed my father by the arm, and they were gone. I was alone in a cafeteria full of freshman.

Of course, just as it happened in Kindergarten, I made friends and soon it was as if I had been there for years. I even became pretty popular. In my senior year I earned the prestigious role of Housemaster. I got the big room on the dormitory's first floor and a meal ticket in exchange for taking care of forty members of the class of 1989.

I decided that I would try to help them get over their away-from-home loneliness by remembering their birthday if they had to spend it on campus. Nothing complicated. Just a colorful poster announcing the big day with balloons and glitter pasted to their door. On these days I'd get up early and quietly and anonymously create my altar to their big day.

One Saturday morning I had two birthdays. April on the first-floor corner room was easy. She was an athlete and could drink just about anybody under the table. She could sleep through the rowdy goings on that got the rest of the kids up annoyed and bed-head disheveled.

But Andrew was waking up to his 18th birthday in the corner room with an awkward door on the second floor. I was trapped if the door flew open. I could hear talking coming from inside. And I remembered. Andrew's roommate Lenny had a visitor this weekend. His little brother, Isaac was in town. Isaac was one of those spoiled younger siblings who detested his older brother and wanted to be nothing like him or want anything to do with him. But he adored Lenny's friends. I could tell what was up when I watched them in the Quad. Isaac broke away and ran toward a group of older boys on their way into the dining hall. Lenny called after him, certain that those older boys would get rid of pesky Isaac with a paralyzing punch to the arm. Isaac turned around sharply, his eyes narrowed into slits of hate and his tongue jutted out pink and spiteful.

When Andrew strode into the dorm room in his bike shorts his ten speed on his shoulder, and his bike riding shoes clicking on the linoleum, Little Isaac hopped off of his brother's bed and stuck to Andrew like fly paper. "Those shorts are ugly," he sneered. "Are you going to wear those shoes around the room?" he got even closer. "It's irritating."

Andrew knocked fast and hard on my door Friday night and flew in not waiting for an answer.

"Shhh…" he placed his finger over his lips and whispered, "I'm hiding from Isaac."

"He's having a little trouble with his sexual identity," I explained. Something about being a Housemaster made you part-time therapist and social worker, too.

"His WHAT?" I was not making Andrew feel any better about his new friend.

With the balloons in my hands taped up and ready to go and the poster flecked with stars and glitter I stood for a minute to listen to the voices on the other side of the door. It was Isaac, barking questions to

Andrew about who he's kissed and if he's ever touched a girl down there. I could hear Andrew groaning and Isaac giggling. Isaac's voice faded in and out as if he were pacing somewhere in front of the door. I prayed he would be so preoccupied with Andrew that he wouldn't hear me stick the balloons to the door as they squeaked under the pressure of my fingers. I had the poster up when the balloon that I suspected I had over-inflated squealed and whistled out of my grasp. SHIT. The door flew open. It was Isaac, suddenly looking eight feet tall as I was on my knees scrambling to grab the balloon that was evading me. He looked down at me terrified, and then slammed the door.

"ANDREW…there's a BLACK garbage lady outside!!!"

I was undone and did not catch the balloon or finish Andrew's birthday door decorating. Here I was a senior at Johns Hopkins University—a virtual grown up charged with minding this building full of freshman. But seeing me kneeling on the floor outside of his brother's dorm room, Isaac couldn't get passed my skin color to see me as anything but a cleaning lady.

I was the first black woman English teacher at an Episcopal private school in DC the minute after I'd graduated. I became friends with the Poet

211

in Residence. At dinner the night before with my Panamanian cousin, we discussed the country's recent ethnic conflicts arising with the influx of Jewish immigrants. The Jewish Poet argued her side, that Jews and blacks have way too much in common for there to be strife. But the next morning walking through the halls I countered with Jews being able to maneuver in closed circles of skin color in which black Panamanians were kept on the outside. She argued that blacks should be more sympathetic to Jewish struggles.

I was in a black linen suit with a bright red silk top, carrying a black Coach briefcase and I was wearing my favorite Joan & David peek toe pumps. The Poet wore an old peasant skirt and an even older sweater. She had flattened the back of her ballet slippers and had transformed them into scoots. While we were far from angry, the discussion through the hall of the dorms was getting more and more heated. We didn't notice the popular, tall handsome teacher approaching us. Josh was a young minister whose young family lived on the Close. His father taught at this school before he retired.

"Hi Laura," he nodded at my companion. "Good morning, Mary." He nodded in my direction.

212

I continued. Josh had momentarily made me lose my train of thought. But it was back. "But Laura don't you think the…"

"Forget it." She was looking at her feet, shaking her head. "Just forget it. You're right about everything."

"What?" I turned to face her. "What do you mean, forget it…"

"He called you MARY." She took a deep breath and looked at me.

"Yeah…I know," I wanted to get back to Panamanian gentrification and tourism displacement and what it meant for poor folks. "I don't think he's ever bothered to learn my name…no big deal."

"No, he called you Mary."

"Isn't that the name of the black woman receptionist in the office of the main hall?" I said, way too calmly for the Poet. She often wore a black suit. "You know what they say. We all look— "

"Yes, but what you don't understand is that we are in the dorms," she was exasperated and frustrated that I wasn't getting it. She started frantically scratching her palms. Her hands itched with eczema when she got upset or unnerved. "He called you Mary because he thinks you're Mary, the dormitory maid." The image of Mary flashed through my brain. Yes, I had seen Mary that morning on my way through the dorms to the dining

213

hall for a cup of coffee. She had a fairer complexion than I had and was about 20 years my senior. This morning she had her head tied with a paisley scarf and was wearing a denim shirt—soft from many washes—and a pair of beige capris. "He thinks I'm Mary?" I asked the poet.

These were the types of incidents that took my breath away. As much as I tried to act "white", people were always mistaking me for a "black" person. I'd been perfecting this rejection of the stereotype for years now. I was in the orchestra at school. After four hours of football on Sunday, I turned to PBS and did not leave my seat until Alistair Cook said, "Goodnight"

I was considered a freak by some of the black kids at the school who claimed I talked "white". Behavior that would get me beaten by my parents was the very behavior that would have kept me from being beaten up by this small clique that had determined that their definition of "Black" was the only one. Not conforming was going to earn me a bloody nose.

I was surprised to find that there were a number of people who were buying into it. Black or white, it made no difference. This seemed to be a strange point of agreement. I wasn't living up to the stereotype: a

214

happy-go-lucky underachiever, with loose morals, a constant craving for fried chicken and an inability to use words to resolve conflict.

Hollywood was an influential accomplice: killing off the "good blacks", while the others, good until the climax, turned on the white hero. Saturday morning cartoons had black kids making instruments and spaceships out of discarded radiators and lamp shades. I couldn't imagine my microbiologist mother, who didn't let us outside in our bare feet, letting us anywhere near the local dump let alone allowing us to put our lips to anything tossed in there.

Grown up and working for a living in a suit and heels, I thought those days were behind me. I was hired as the communications director for an association in DC. "Acting white" was paying off in three weeks of vacation and a nice fat salary. There was one big drawback. My boss wasn't happy with my work. He called me into his office. "You're black." He reminded me. I pulled at the sleeve of my herringbone blazer to get a better look at my arm. I agreed. It's true; although, I hadn't thought about it all day. I guess sometimes I forget that I really am black and that's what people see when they look at me. "You're black," he said again, carefully making sure I understood that this was something I had to stop forgetting.

"Everyone involved in this association is white." He waited for me to agree. I did. "There is no way you can communicate: hear their message and convey their message." If I remember correctly at this point my jaw was starting to drop. He was undeterred. "You understand, I'm white like they are," He made a point of meeting my eyes. "Everything you do in this office has to go through me."

Is it any wonder I left this job and began a much longer second career in a professional kitchen? Here I labored for 10 hours a day in the basement or a tucked away fluorescent lit corner of a building where it didn't matter if you had a perfect smile, a beautiful body, or fair skin so long as you put those plates of food up in the window just as the chef told you to. I could be as black, or as white, or as nothing as I wanted to be in the close, hot kitchen of a restaurant.

That is until I opened my own place and was soon under the microscope of a young and hungry dining community. I had lost the anonymity of working under a chef. Now my name was in the paper. Photographers came to take my picture. With the entire city knowing what I looked like, my behavior was being re-examined.

The first photography session made me realize that it was naïve of me to think that race was not an issue. My first open kitchen was at a restaurant early in my career. Cashion's Eat Place was a sprawling place considering its Adams Morgan, DC location. The place would fill up fast on a Saturday. And in the summer, the 20 outdoor seats were taken all night long. We cooked like maniacs, dripping sweat and cursing. When there was a moment to look around, I would guzzle my red Gatorade and scan the dining room. There were dozes people in the room, and I was the only black person in the building.

I left Cashion's to become chef at Evening Star Café. It wasn't until my picture appeared in a local magazine; did I see black people in the dining room. I went to their table. "We saw your picture in the magazine," they were as proud of me as if I was their daughter. "We came all the way from Gaithersburg."

Black folk from all over town crowded in front of Colorado Kitchen early on a Monday morning. It reminded me of the scene from *It's a Wonderful Life* when George and Mary give up their honeymoon to calm the distraught depositors by doling out their travel money after the stock market crash. This crowd had seen the article in the morning paper. My smiling black face got them to the long-forgotten storefront that was now my first restaurant as chef and owner.

I basked in all of the attention from the local black community. They filled the dining room promptly at 5pm. Then the complaints started filing in. Folks had been misled by the newspaper. Expecting soul food, they'd gently put their menus down, say a few words to each other and tell the server on their way out, "We thought this was going to be soul food." No one wanted the white server. Then there was the confusion about the ownership. Is this black or white owned? This question was often answered by Robin, my white business partner, with a simple, smiling "yes."

But it took the angry call from a customer that made me realize I was just not black enough. "So, I can't get carry out?" I had prepared a speech for this as soon as I decided there would be no carry out at Colorado Kitchen. When my daughters and I moved into the neighborhood we trolled the commercial areas for a place to have our Sunday dinner. Subs and Chinese Food served in foam containers from behind bullet proof glass, was all we found. We often spent Sunday in the white neighborhood where they were going to school. In our new 'hood, meals were taken on trash

218

cans and bus stop benches with broken plastic forks. We told our customers to sit your butt down and eat.

My father used to chide us for eating standing up. "What are you a horse?" I took it personally that people thought the "No Carry-Out" option was a bad thing. Besides, I took a certain amount of pride in how my food came together on a plate. The sauce under the fish, not over it. The turned potatoes glazed with butter and browned alternating with similarly colored glazed turnips. I couldn't imagine what would happen to all of that in a hinged foam container. "You mean if I can't eat it there, you won't give it to me to carry-out?" No matter how many ways the question was posed, the answer was still NO.

She called again. It was a Friday night, and the August heat was clashing with a cold front. The sky was turning a creepy gray and the trees were whipping at the power lines. "I can't believe you are not offering carry-out," she said. We had been open just about a month, but I refused to cave in on this one. I had a vision, no, a responsibility to control how my food was delivered. "Obviously you know nothing about what is going on in the world today," she was trying a new tactic. She told me about two

219

income households and busy single parents. Then she hit me with something I never expected, "You're doing a disservice to your race."

Later that year the criticism wasn't as harsh. A black woman had finished her brunch and walked over to me. "It's good to see a black-owned restaurant," she smiled. "We see so many of our black-owned establishments disappearing," she explained. I hated that she would suffer horrible cooking in a black-owned place, especially if I were the owner. I couldn't help but answer, "Perhaps those places are disappearing because the food isn't very good." She was shocked at my answer, but I know firsthand how tough this business is. People get old and their success put the kids through school and in professions far more lucrative and less exhausting. Cleaning slows down. Imagination ceases to be worth it. Good enough is acceptable. And the fryer oil is just too much trouble to change. The appetite for chains has forced many of these mom and pops to step aside. Segregated neighborhoods had nothing but these old stores, now with a shiny new KFC, and a shinier McDonalds moving in there's no longer any reason to pay more than 99 cents for dinner. I tried my best to reassure my customer. "I know plenty of white people who can cook."

I've always believed that only in the smallest way should how you look dictate what you do. If I had my heart set on being a model, nothing would stop me—just that my career would probably be limited to the bra section in the plus size catalog. The runways of Europe or for Vogue, I wouldn't stand a chance. But I never thought about food as a segregated profession. "Black folk get your skillet and stand over there. White people hold on to your brazier and stand right here."

I have to admit, I continue to be a bit naïve. I'm sure if a psychologist asked a representative cross section of study subjects what came to their minds seeing a black woman in an apron and what words popped into their heads; the white guy in an apron would get a much different set of words. Ask the black subjects who they want to see cooking for them. Many of them would pick me, without knowing my background or training or that the first time I had grits I was a sophomore in college.

It is my failure to accept this about my customers that leads me to take notice of the biased-based presumptions to which I'm often witness. We hadn't been open very long when I noticed an older black woman and her daughter. They were coming once or twice a week for breakfast. Other times, the mother, Irene, would be sitting in one of our red Naugahyde chairs later that week having dinner with her husband—a minister. One night she came in by herself and sat at the counter. She ordered a bowl of soup. Soon her daughter joined her and the two sat and shared a chocolate tart. Robin refilled their coffee from behind the counter and took a phone call. We got busy that night and, while I liked to watch the dining room, I soon got too busy to keep my eye on anyone.

When I unlocked the door the next morning and started the coffee brewing. Irene and her daughter came in pretty soon after I had. I brought them the plate of eggs they were sharing and started to get today's soup on the stove. But Irene stopped me. She was hoping we could hire good people.

"Did Robin hire that man she was talking to on the phone?" she asked. I was stunned. I don't think she knew my name and I'm sure I'd waited on her 10 times as much as Robin had.

"What was that?"

"Robin was interviewing a man over the phone," she explained to me. "I know she's having trouble finding experienced staff. I was just wondering how it was working out for her." I was floored. Did Robin really talk to this customer about what was going on with us and this ridiculous idea we had to open a restaurant in a transitioning neighborhood where customers and job applicants didn't feel that they were safe after dark? I guess my disbelief was showing on my face. How did this woman get close enough to Robin to have her confide in her? I didn't know what to say. Nonetheless, misreading my slack jaw and reluctance to answer, she forged on.

"You know," she said trying to get passed my obviously very low IQ, "Robin," she repeated, "the white lady that owns the place."

Black and white customers assumed that my place in the restaurant required that I say, "Yes, ma'am." When a local critic published a letter I sent to him defending a chef's right to do food without customer interjection, people came to the kitchen and asked me to step aside so they could give my white business partner a piece of their mind.

Word got out that other places were coming, other restaurants were on the drawing board, a sad face would inevitably approach, "Who is going to cook here?" I'd explain that I don't always do the cooking. I train people to cook my food after I've developed a menu and recipes. Blank stare. I'd continue that this is the easy part. The hard stuff is sitting across the table from the landlord and trying to get him to come down another $5 a square foot.

Every restaurant that opens will be a new and interesting lucky happenstance. I'll never be looked at as the sage businesswoman who knows what she's doing. I never get used to the "Oh how cute" and the "Oh look at you" or even the "Listen, you're never going to make if you don't take my advice and…" I've got to be young, green, inexperienced, and needing a pair of sure white hands to guide me no matter how much gray hair I've accumulated.

We've all heard that women who insist on having things a certain way, are called bitches. Strong willed, demanding, egotistical—are perfectly acceptable qualities in a male chef. A woman chef with the same qualities must be getting her monthly visit from her friend. Cinch it up a notch for a black woman. A black woman chef is best received when she is both pandering to what is considered the black palette (macaroni and cheese and fish platters) or if her first and foremost personality trait is humility. I have to pretend that I'm not arrogant. I'm neither thinker nor problem solver.

Not everyone has gotten past the images of Aunt Jemima, Rastus, and Uncle Ben. All smiles, eager to please, and devoid of all feelings of self worth; they were a wonderful crew to have cooking for you. You could spit it out right there at the table if you didn't like it or send it back dozens of times. No one went to the trouble of doubting the sincerity of the grin. I'd like to think Aunt Jemima was just letting them go on thinking "whatever" until her rage boiled up inside and she cooked their last meal with rancid fat and sausage left in the danger zone over night. There was no way they could get away from the outhouse to chase her down as she made her escape on a mule. Or perhaps, Jemima and her contemporaries were bigger people than even I imagined them to be. Maybe they lived my mantra: the food is more important than your feelings. The food pleased Rastus so much he didn't give a shit who he was cooking for. It was bacon he handled with care and devotion. It was the buttermilk rich and tangy that filled his heart with joy. He could get passed having to say, "Yessuh," so long as the corn was sweet that season and the turkeys were fat.

I'm not as gracious as Rastus and the stress of the day might show on my face. I've been told that I don't smile enough. We were taught a great many things in culinary school, but I don't remember being instructed to make sure I'm smiling while I whisk the clarified butter into the hollandaise. During my first years cooking, the Chef never chastised me for not smiling and facing the audience while I reach into the 500-degree oven to pull out the sizzling duck breast.

I've got thinner skin than Jemima. Even though I've got a very tongue-in-cheek Monkfish Schnitzel on the menu, my cooking is still described as soul food. It's become an argument that even this first-generation American, born in New York can't win.

I'm a black woman in a professional kitchen. Nothing I cook could take any smarts or sophistication. I'm just doing what was easily learned from being forced to help or tag along to Miss Daisy's. I'm not bitter over the lost childhood, just grateful that I scored a future out of it. Despite the expensive chef clothes, I'm a domestic.

That's why I struggled over the decision to add fried chicken to the menu. I perfected my recipe adapted from Craig Claiborne's making family food during my first year in the pros. And when the oven went down at Evening Star, I substituted the beloved roasted chicken for the fried. It didn't go over as well. But there were a few customers who asked for it. It appeared every once in a while, on a Sunday night at Colorado

Kitchen as just another representation of classic American cuisine. Still, I hesitated to make it the mainstay of a renovated General Store. An amusement park was built around Mrs. Knott's rendition at the Berry Farm in California. Fried chicken was an iconic symbol of the American get together. In good conscience, I couldn't leave it out. If I were to live my mantra, the food had to be more important than *my* feelings

But I wasn't comfortable with everything that could possibly come with me frying chicken. Customers would see it on the menu, glance up and catch a glimpse of me in my chicken-blood-stained apron and say, "Oh yes, of course." Nodding at each other in agreement, "we'll have the fried chicken." And all day that is all that would sell. The corn bread and collard greens just sealed the deal. I had to let go of all of my own feelings of race and what people expected of a black woman chef.

Black women got rich off fried chicken. They'd be at the train stations in the years when Wilson was president with baskets of fried drumsticks to sell to hungry travelers. With all of that chicken money they bought houses, put kids through college. They worked long hours certain their hard work would mean that no one—not they or their kids would have to make a living in front of a hot stove ever again. These women may not have had formal education, but they were resourceful and cashed in on the skills they had. There would be mortar boards and office jobs and black women with initials after their names. There are so many choices out there. Who the hell is foolish enough to even consider going backwards and cooking for a living?

Fried chicken was going to bite me. No one was going to call me chef anymore. I was going to become the big-breasted and thick-legged Miss Gillian.

"You got fried chicken today, Miss Gillian?"

"I always got fried chicken for you, suggah." Tyler Perry is going to play me in the made for TV movie.

There was no money in the corporate account by the time The General Store opened its doors. The creditors had their hands out. In the line at the counter were process servers on delivery. Something had to bring the crowds in and keep them coming. I convinced myself that a white chef with my recipe wouldn't flinch. Just serve the blasted chicken. If I couldn't get past race, how did I expect anyone else to?

I recalled all those times in the kitchen where the new delivery driver looked around for the one in charge. He'd take the invoice to the only white man in the room—my dish washer, or the cook I was training.

There were the customers who assumed I played a lesser role than my partner and restaurant newbie, Robin. "The food always comes out better when you're back there," said one regular customer during one of those busy, short-handed Friday nights where the woman I dragged into this business—my Frankenstein monster she's been called—ran from kitchen to dining room to work the salad station and then bus a table. "It's really not me," she explained, from the kitchen I could see the knot of confusion in her brow. Her hands full of dirty plates she used her chin to point in my direction at the stove, "She's the chef. None of this happens without her." They smiled and nodded at her; with that smile and nod you give to someone stretching the truth; as the special-needs child, usually relegated to bringing Gatorade to the huddle, returns a kickoff for a touchdown at the last meaningless game of the season. Perfectly fit players fall and stagger around him, unable to bring him down. The bleachers empty onto the field and he's hoisted up onto someone's shoulders. I was that special needs kid Robin allowed to "run" things: cute lil' black girl, who needed the wiser white woman's guidance to get through this restaurant thing. All I had was this natural gift...I could mash a potato...sure could. And boy could she fry some chicken. For too many who should have known better I played the Monkey to Robin's organ grinding.

And with Robin out of town and the restaurant gone, I could do nothing but throw myself into this river. Hadn't I been the dumb one that pulled the string thinking I had the world at the end of it? There was nothing more to do but let my lungs fill up and drink it all in—the mud, sticks, whatever was floating in here with me. Put an end to it.

Chapter Seven

Alternate Adding Wet & Dry Ingredients

I couldn't breathe. I soaked up and sucked in as much Potomac River as I could hold. My head full and pounding in the dark water my own thoughts had quieted. It was just a dull hum now

The fried chicken, golden brown and delicious, lived up to its hype. Buttery, garlicky and crisp-skinned, it had everyone talking and took center stage in every review and TV segment.

"Everything she makes is great," servers would say to disappointed chicken fans that had come after we ran out.

"We'll come back." They are soon down the stairs and in the parking lot without reading the menu.

It was as if I was the one who had set fire to the love letter at the campsite and the dry grass caught before I knew it. Yosemite was burning bright enough to see from the space station. I was called out at the movie theater or in line at the DMV, "We love that fried chicken." Talk of my great hollandaise was silenced. Nobody gushed over the crab cakes anymore. Fried chicken was now my calling card and the reason anyone bothered to see me.

Then the Food Network called. First it was Guy Fieri, blonde tipped and full of enthusiasm. And although they tried to keep it a secret, I was making chicken in a banquet hall about to be surprised by Bobby Flay who challenged me with his best batter fried. The exposure brought us crowds at The General Store that we'd never seen.

"Hi, we're from Florida."

"Are you in town visiting family?"

"No, we drove up after seeing you on one show, and then the next."

The shows were aired over and over on a weekend. And with my appearance on CHOPPED soon to follow, we began calling it the Gillian Trifecta. We could hear Bobby Flay's voice scratchy from a TV in the background during a phone call.... "Are you still open?" And we knew what was coming. There was barely enough time to run to the cash and carry and pick up two cases of 8-cut and brine it before the parking lot was overcome and faces pressed against the glass of the front door.

But it wasn't enough. We still owed the attorneys, and there was the back rent. I had been on television more times than any chef without a regular stand and stir gig, yet I had no money. As busy as it was The General Store was still a black hole. Renovating a 19th century store owned by trigger happy landlords had us opening the place in debt well over my chef hat. And as I watched case after case of chicken disappear things never seemed to get better.

***

Before we got there the building had survived three fires, charred beams under the new roof told a tale. There was hardly any plumbing, no insulation, a floor with deep hills and valleys, and electrical wiring that wasn't safe enough to charge a battery.

I let out a bubble of a laugh as I spun around in the undertow of the treacherous river. If only I had jumped before, when the landlord

233

suddenly turned ugly. Instead I imagined opening the car door whenever Robin was driving. I set the child lock to resist the temptation to tumble out onto 395 while she accelerated to 65. It would be selfish and messy. *It took this silly job on this miserable boat to bring out into the middle of this river to make this cleaner exit.*

When our contractor uncovered another costly issue, or the county would not grant our Certificate of Occupancy without more parking spaces, or the utility decided we needed to pay for the installation of a new power pole; the building owner was relentless. We were still months from opening and we weren't paying rent. We tried to talk him out of his latest lawsuit. There were gaps in the sub floor, no room for the HVAC system, and the landlord had dug the floor four inches too high to create the useable prep space.

"Theo," I pleaded, "you had to have known the building was not fit to lease."

"Thstill," he said through a forward thrust lisp. "you thstill have thto pay rent."

"You know we can't." Robin tossed the thousands in contractor bills we were struggling to pay on to the table. The stack wobbled the nearly empty cups of coffee.

"Wellth sthen the courtsth will award me possethion of the premisthisth," he waved his hand. The amount of money we'd spent was meaningless. "Tsthen I'll have the powa to take tsthe thspathe when I want." I felt instantly angry, scared, and powerless. Backed into a corner because of a dumb piece of paper I'd signed, convinced Robin to sign. My head was spinning, and I couldn't bring air in. We'd spent almost all of our SBA loan and we hadn't even finished. And all he wanted was the power to take it all away whenever he felt like it. We'd been tricked. We were alone in a dark room and someone had come in, the only sound was his heavy breathing and the click of the dead bolt.

"This is rape." I said, my throat so dry there was no volume, but the quiet around the table helped lift the words. My lips had turned dry as molted snakeskin and my throat was dirt during a drought. "Is this what rape feels like?" I just wanted to know now. The commotion at the table snapped me out of it. Theo had stood up, the effort of anger and hastily lifting his big body made his breath come in short, hard, bull-like puffs.

His lawyer was grabbing the files and pulling him from the table. The coffee cups toppled now, and cool brew and half & half flowed onto Robin's stack.

"Thid you juth call me a rapith?" He was angry. He hadn't been angry about the rent not being paid. He was angry now. Our not paying the rent was exactly how he wanted it. We had paid for the power pole, the new floor; insulation was behind the walls and in the rafters. The electric and plumbing were just about done. We'd filled out the paperwork for the parking exemption and the last of the drywall had been delivered. The ventilation had been completed including the iron ladder and platform the county wanted us to build around the exhaust fan on the roof. But as we sat quietly at that table, the spent coffee cups and our stack of crumpled invoices scattered and stained, we agreed to walk away and let the rapist have it. We'd lay there without tears or protests; quietly thinking of flowers or bread and butter while he rammed his "powa" in and out of us. Okay, straightening our blouse and pulling our skirt back down over our zipper scratched thighs, and strode out of the room seemingly unaffected, but knowing we'd never be the same again.

When we let go of the old building and the idea of opening the General Store, we called the contractors. I had my finger in my ear so I could hear the dry wall guy, while Robin talked to the electrician. We unlocked the door so they could get there supplies and equipment. It was over. A road trip to my publicist in Pennsylvania and we felt free. We sang along to the radio and I went the whole ride without wanting to open the car door and fall out onto the highway tumbling along at 60, then 50, and then 10 miles an hour as the car sped past me; a bloody heap of broken.

We'd sell whatever we could and get jobs. Robin had started walking dogs and I was willing to dust off my hack license. We owed the bank a lot of money. But our happiness at that very moment was priceless. I was learning to accept defeat and how to raise the white flag. There is no shame in retreating, I told myself. I could live to fight another day.

They were watching the whole time. Maybe from somewhere in the forest that surrounded us. They quietly wondered as trucks and vans maneuvered the sharp curve of the main road into the parking lot. Men in Carhart coats and insulated denim dragged coils of conduit and sheets of drywall out of the building. A steady stream of contractors emptied the almost-renovated restaurant. We were over $100,000 in and turning back.

237

A shiny exhaust fan graced the roof. A new power pole juiced the outlets for heavy equipment. Three new bathrooms were plumbed and fixtured. And the warped and hilly floor had been pulled up and replaced by yet to be varnished planks of rough sawn oak. It was so close the rapist, his slow and bumbling little brother, their white-haired realtor/errand boy could taste it. We could taste it too. But to us it was less chocolate ice cream and more warm bile. The most crucial things were missing and at this point seemed incredibly remote: the final ok from every agency (Fire, Health, Building) that would lead to a precious Certificate of Occupancy. It was what everyone wanted. But right now, today, it became something Robin and I no longer tossed and turned about and clenched our fists to the skies over.

The euphoria was short lived. For less than 24 hours we became two carefree middle-aged women who didn't have a restaurant sucking the life out of us. The phone rang and it was the attorneys.

"What's going on, ladies?"

"We're done. They want the space back…"

"No, they don't." he said. "They've been watching your contractors clear the place out and they're ready to work with you."

238

"But…" I wanted to tell him how happy I was to have taken off the hair shirt of The General Store. I wasn't listening to him. I was imaging my shoe in a wooden box that got smaller and smaller. My arms were tied to one horse, my legs tied at the ankle to another horse facing the other direction. This horse stretched and shook his head, rattling the bridle and grinding on the bit between his teeth. He was ready to go and wouldn't need the sharp slap to his rump. I was focused on staying as still as possible.

"….and then there's the bank. You might want to reconsider and try and work this out."

It took four more months--Priming, painting, tiling, sanding varnishing. We failed inspections. Fire safety insisted we close in the stairs until we pleaded, and an inspector took a second look and allowed us to take down a wall instead. The building had barely survived three fires. Faulty wiring, the illegal preparing and serving of food, folks seated beyond legal capacity. The building inspectors had their eye on us.

Nonetheless, we were close. The exhaust system had failed inspection. I grouted freshly hung tile alongside the stainless-steel wall behind the equipment an hour before the re-inspection. Robin brushed the glossy blue on the trim. And then we poured and spread a thick coat of varnish on to the floor. Our bones ached and we left that place every night barely able to stand upright. Sometimes a neighbor would barge in, attracted by the bright lights around the pale blue building that had been dark for so long.

"What's this place gonna be?"

I rose from the newly tiled floor of the kitchen; my knee pads pinching. I had on t-shirt and sweatpants stained with tile adhesive and black grout. The booth benches had been delivered and the old post office counter was in place where folks would step up and order.

"You mean you can't tell?" I wiped an itchy dry spot of grout off of my chin with a clean spot of my glove. "It doesn't look like a restaurant about to happen?"

"You'd better get a sign," they usually let out with a sneer. We'd see more strange behavior as the year went on. A woman came in at closing to buy a loaf of bread because her mother was in town and rejected her whole grain staple and insisted on the plain white, she'd grown up on. "I've got to have it for her for breakfast." She was frantic.

"I know we called the place The General Store," I explained, strangely afraid of her. "But we really aren't a store." She stormed out cursing.

Then there were the mysterious folks who came in and went straight for the shelves, sliding my olde timey knick knacks and ceramic chickens around like they were searching for something. They'd head to the back room and I could hear them sliding objects around, moving furniture. Finally, a customer in on the joke revealed that his neighbors were searching for some of the antique figures that lined the shelves when the old owner sold antiques amid the mess and ruin. A little ceramic elephant, the sad face of a clown; he wouldn't budge from the marked price. Had any of these been left behind they would surely have been pocketed and then would have appeared on eBay.

"But the place has been gutted," I told a woman who was biting her lower lip in disappointment. She looked through me and was out the door. "…. there was nothing here." I said to her back now well beyond the glass of our front door.

We had decorated the place as if it were an active general store— the buildings original purpose in 1893 when it sprung up with sticks of pine

241

and oak siding. The iron hook by the train tracks (the rumble of the commuter and cargo lines rattled the windows) still stood. They hung the mail from that hook so the train conductor could reach out and just grab it. We posted wanted signs from the times, old newspapers, and old letters and post cards from the antique stores across the Potomac.

A particularly fascinating set were from a spinster in Ohio whose family had made it big in the sealing wax business. She died on the family estate years ago, alone and with just one servant left as the sealing wax business waned. Her brother and sister both married and left her alone to care for the aging parents. The sealing wax king and his wife quietly and without warning died within a few days of each other. And there she was doing things as mundane as signing up for a women's club, inquiring about the delivery of her fur coat, or writing to a friend about to disembark from a cruise ship from New York's Battery.

We marveled at the instructions to the postman, "Please deliver to Dock A tonight." The letters in the downstairs bathroom were more interesting: a young woman was sent to a sanatorium after her father objected to her fiancé. Letters down there pasted to the wall insisted on immediate payments and complaints about deplorable service, the last word from a parent bent on disinheriting a wayward son were finely crafted with perfect grammar and succinct word choice that kept it civil but could still make the reader clutch her pearls.

But there was something neat and relatable about the sealing wax heiress' fine hand and letters imploring her friends out West to support Barry Goldwater or introducing her cousins to a friend's new wife. We were charmed by them and often sat at the table by that wall to imagine what her life was like and recreate her day to day in our imaginations.

The letters pasted around the building was one indication that we invited our own misery. Another was the Nickelodeon. When the concept vibrated out of the walls and into our brains we imagined bringing this General Store to life with all of those things somebody might find should they tie their horse up at the front of the building and come in to post a letter, purchase flour, sorghum or a few yards of gingham for a new apron. Our wild imaginations and business model of making the concept permeate the building for a unique dining experience; Robin and I were convinced the store's music system had to come from a Nickelodeon. We'd about given up on acquiring one, but Robin out antiquing in Hagerstown stumbled upon an old player piano with 5-piece band behind a glass frame under the keys and a chad cut roll of classic American tunes when you flipped up the lid. We couldn't believe the price. We had almost settled on a $9000 accordion on barrel that played itself when you deposited a quarter. This was an entire, functioning piano with drum, cymbals, tambourine, cowbell and accordion for $7500. This was a bargain.

The varnish had dried. The furniture was in place. Robin took a razor blade to the windows to scrape the paint. I vacuumed and rubbed tacky paper everywhere to get the last of the paint dust. Robin's idea of having a cigar Indian morphed into a chainsaw cut bear and finally to taxidermy. We had a stuffed black bear and a lazy raccoon to solidly bring the atmosphere of the building back to the 19th century.

Then the call came: the nickelodeon was ready. We rented a truck and headed to Pennsylvania to get it. We drove through a rainstorm to a rural Pennsylvania town that didn't even have a spot on the map. The directions to his workshop were sketchy. It was as if he was counting on us giving up and turning back so we'd hire the crew he recommended. But $200 to rent a truck and drive ourselves was more than we could afford right now. We certainly couldn't pay $550 plus fuel for hired help. We hit a deer on the way. We lost GPS and phone signals 100 miles out. And the dark and rain made the roads slick and hard to stay on. We followed the lights of a house in the dark. Robin went to the door with her hair and clothes soaked to her body. From the cab of the truck I watched a woman upstairs dim her light and hide behind the curtain. We tried the next house. When my partner had not returned in what seemed like forever, I imagined she was being tortured and assaulted. What were we doing? What were we thinking? My anxious breathing fogged up the windows as I was sure she was in there being forced to perform sex acts on an old man and his disfigured son. They had her in the barn by now and if I did see her again, she wouldn't be the same and we might as well forget all about this player piano and this restaurant because she'd be a shell of her former self and in no shape to manage the store.

The driver's side door swung open with a groan and the sound of rain spattering the mud was suddenly deafening again. I opened my eyes to find her, rainwater dripping from her ears and chin, sliding into her seat. She opened her hand where she'd crumpled a map scrawled on a torn page of a yellow legal pad. We rolled down the muddy road straining our eyes to focus on the dim beam of the head lights. Then there it was; a large, paved circular driveway, a barn on the other side. One door was open, and we could see wood, odd tools hanging lit by rows of fluorescents.

"I never thought you'd find me," he seemed disappointed. Before long we were back on the road and arrived at the front of the restaurant, backing the truck as close as we could to the front door. It was two in the morning when we let loose the rope securing the player piano to the inside of the truck. We slid the ramp down and panicked. The ramp supported only two thirds of the pianos base, about six inches and a set of tiny wheels hung over the side. We were exhausted, no longer trusting the fates, and battling the image in our brains of the piano—that took five years off of our lives and yet wasn't even in the building yet—was going to topple over and explode into pieces. It took almost an hour to have the courage and faith to slide it into the building. We held each other collapsing into grateful sobs. Maybe after this, after this one thing stuff would start to go our way.

I'm no longer too embarrassed to admit what I hoped the player piano would do. I was hoping it would charm folks into liking me. I was done with being hated and disliked because rumors and fantasy had people distrusting the gifts I was bearing. Here I was trying to get people to like

246

me. I thought bringing this disaster of a building out of the way of a wrecking ball, decorating it with flights of fancy—I know I've never come across a working nickelodeon before and I haven't since—folks would say, "There she is. Isn't she wonderful?" Instead of, "Is that her? Why doesn't she ever smile?" How many restaurants did I have to open to convince them?

There was a bayonet to our backs when we opened the doors to The General Store. The landlords, the bank, our attorneys had a huge stake in what happened in that cash drawer. Negotiations to end the court battle meant we'd be paying off back rent with an added $4,000 on our monthly payment. We owed the bank for the construction costs, the lease on the equipment, and we owed the attorney thousands of dollars and our thanks for helping us to get open. Hooray. Robin and I no longer imagined that owning and operating would propel us out of the working middle class. We might as well have had shackles on. Bills weren't being paid; the mortgage payment was late.

We announced opening day with emails to our Colorado Kitchen regulars and crossed our fingers. Sometime after 11 am the door flew open and dozens of people I've never seen before flooded in. A woman grabbed

247

one of the chairs from around a table and she danced with it across the room to place it in front of the player piano. A crowd had gathered around it as her husband began pounding on the keys. His entourage started bellowing over the crowd noise. They were trying to make it a party, their party. I hesitated. I couldn't let this happen. They argued with me. But I insisted. No hands on the keys. Put a quarter in it. Let it do its thing. Please no singing, we have people trying to order and we can't hear them. The crowd was divided. There was a contingent that really came to eat.

And then there was another who wanted to stake their claim on the place. Come and go when they pleased. Plant themselves in the back room and bring their own food and alcohol to say goodbye to a neighbor who was moving or celebrate the new ordinance that silenced the trains whistling through the crossing outside our door. They had watched this building burn three times, they'd been in it to finger figurines and eat food from a kitchen not sanctioned by the health department. And somehow, they were convinced it was theirs and my new quick serve restaurant existed by their grace. They wanted to be able to fold their arms and tell me what should be on the menu and how much I should charge.

They were counting on my gleeful participation as their children pounded on the keys of the piano or ripped young shoots of basil out of my herb garden. I had to give up my own ego to be a part of this. The food and concept weren't enough or wasn't even a consideration. I needed to sign my rights away with the blood of my index finger. The food was great. The beer and soda selection were unique and varied. The downstairs tavern had televisions and games. What more did they want from me? I added vegetarian sandwiches and let people pay to pick the parts of fried chicken they wanted. We did cool things like play nature sounds through speakers hidden in bird houses. But still after all of that reactions ranged from nonplussed to "can you turn that off, the thunder sounds are scaring my child."

That first day I trembled and went through the day as if I were watching it on an old tube television. The knobs were broken, or I'd have changed the channel. We stayed open as long as we could—until there was no more food. I quelled my nerves and fear by diving headfirst into a menu rework and an examination on how to do it better. The thing I like most about this business is shutting the door at night and starting the next morning with a new vision on how to improve upon the day before. I can change the food, answer the cries for more pedestrian beer selection, allow

249

people to order the tavern specials in the upstairs dining room. Changing who I am, that's another thing altogether. But we soon found out, that is what Nightshade Barbra and her crew wanted.

Barbra came in the minute we opened day two. Today's pies were in the oven. Plenty of chicken had been fried, finishing in the oven it would then go into the warmer with the trays of buttered corn bread. Greens, chili, tortilla soup were working. It was 8am and we held out hope that breakfast would be a neighborhood thing and we could sway the locals with crullers and muffins and a breakfast sandwich that I had been working on for years. Inside a lightly toasted ciabatta roll were softly scrambled eggs, a crispy layer of hash browns, and a customer's choice of vegetables, cheese, bacon or sausage.

"What is this place?" she asked. I was alone at the counter as Robin was rolling pie crusts and filling muffin tins in the prep kitchen downstairs. Bacon had come out of the oven and muffins caught the sunshine with their sugary tops. I smiled at her. Was she serious? I slid a menu to her over the glossy varnish of the counter that I had sanded and brushed shiny just a week ago. She blinked her eyes at me but did not relent. She needed an answer.

"You really can't tell?" I was sure she was kidding. Silence. "It's a restaurant." I felt silly for answering.

"Well, you should have a sign." Was that it? Was that why everyone was kind of mad at us? Rolling their eyes. Tsking. Waving us off as you would a gnat, an amateur. Were they thinking when they drove by the brightly lit building (the county insisted we place bright outdoor flood lights at the front and side entrance), these two women are a joke? Sure, they made that shell safe enough for the fire inspector to let people in there. They've got a taxidermy bear and raccoon in there, a player piano, seating for 40, bird houses that play sounds and music, a cozy little bar downstairs that's dark and moody from those black out curtains. The word "SIGN" now makes the hair on the back of my neck stand up.

I had prepared a speech: "The fact of the matter is that signs are expensive. Oh sure, we can slap anything up on the building to read "The General Store", but we've spent a great deal of time and money to come up with a look and feel that a giant home computer generated banner would only mock all our efforts. This building didn't come easy. We have several large loans we're working to pay back. Our monthly rent has us sweating every day. A sign is just not in our budget right now. We've spent hours

251

picking colors, traveling to Egypt to bring home a nickelodeon, finding a taxidermist to stuff a bear and raccoon, crawling around in the attic to wire speakers for our nature sounds. Yes, we've thought about a sign. There is very little we haven't thought of. Yes, we plan on eventually getting a sign. But the bottom line is that all these questions are asked by people standing in the building who have obviously found their way here. We do appreciate everyone's concern for our success, though. I never did say this. Although it was on the tip of my tongue.

"What can I get you?" I uttered quickly to break the silence. I poured her a coffee and gave her a minute to read the menu. Her potato allergy made her hesitate to order the breakfast sandwich. "I'm allergic to nightshade plants." I'd never heard of such a thing. And I listened as I made her sandwich without the crispy potato layer. She told me about how she'd changed her diet and rid her body of arthritis. But she was still prone to bouts of depression and anxiety. She blamed the tomatoes, eggplant, and potatoes that had been part of her largely vegetarian diet.

I made Nightshade Barbra that sandwich every day. Then there was the morning she came in and found a line and customers waiting for their orders. I poured her a coffee and sent her on her way. We could settle

252

up later. She mouthed a thank you and disappeared in the crowd of winter coats at the door. In a minute she was back, red faced and flustered. She had an empty to go cup in her gloveless left hand. She blinked her eyes dry—glossy from the wind or stress, I wasn't sure. "I dropped it…." She whispered. She looked as if she'd seen a ghost. I wondered, as I poured her a fresh cup with a chuckle and a pat of the hand to put her at ease, if her husband beat her.

It wasn't long, after we opened that a small band of customers became regulars including one tall brooding woman who joined us weekly, ordering in a husky voice eyeing us to see if we could tell that she preferred the company of women. One afternoon, she finally found something in the old building to make her smile. "Those letters," she said cheerfully to Robin, "I know who that is, I know her family." Robin could hardly take her seriously…. the family is from Ohio, she thought to herself. "That's great," she told her.

"Catherine Walls' niece is a friend of mine," I'm going to bring her in tomorrow. "She is going to love this." For the first time she did what so many other customers didn't—she acknowledged us and spoke to us. She didn't eye us with suspicion and wariness that so many others did, opening the door slowly and drilling their eyes into me as I plated their fried chicken or occasionally manned the POS. The rumor was that I never smiled and had a mean streak. The strict dining room protocols against seating a pair at a four top at the 48-seat Colorado Kitchen had labeled me. The limited storage space in the 300 square foot kitchen back at the now closed Colorado Kitchen meant I wasn't too eager to make substitutions and I didn't believe in kid's menus. I became the chef "who mistreats her customers."

But something strange started with a bomb scare. It came right after we'd banned a customer from Colorado Kitchen. He had been in the dining room enough times to have watched Magalee grow form pre-teen to young lady. And when he whispered and gestured something creepy to his dining companion, Robin showed him the door. The bomb scare was a harmless interruption that delayed our Sunday Brunch. The police showed up and looked around, confident it was a prank. We moved on. Forgot all about the creepy customer. Colorado Kitchen was gone. And we went through a difficult labor that almost killed us and gave birth to The General Store.

And things got weirder and a little too sophisticated than just a prank that might have been carried out by the creepy customer. A pounding on the door got us out of bed early on a Monday. Someone had called 911 and reported hearing gunfire from 630 Otis Place. Everyone present, not bleeding, and accounted for; the cops left satisfied that there had been some mistake. We thought nothing of it until our neighbor came by the restaurant to tell us that the police had been by and had been called to investigate shots fired again at 630 Otis Place. "This is the third time they've come to my door looking for you guys," she said. Were we being "swatted"?

This all culminated on a night I was so tired from a busy day that started at the poultry supply at 7am and ended with a drive home at 11, my head snapping back and then forward as I fought sleep. Another pounding at the door got us out of bed at 2:00 am, Robin flew down the stairs and I peeked out of the window—the street, the house was glowing red. I thought 630 Otis Place was engulfed in flames. When I parted the blinds, I saw them all down there blocking the street: ambulances, police cars, fire trucks, tactical vehicles. No sirens, but red and yellow lights making more than enough noise. This time the caller reported an active shooter, hostages, and casualties. I stood at the door while the police looked us over in our pajamas, their guns drawn. How close had they come to shooting one of us?

One man stood out in the commotion. He was there on the sidewalk while the officers waved the squads off. Trucks pulled away and rumbled bright but quiet through the traffic light. He pushed his glasses up off his nose as he stood there in khakis and a windbreaker, staring at the scene and our house. I didn't know this guy and didn't think anything about him standing there until I realized it was just passed 2:00 am.

I wondered about the nature of people—what makes someone dislike a stranger to this point? Was this what my making food drove people to? The folks at this new store had heard all about me. They came in the door waiting, expecting me—the mysterious black woman under a chef hat—to show a flash of temper. To "swat at them with a rolled-up magazine" as was once reported. They expected me to refuse to make something for them, to not acknowledge their smile, but snarl at them instead. We were almost a month in and none of them smiled at me. What they didn't know is that I was really at the General Store against my will and if it weren't for the gun to my head, I'd be happily working at a diner somewhere breaking eggs over a flat top grill. I spent most of the day dodging bill collectors and hoping that the guy in the trench coat was not here to serve me a summons to appear in Landlord-Tenant Court.

I had forgotten about the woman who had smiled at our collection of letters until the large, masculine woman appeared at the door showing all of her teeth in an uncharacteristically wide grin as she led a tall, scrawny, bottle-red head into the dining room. She paused at the counter to ask for two fried chickens with mac. She slapped her credit card on the counter with a wink and a confident hitch in her step—almost skipping. She took the niece to the table framed by a powder blue wall where her aunt's letters were affixed with Mod Podge. The big grin was gone by the time Robin brought them their food. Catherine's niece was in tears as she plopped her big bag onto the table. She shoved the spare glasses, keys on a ring and checkbook wallet out of the way and grabbed the bottle of Xanax. She squinted and glared at Robin through her tears.

"How could you?" she shrieked and ran into the bathroom with the bottle of pills. She was shouting loud enough that we could hear her at the front door. "This is a violation." She returned from the bathroom, tears staining her face. She clutched a soiled tissue in her fist and popped a long

257

finger out to wag in Robin's face, "This is a gross invasion of privacy and I demand to know how you got your filthy hands on my Aunt Catherine's letters."

"EBay," Robin told her, "We bought dozens of letters. None of them from your family really say anything person— "

"I want them." She shouted. She stormed back to the wall and stood there, her hands on her hips. Her large companion seemed quite manly now, unable to calm the hysterical woman or talk sense into her. Meanwhile, Robin had been downstairs and got the remaining stack of letters from the Sealing Wax clan. The niece confronted her at the counter.

"I've got a young man from El Salvador who works for my husband," she looked steely eyed at Robin, rubbing her palms dry down the length of pinstripe wool on her thighs. "He is going to come in and take this wall." After seeing the look of panic in Robin's face (there was plumbing and electrical in that wall), she offered, "I'll pay for the whole thing--removing the wall and replacing it." She had, with the Xanax in her, arrived at a neat solution and now dried her eyes with the soiled tissue. She dotted the end of her nose with it before she put it in her bag and zipped it shut.

"These are all we have left from your aunt's collection," Robin handed her a rubber-banded stack of 30 or 40 sharp letter opener sliced envelopes, some of them were empty. Some were bright white with a striped red and blue border or pale blue feather light onion skin *par avion*. The woman snatched the stack from Robin's hands as if she were grabbing her purse from a street urchin who'd picked it up after she'd dropped it. With that, "I didn't drop it, you pick pocketed me," kind of look.

"He will be here to take that wall down first thing Monday morning." She stormed out and was in the parking lot and gone. The slow closer on the door that we had installed and reinstalled had not shut the large old wooden door before her car was turn signaling left at the light.

Her friend still sat there stunned. She sat at the table where the red headed kin to the Walls family had left her. Her chance to score big with her friend had blown up in her face.

Then the anonymous letter arrived, telling us to clean up our act. The neighborhood that surrounded us was comprised of four different communities. Each had their own private list serve and chat page and two women running The General Store were the main topic of conversation every day. The food was not enough. And it would never be as far as this contingent of haters was concerned. Robin read to me the ugliness that was swirling around us: I never smiled. We were rude. We scolded their children. We never listened to suggestions. Where was the sign? There was a name signed at the bottom of that letter recalling dozens of dining room tragedies. It was Barbra, Nightshade Barbra. She was now dead to me. I no longer stopped what I was doing to greet her and bypass the counter girl to hand her her special sandwich. I put it in the window like all of the rest.

The saving grace was that our regular customers from Colorado Kitchen found their way to our new digs and we often had pleasant days where the room was filled with happy, familiar faces. But then there were the folks made curious by the community conversation and then found my pouting work face meant absolutely nothing to them. The chicken, that spectacular fried chicken was what they came for. And some of them came for lunch on Tuesday, dinner on Thursday and then again on Saturday.

Still there was the couple, stoked by the list serve, who came in looking for an opportunity to say, "My word. It's exactly how Barbra described. I've never been treated that way at a place where I'm spending my money." It was early in the evening and we were plugging through a smattering of orders on a Tuesday night when they came in. The woman wore a large brimmed hat that covered much of her face, but her husband was scowling. He stared me down from the customer side of the counter. I was frying shrimp for a po' boy and I could feel his eyeballs burning into my neck. He looked like he wanted to hurt me. I swallowed hard and slowly turned my head to see if he was still looking at me. His forehead melted down into his brow and his eyes narrowed. I tried to think, to remember, "Do I know this guy?"

The woman ordered demurely, politely asking our counter girl for a this and a that. The man still scowled at me. Then he turned to the girl and barked. We quietly put up their food on the aluminum trays that in our imagination might have done for dishware back when the shopkeeper served a bite or two for his customers' long horse-drawn ride back to the farm. Our runner placed the food in front of them. He was on her heels and back angrier than he was before, "I also ordered a cheese steak!" he shouted. He stood there; arms folded. We had intentionally not made his sandwich. And he was going to stand there and watch me and make sure I didn't spit into it.

It wasn't long before the encounter was memorialized in a review of the place. But it was more a review of Robin's and my behavior. We hadn't smiled at them. I hadn't come from behind the stove and greeted them. The food was good, but how could customers come to The General Store and endure this mistreatment? She had given voice to the list serves. We were bitches and had no business running a restaurant. It was a theme that spread as if sparks from a dragging muffler had drifted with the dry wind to the parched grass at the side of the road. The forest was on fire. Chef Gillian, the chef who mistreats her customers. The magazine article, when we finally got our hands on it, lead with two-inch-high type: *In the Shadow of No Smile.* Not knowing the tone of the piece when the photographer came, Robin and I stood by the original post office counter at the front of the room wearing toothy grins. He had said, "Smile." as he opened the shutter. And we did.

The phone calls made all of this meaningless. There were the producers from *Chopped*, the folks behind *Diners, Drivers & Dives*, and then Bobby Flay's Rock Shrimp Productions that produces *Throwdown.* But before all of that I got a call on the quiet of a late Tuesday night. My father's cancer was back. It was in his bones. And as much as we held out hope that he would beat it again, all of us knew it was a long shot. The magazine, the list serves, the people who wanted me to smile; I didn't care about any of them anymore.

Chapter Eight

Bring to a Boil and Reduce by Half

This business had taken hunks of my life. I missed school plays, PTA meetings, birthdays. I had only gotten to see my father three times before he died. I ignored the calls from the woman trying to nail me down for an appearance with Bobby Flay. I was sitting with my mother and sister with the funeral director. She was sending my phone into wild vibrations a minute apart. I finally excused myself and took her call and agreed to be on a new show on the Food Network called Fried Chicken Kitchen which would morph into a fried chicken showdown with Bobby Flay.

I broke down when I was eliminated from *Chopped*, unable to push down the sobs that were bubbling out of me like hot cereal overcoming a lidded pot, the weight of my father's death still heavy on my heart. It felt like it was beating a soft dull thud three times a minute. I left New York and went back to the restaurant and picked up right where I left off clawing my way through the days, and grateful for the solitude of the weekends where bill collectors took the day off and courts were closed.

I dragged through the day like a sad robot, cutting greens, frying chicken, stirring chili. When a man my father's age or older would come in and scowl or frown or complain about our lack of cheap beers or scold staff because I'd run out of chicken; I could not contain myself. I had to fight back tears of anger and crushing sadness, "Why is that man still alive?" My father spent his life lifting people out of terrible situations (he brought homeless men from the brink as a social worker and helped them create new lives.) He loved people and he would have flirted with my staff even if I'd run out of chicken. Scowl, frown, or shout? The thought would never have occurred to him. "Why is that man still alive?" I'd choke. "And my father is gone."

Taping the Food Network shows, making the list in the local paper of top new restaurants, a feature story in *Southern Living Magazine*, being voted Hottest Chef by *DC Style*—anything positive or negative had been eclipsed by my father's death.   The bayonet in my back poked me just hard enough to get me going each morning. Every day seemed impossible. I recalled a story Potocka once told me about a drive with a guide through the African bush interrupted by a flat tire. The party laughed when the driver opened the car's tool kit to find just a spare and a screwdriver.

"You don't understand," the driver was shaking. "We need to change this tire. There are bandits in those bushes. They'll kill us all."

I've asked her dozens of times, "How the hell did you do it?"

"I don't know," she'd squint through her cigarette smoke, "We just did." Here I was with a flat in the African bush and I didn't even have the screwdriver.

We weren't any closer to seeing the light at the end of the tunnel. What made it worse was that we were doing it all amid scowling faces and customers wanting more from me than great fried chicken. A guy we hired to tend the tavern downstairs allowed people to think that he owned that part of the business.

"If I didn't go along with it," he apologized, "they would have walked out for sure."

And then it was like a cork was pulled out of the bottle and in the blink of an eye we had a Food Network television generated fan base. We were swamped.

***

The restaurant filled up and cars with tags form Illinois, Texas, Florida, Tennessee were clogging the parking lot and taking up the shoulder on the winding county road. There were people eating standing up and we had no room for the mean-spirited neighbors.

This went on for weeks as shows were aired and re-aired. Our numbers doubled. When I beat Bobby Flay with my fried chicken recipe, they tripled. We caught up on the mortgage, paid off the equipment loan and celebrated our anniversary with a feeling that maybe this could work after all. Still, our feet were over the fire. There was almost $200,000 in loans, back rent, and legal fees. And as we robbed Brad to pay Tim, there was very little left to go around. The bulk of the money went to rent with ROI projections stretching into the next century.

The smoke would clear, and we would slow again. We had stopped doing breakfast, so I no longer had to go out of my way to shun

Nightshade Barbra. Mop buckets and degreaser would come out for an early close. Then the phone would ring.

"Thank you for calling the General Store."

"Hi, are you open right now?" the voice was sharp and loud as the caller tried to talk over a shouting Guy Fieri or the cheers from when Bobby capitulated. The background noise meant a busy weekend and it would start all over again.

With the media attention my hamster wheel flew into overdrive.... a head spinning 3000 RPMs. But it was still a hamster wheel. Up at 7, to the cash and carry at 8 (we'd bounced so many checks almost all of our purveyors had cut us off), unload cases and cases of chicken with a fold up hand truck from Costco. Fried chicken ready at 11:10 am; almost too late for the angry mob at the door and the constantly annoyed folk who would ask crazy questions like—

"Do you grind your own pepper?"

"Of course."

"I can't eat here; fresh ground pepper always has nubbins in it."

And— "How come I can't buy just one cookie, I'm a diabetic?"

Or— "Excuse me, why aren't I being served?"

"I'll be right with you ma'am; I'm just going to bring this table their food."

"Still, I've been waiting."

"I know and I apologize, but right now I'm the only one here."

"Well, that's just too bad."

Also— "I want a breast with the $3 chicken snack."

"I'm sorry you can get a breast for $6 but the snack only comes with a drumstick."

"I'm a nurse and I'm not accustomed to settling and I don't expect to settle now."

"So, would you like the breast for $6?"

His slicked back hair was a giveaway, as was his monochrome outfit. He didn't have the free flowing unkempt of Forest Glen accessorized with patchouli and sandals. He was the process server, the one we feared most and expected. Any day now. Any day.

We were back in Landlord-Tenant court. Because we were behind on our sales tax, the county had dissolved our LLC, which strangely meant we could represent ourselves in this losing battle. I threw everything at them at the first hearing: claiming the landlord was a competitor and trying

269

to shut us down. I argued to the judge that we were served just 10 days before our hearing and needed more time to find an attorney (which I knew we would never be able to afford). It was a surprise little victory for us— we brought a butter knife to a gun fight but still managed to draw blood from the landlords $200 an hour lawyer. And it bought us a 30-day postponement, in other words, another $36,000.

We left quietly. Taking only the wooden signs that hung outside, and around on the trees directing folks who were often stuck at a light on that winding road that we had fried chicken and homemade pies. And the raccoon. Robin went to erase our chalkboard menu and found that someone—the landlord most likely—had scrawled "86 Robin & Gillian".

Rumors swirled; social media smoldered. I was untouchable. A chef job was impossible now. I'd been marked. The stench of failure was all over me. The more I struggled and wiped, my hands and clothes were all the more covered with the sticky blood of murder.

The remote corner of Southwest DC was a miraculously safe refuge. No one had heard of me. The docks might as well have been a different country. There were cooks and chefs who had no knowledge of the goings on at the restaurants everyone praised and bashed in food loving circles of the nation's capital. On paper I was a line cook again. My years of experience could not be ignored, and I was in charge of preparing and serving food on a 30-person party boat that turned laps in the Potomac. It was $14 an hour with overtime. There were days that I got on that boat at 3 in the afternoon and walked home from the dock at 4 am.

I lived a life in the shadows. I hid my face behind my collar. I replaced my signature floppy white toque with a black bandana. I was just another working slob. That's the message I shot out of my eyeballs and posture when I suspected a flash of recognition from someone sharing my train car. A bartender on one of the bigger vessels opened her mouth when she saw me. She turned away, and then looked again. I remembered her; she'd come to Colorado Kitchen looking for a job. We were turning tables and turning folks away with a 40-minute wait and word was out that money was to be made. Unlike those slow first months, we now were in a position to be choosey.

"Aren't you..." she started. Wagging a finger at me as if I was bad and I was cheating.

"I cooked there for a couple of weeks," I coughed and sunk lower into my shoulders.

I feared the appearance of a regular customer. I had plenty of close calls out in the street. I slowed my pace or turned and took the long way. One of them might make it onto this boat. The food that came out of that kitchen made me ashamed. There were no fresh herbs. Fish was stored in freezer burned planks in an iced-over fridge that had to be slammed shut but rarely was. Plates and silverware were soaked in a tepid galley sink in between courses. I dreaded any conversation about it. Clocking in, clocking out. I didn't want to think or talk about the ugliness in between.

My miserable day could start with me walking past the neighborhood crazy.

"You got a light?" She would say with a sour expression. When I'd tell her no, she'd say, "You lyin' bitch." Sometimes she'd be on the corner when I came home and with my head hanging from fatigue, I wouldn't notice her until it was too late. It's 4 am by the way.

"You got a cigarette?"

"No, I don't smoke."

"Why you lie to me, you fuckin bitch?" her face contorted with hate, she'd shout loud enough to cause lights in houses down the block to flip on. I was miserable with an extra helping of downtrodden. I avoided everyone. I had nothing to say that wouldn't be choked with sobs.

That rainy night was the answer. The food waiting in the warmers as the boat sat out the storm was an abomination, but it was all that we had to serve. I didn't want to be in this chef coat while that food was being served. I would expect, I would welcome an uprising. The raw red wine stench of the sauce the sous chef made had taken over the galley. Everyone needed air. I drifted to the rear deck. The front salon was crowded with party goers. The bar was open through the storm. Drinks were strong. The plan was that no one was to leave that boat, impatient and hungry. We charged by the person. The rain had stopped and sloshy folks in suits and heels leaned and lurched their way around the ship. A crackle of the speakers and then the boat lurched to the side, backed up, and slowly turned away from the gray slabs of weathered wood. We were underway.

. By now I had talked myself into swinging my legs up so that I sat on the railing. In a minute I was in the water, the boat pulling away from me, the hooting and hollering from the crowd distant and sounding like the

273

cries of a dozen sea birds. There was no flash of "Oh no, what have I done?" Just the, "How long is this going to take?"

The water trembled. And there was that sound again. My ears had gone dead. I felt the hollow quiet of what I assumed what being deaf was like. But there it was again. It was definitely a sound. Was I swimming or was the pull of tide or undertow taking me toward it? Anyway, it was getting louder. I'd heard it before. I could almost place it. But I knew it was a sound I hadn't heard in a long time. I tried to name it. It was on the tip of my tongue. There it was again. Louder this time. Was someone shouting? Perhaps the crew noticed I was gone and was looking for me, shouting to me from the deck and shining a light onto the green water. But none of them knew my name, what could they possibly be shouting? Certainly, none of them would be calling me "chef." "GILLIAAAAHN!" I could have sworn I heard my father calling me.

My father used to call me when he'd come home from work and I'd be too busy with my nose in a book or waving a pencil at the stereo to the down beats and holding my palm out to quiet the cellos of the St. Martin in the Field Orchestra to pianissimo to notice.

He'd shout until I answered, "What!"

274

"GILLIAAAAAHN." Louder this time because WHAT was not an answer in my father's world.

"Yes, Daddy?" I'd be saying, correcting myself, as I stumbled down the stairs. First there'd be the teenage wobbly neck, foot stomp pout. But then I'd remember…wait. Daddy's home. I'd snap out of it and I'd tumble down the stairs straightening my spine and making as much noise as I could as I stomped down to the foyer. He stood at the banister, slightly pouting and maybe stifling a laugh.

"Well…" His perfect Windsor knot was pulled loose and his sleeves were rolled up just above the wrist. He still had his car keys in his hands. His suit jacket on the hook of his index finger over his back or resting on the shelf of his forearm his big fist pushed into his hip.

"Oh…. Good Evening, Daddy." No matter how many evenings we went through this ritual, I still seemed to forget that if I wasn't at the door to greet my father when he came in from work, he'd make me.

"Good Evening." He'd look at me seriously. A slight nod and I was dismissed. And he'd stride into the kitchen, sometimes deftly slicing a chicken into its parts before taking a minute to change out of his dress shirt and slacks.

"GILLIAAAAHN!"

I couldn't see him, and his voice was strong and loud as it was before cancer weakened it.

"GILLIAAAAHN!"

I could hear the laughter behind it. He was watching me swirl around in the cold water and could not hold back a chuckle.

"What are you celebrating?" My father usually asked me this when I was doing something stupid; like the time I was headed out to catch the train and stomp around the Peppermint Lounge to Duran Duran with my friends. I had on one red sneaker and one black. I had on a leather skirt and a vest I'd made from tin foil and a trash bag. I was back at home in high school and I looked down at what I was wearing. But this time there was no foil vest. It was a tan bra and waterlogged hound's-tooth chef pants that had slid down to mid-thigh. I could see the bright white of my socks. My heavy work shoes were gone.

I didn't have an answer. I was holding back tears. I've not cried very much in front of my father. There was the day after my high school graduation when we left the vet's office without the cat. He'd brought Serena home, a chubby little Siamese he'd found in the parking lot, when

I was in the second grade. Ten years later her lungs were full of tumors. My father drove, and I sobbed quietly with my forehead pressed against the glass of the passenger window.

I tried not to cry now. I had hidden from my father just how bad it was. He was too sick to watch. But one afternoon I kicked my shoes off and stretched out beside him in the bed where he was suddenly so small and gray, a bed he rarely left. I told him of Guy Fieri ("Who is he?") and that they wouldn't admit or deny that the show they wanted me on next was Throwdown. As far as he knew things were going great. But when he shot up to heaven that morning in June, he probably looked down at all of the handwringing that was going on in the General Store as if the roof had been torn off.

"Huh…. what, what?" My father's way of urging me to speak…. surely, I was answering him, and he just couldn't hear me.

"It's not good, Daddy." I managed. I was sobbing like that day the vet took my best friend from my arms.

"It's not good?" He drew air and saliva through his teeth before rumbling the water with another laugh. "It's supposed to be good?" a typical Afro-Caribbean philosophy of you'll never be disappointed if you

277

expect the worst. "Did someone tell you it was going to be good? Someone told you that it's going to be good, all of the time?" This is the line of questioning that Afro-Caribbeans use to prove a point—making your argument sound utterly ridiculous—a foolproof motivational technique.

"No, but…"

"Well," he laughed again, "it will never be good now." The sad irony of this made me laugh, too. "It can stay *not* good. And that would be fine." It was as if he turned a light on like the one in the hall that he'd turn on as I came running down the stairs to wish him good evening. "But what if you're missing a chance to make it good?" The light flickered and blinked and finally steadied, lighting the surface of the water.

"It will never be good with you down here." He said that in a tone that came with bad news or when I knew my father was serious. The last time he used that tone of voice was when he said, "Don't marry that guy." And I didn't listen.

"It will never be good with you down here." He said it again. The light shining on the green water flashed and flickered on the debris brought down by the storm. Webs of leaf covered branches and splintered limbs bobbed and spun with their soggy ends beneath the surface. I took hold of a limb with my swollen fingers, wrinkled and water-logged. I pulled my face to the surface and coughed up lung and stomach fulls of the murky river.

Chapter Nine

'Til Stiff Peaks Form

The psychic had come highly recommended. But I regarded this afternoon; sitting across the table from her while she checked her voice recorder, as entertainment, a distraction. That is until her eyes fixed on me and the room grew eerily quiet. "What happened when you were 47?"

I saw my father again one night after preparing for a tasting. I was auditioning for the position of head chef at an arts retreat with a house string quartet and barn that had been converted into music and dining hall. The old farmhouse was now a 15-room inn. I was serving a 3-course dinner to 15 members of the board of directors. My oldest, Magalee, home from college and joined me. Since Colorado Kitchen she'd worked as a server at some of DC's hottest dining spaces. She had grown into an accomplished performer in the dining room. Expertly opening bottles of sparkling wine and running service like an old pro at a Jersey diner.

They gave us a room for the night. We'd prepped all day, and then retired late to a room in the old farmhouse with two twin beds. It was the off season, so the grounds were deserted. The little light from the hall was just enough to illuminate the paintings in the stairwell. Portraits of Barbara Villiers and Peyton Randolph watched as we took our bags to Room 5. We were to sleep under the watchful eye of Evelyn Byrd.

I had been cleaning trout and boiling lima beans, while Magalee polished glasses. I fell asleep in no time as she caught up on her inextricable laptop. I dozed off to the easy rhythm of her hunt and peck. It was a restless night. The old farmhouse creaked and moaned, and wind scattered leaves down the chimney. I could swear I heard Evelyn's heavy sigh. Terrified, I peeked an eye open to make sure that she wasn't walking about the room in rustling petticoat that sounded just like crisp leaves falling into the fireplace. I was going to ask her to please find her way back up to the painting, but my throat was so dry it hurt to inhale, and my teeth were chattering. The blue light from Magalee's laptop, closed and charging under her bed, cast a discotheque beam across the floor. Evelyn had gotten down from the wall and was rustling her petticoats when I heard my father's laugh. It usually started in a low rumble, then the cartoonish heh heh and one couldn't help but join in even if you'd just entered the room.

If it was something really funny his laugh went up an octave and you knew tears were coming. The first time I heard my father laugh himself to silence and tears was during a play my oldest sister Allison wrote and directed. At age 3, I had to learn to read to get the lines she'd carefully written out for me that I was to perform in my Halloween costume that I'd already started to grow out of. It was a rabbit costume complete with smiling-bunny-faced mask. I was hopping about and narrating while my other sister Tracy—a princess who had fallen face first out of a tree—had to deal with the consequences of her habitual spying. Allison, the forest fairy, was the only one who could restore the princess from her spinal injury paralysis, but also the only performer whose face was visible to the audience. This show of vanity in his eight-year-old was not lost on my Dad.

I followed the blue light and the sound of his laughter and there he was, standing in the doorway. He wasn't the shrunken figure I snuggled next to in his sick bed. He was the big shoes and loud laugh and booming voice that I grew up fearing, loving, and missing. "Daddy," I was finally able to speak. He was still laughing. Evelyn had not gotten down from the painting after all.

"Can I get one more hug," He smiled and nodded and held his arms out to me.

***

I didn't get that job. A Google search revealed negative press that went to war with the good stuff…NPR commentator, years of experience, great reviews, published author, Food Network appearances all eclipsed by witness testimony that I never smiled and had testy exchanges with innocent customers. I didn't get a lot of jobs. Although a lot of entrepreneurs called me for insight, site selection help, menu advice, and help establishing health department protocols.

One young, ambitious couple enlisted my help to build a classic American diner in a small town outside of Edinburgh, Scotland. They wanted a great burger, omelets, chili, meatloaf, pancakes, cornbread, apple pie, hand-cut fries—the menu got bigger every day. They took to heart

283

every suggestion from strangers and were intrigued and inspired by everything they ate. They had ordered a plug and play diner interior and invested $1500 in an old juke box that they weren't sure was working. The single story 800 square foot space had room for 18 seats and very little storage.

It all started when an older couple on vacation from Kirkcaldy sat at a booth admiring the menu at a Denny's. The Morone's, comparative newlyweds with two small children, sat in the opposite booth, "If you're thrilled with Denny's, you haven't seen anything." The sentence sparked a conversation, which led to the four sitting and eating and talking until the manager, mop in hand, had to ask them to end their evening. The Scottish couple was spellbound by the easy satisfaction that came from a hamburger, the sweet slap of happy that is on the fork with the apple pie; the bold, brash, 'Mericuh, that diners represent having sprung up in discarded train cars and open air shacks across the country. Scotland, with its own brand of live free, drink scotch would embrace this dining history and home-style cooking.

There was talk of a monthly salary, private accommodations, and a work visa so that I could live, work and travel without fear of deportation, plus an opportunity to grow with the young partnership and be on the ground floor as culinary leader.

I designed a tiny kitchen in a 150 square foot space, tucked between a cinder block party wall and the typical diner style counter. I specified equipment and reached out to purveyors across the pond. I found a place that would grind our burger meat, a bakery to supply glossy brioche buns, and an Indian food supplier (the only place to get corn meal).

I'd submit my equipment list to find that a food warmer was replaced by a baked potato station. The Scottish partners also altered the plans to include a wine-cork pull drilled into the small counter, eliminating a bar stool. Sinks and food storage shelving in my drawings was replaced in favor of beer chillers and liquor racks. I forwarded the partners a copy of the local health department requirements that highlighted restrictions on un-permitted liquor sales. In return I got a list of more menu items and an insistence that I look into placing a soda system which required a rack for syrups, CO_2 tanks, chill plate and additional plumbing. I was beginning to think that I was the only one who knew that 800 square feet wasn't very big. I was a little shaky about spending a few months in Scotland, let alone moving there to join a foursome with a childlike understanding of the business.

The Morone's met me at the airport with a change of plans. There was no money for lawyers and no money to secure visas. I was instructed to sit with a woman I had met briefly weeks ago who would serve as the general manager of Scotland's first American diner. We were on holiday together, so we did not have a return ticket. That was our story. Customs agents were going to ask us why. Our plans were open ended—two girls out for adventure in Scotland and then who knows. That's just how we roll.

The agent eyed my passport. She was sure I was going to hide out as an illegal in the UK and never return to my life of sorrow and squalor in the states. Free health insurance, great standard of living…. who wouldn't want to stay? I asked her to Google me, "I'm a celebrity chef back home," I wagered. "I've got to go back." I told her that my daughter was in Thailand, I had friends in Germany. I wasn't sure what I was going to do after Marcia, and I had gotten Scotland out of our systems. Where were we staying? Uh…. let me think. She wasn't buying it. I was trying not to be nervous, but she had that proper British accent that made me fear disappointing her. Surely, I've got something to show that my visit was on the up and up.

"How much money are you carrying?" She asked. I had read that if you come to another country under these circumstances with no cash, you're going to be detained and sent on the next plane back, in cuffs, accompanied by a marshal—a 14-hour perp walk. I pulled a debit card, two credit cards, and $600 cash out of my wallet. She put it aside and asked my travel companion to step forward.

"Hello, ma'am." She was tight-lipped and expressionless. "Can I ask what your occupation is?"

"I'm on disability."

"Really," one of her eyebrows shot up. No one had ever admitted that in her queue ever. "How are you able to afford rent and living expenses?"

"I'm getting public assistance and I live in rent stabilized apartment." If there was a table, I would certainly have kicked a broken tibia into Marcia's leg. If anyone had cause to abandon her desolate life in the states in favor of free health care and a plum Scottish welfare check it was Marcia. Immediately I wished I had gone solo.

The Morone's were standing on British territory and watched the agent count my cash and question Marcia. I had a former employee who had graduated high school in Maryland and was going to nursing school and working at a restaurant part time. A South African national who had overstayed his student visa, he was taken off of a Greyhound bus near Buffalo. The social media frenzy, the campaigns to Free Dylan gave immigration concern and he was held in detention until his departure. As far as I understood, detention was a fancy way of saying jail. And it appeared that's where Marcia and I were headed.

"How much cash do you have in your possession today?"

"I have $1.75" Marcia sighed. We were doomed. They took my cash, cards, passport and Marcia's passport to the back and asked us to have a seat. I excused myself and went to the bathroom. I was certain it would be my last private bathroom opportunity until I got back home.

The Kirkcaldy couple was there to answer the phone and vouch for me and Marcia and we joined the Morones on British soil. It was 2 am when we landed in Edinburgh. I was a nervous wreck and exhausted. A woman greeted us at the house. She was the hired caterer who'd stayed up and waited for us with food she'd warmed in the oven. I watched Marcia

288

and the young family eat. The airline had lost my luggage, so I had no clothes and a borrowed nightgown. Mr. Morone had not converted any cash. He took a few Scottish bills from me to tip the lady and used my plug adapter to charge his laptop. While I'd spent a little over $200 to buy a European cellphone, he fumbled with a SIM card in his and it still didn't work. He took my phone and called the old couple.

The Morones were fully committed. They had brought their two young children and sold all of their belongings and had given up their lease. They'd bought a used car and leased a house on Black Street. I had a mattress on the floor of the room closest to the kitchen and the front door. This was as private as my accommodations got. The door of my room didn't lock and the toddlers in the house didn't have any notion of personal space or privacy. I'd leave for a minute and find them tearing into my hair products or breaking my granola bars into pieces all over the floor. Mrs. Morone hid the trash can so butter wrappers and empty juice boxes would not wind up in the foyer or on the bathroom floor.

Mr. Morone picked up the used car he found on Scottish Cragislist—a left drive Ford Escort with wood trim. He and I were headed to the space. He told me at the airport that so much work had been done and he had pictures of the sign being installed and the electric almost complete. The old couple had been painting and cleaning and once the diner interior was delivered, they had men who would snap and screw the glossy reds and creams to the walls and slide in the chrome trims. The chrome banded counters and puffy red Naugahyde booths would be placed and we'd open in a week. I didn't hear anything about the equipment.

"Oh that," he said, bouncing the passenger side wheels into the curb as a bus sped past us. "Yeah, we're going to have to take a look at that." Jaime Morone was a 30-year-old teacher from Los Angeles who had big dreams. The commercial districts or High Streets of suburban Scotland were going to make him rich. He told me that his plan was to be sitting in a chair on the Riviera watching his wife walk around in a bikini. I guessed that she might be a little over 300 pounds. I tried to blink the image out of my brain. I held on to the notion that I could maneuver my way through the municipal codes and temper this partnership's lofty ideas.

"The other teachers laughed at me when I resigned last week," He was trying to find a place for his Garmin, but the car's cigarette lighter was gone, and its power source disabled. He tossed the little black machine and its squid trail of wires into the back seat. We pulled into a driveway beside a woman out walking her dog. He asked for directions to the High Street.

"You're going to go down this hill right here and take a right. When you get to a church go left. Follow that road." She surveyed the old car and smiled, "You'll be there in a minute." He thanked her and we were off, but at the end of the hill he went left. We drove around aimlessly through the Scottish Countryside, rumbling by old petrol stations, small farms, asking directions and not taking them. We had been at it for 2 hours and the old couple—apparently waiting for us there—called my phone out of concern, or maybe fear that the Americans had changed their minds, or maybe run out of money. The old woman got on the phone and gave Mr. Morone (he insisted he was going to make staff call him that out of respect) step by step directions. We were on the High Street in no time and in front of the small space that was on its way to becoming a diner. There was no sign. In fact, the façade was crumbling tile and exposed cement pocked rebar. Plywood had been propped into the spot where the plate glass had been broken. The old couple had been busy slopping silver and red paint on the wood trim that would frame the fiberglass wall panels of the diner kit. I'd painted Evening Star. I'd painted Colorado Kitchen. I'd painted

2,400 square feet of walls and trim at the General Store. I had become somewhat of paint snob, I guess. I tried to hide my dismay with a cough. I looked at the dried drops of silver that clung to the edges and the streaks of wood showing through the red. Jaime could not contain his excitement. The painted trim meant they were that much closer to opening.

"Wow. Great job George." He said, embracing the big old man who practically absorbed the skinny high school teacher in his massive arms and belly. The old woman was busy with the jukebox. She had peeled the old newspaper off of it and was rubbing the yellowed glass with an old rag. Mr. Morone and George talked about the job ahead of them. "Does the electrician have much to do?" and "We'll just stall him for another two weeks. We're not going to have the money to pay him until after we open." The old woman had been working to get a municipal grant to pay for a new façade. "The estimate is bit over four thousand for everything. That's not with the sign, ya know." She ran her hand over her nose.

The building was cold with the openings up front. The grant would give them just half of that and the city was months from awarding funds. I wandered around the space during this talk, my innards were being consumed by that gnaw—the feeling I hadn't felt since the anxious days at the General Store. It was a nervous time—dark rings circled my fluttering eyelids and my hair started to fall out. The flash back was overwhelming. I needed air. I went through a small back door (it seemed larger in the drawing and it was beside where I drew in a small dish machine). The door opened up to a few small brick buildings and a retaining wall made of centuries old stones. Beyond the wall was the brilliant dark blue of the ocean. The wind whipped the scarf from around my neck. They had run out of money. I knew what it smelled like and what it felt like. Strangely, they didn't. They were as gleeful as the night in Denny's where they sat amid soiled dishes and crumpled napkins, tucking into their pies and ice cream and hatching this plan. Mr. Morone came out to find me.

"There's not much room in there," I stated the obvious here, "what do you think about a storage cabinet out here?"

Jaime squinted his eyes to the sunlight bouncing off the water, "Nah," he drew the too long sleeve of his sweater across his nose. "The landlord isn't going to let us put anything out here." He was curious about what I thought for the first time, "What do you think?" he was beaming, certain I would affirm his confidence. "Do you think we'll be a success?" Here I was in Scotland with strangers. I had to be careful what I said.

"Well, of course there are a lot of factors involved." I started slowly. "Keeping your expenses low is key."

"Well we jumped at this place because the rent is only $1,250."

"That's good. But," I made a feeble attempt to get in there, to chip away at his hubris just a little. This man had been detained briefly at customs when they found a large box (the largest I'd ever seen) of business cards newly minted as evidence of the empire he was set on building in a country where he'd illegally immigrated.

"And that's why you're here," he said loudly. He pushed the sentence back into my open mouth and down my throat. He held the door open, insisting I go back inside. The wind and cold was too much for him. The old couple was standing in the small space that would be the kitchen. It was apparent that I was in for a talk. I'd had little sleep and it occurred to me the last meal I'd had was about a day ago on the plane.

"As you can tell, young lady," George started, "we've got quite a project ahead of us." He spoke with a rumble that a cough couldn't fix deep in his throat. That and his Scottish bass gave his words a weight and severity that made you listen. "We just want to make sure you're in it with us, right." I tilted my head a bit, unsure, not certain at all what they wanted.

"You don't seem like you're ready to move here." Jaime squeaked in, perhaps sensing my lack of understanding.

"I don't think I can commit to moving until we see how this goes," I don't think I was out of line here, "We've got a lot to do." They had no idea how hard it was for me to use "we".

"Well, this is going to be great," George added. "Everyone is excited, and I've told them the chef is straight from the states and she's got quite a reputation."

"There may be room sometime in the years to follow," Jaime revealing to me now that this conversation was planned and rehearsed, "for some type of partnership incentive. We want you to run this store while George and I are looking to place the second, third, fourth." He smiled at George, anticipating the great times they would have. George had fixed his flat when he ran his rental car into a curb, still confused by the left-hand drive.

He would have many more flat tires as the weeks turned into months. He couldn't go anywhere without George. In fact, we headed to the airport the evening before to pick up my lost luggage. Mr. Morone had gotten hopelessly lost and stopped in traffic on the freeway. Marcia panicked and shouted, urging him to take the exit before we were killed. Mr. Morone called a house meeting on Black Street that night, insisting that Marcia not show such disrespect for him in front of staff (me). Mrs. Morone was the only one who made sense that night as the two of them bickered. "We're all living in this house together, Jaime." She touched his arm urging him to let it go. "Some of those rules aren't going to hold." Later, Mr. Morone confessed that Marcia, his mom's youngest sister, was his aunt and really was hired because she'd been jobless for years.

"What do you say about a house on the Bosphorus," the old woman's eyes gleamed. "Two weeks, you'll just need to handle your own food, but all other expenses paid...airfare, lodging."

"We'll be there," George added, "But otherwise complete privacy." I was feeling a bit dizzy and steadied myself against the red and wood trim.

"Have you been to Turkey?" Jaime quickly broke the silence. A technique I learned from a short stint selling the Baltimore Sun over the phone during a summer taking classes and couch surfing during college. We were told to keep talking, fill the air with your own voice. You'll get a "yes". Just keep talking. The first night I read the script and talked over the objections of weak willed twenty-year olds and feeble old folks who had no more fight in them. I sold 23 subscriptions that night. The manager came buy my cube and handed me a $20 bill, clapping me on the back. I'd won the night and had my name push pinned on to the leader board. The next night a woman hung up on me and I wavered. It was almost 9pm and I hadn't made one sale. I started calling numbers of friends I knew were out of town. My manager clicked into my calls to help me out and fed lines into my ear. I made a sale. It was an old woman; I'm sure she was on a fixed income and had long ago succumbed to macular degeneration. She didn't have any use for that newspaper. I took my pay that night and never went back. The technique was not lost on me.

"I don't think I've ever seen a more beautiful country," Jaime continued, they were all nodding and murmuring about the country and the great food and how wonderful the house was—pool, spa, sauna. They wanted for nothing when they were there. What they didn't know is that I had a sore spot for Turkey. My husband and his family were from Turkey. After our divorce they disappeared and stood by and watched while Hakim missed visits and child support. The country was evil as far as I was concerned.

"So…." I had done the math. In my luggage was a binder full of recipes and the menu. It had order guides and vendor lists. There was even a thumb drive with templates for inventory spreadsheets and menus that could be altered for updates and reprints. I had done thousands of dollars of work already. "I get two weeks at your house in Turkey as payment."

"Yes, yes. Now you've got it," George clapped his big, calloused hands together soundlessly. "Bring your family. I understand you've got two daughters. Bring them along." The old woman was patting my arm with an expressionless face. There was no more to talk about. The deal was done.

"Well, let's go." She said. We all piled into Mr. Morone's little car and headed back to the house on Black Street, the old woman gave directions from the back seat and it wasn't long before Jaime weaved away from a bus.

"Hold steady, my man." George shouted, but it was too late. POP, Hissss. The tire exploded at my feet on the passenger side.

"Dammit, those busses," Jaime reasoned, "they seem like they're too close." George was out of the car and out in the cold and wind without a coat. He had the car up with all of us in it and the tire swapped out with traffic whizzing by him. We were at the house on Black Street in less than an hour.

Jaime had asked the old woman to cook and she set about the ground beef and potatoes in the fridge. "Neaps & Tatties," she cried, peeling ugly, gnarled potatoes with a steak knife. The house was ill-equipped for cooking and company. She served it in the cooking pots. Plates and flatware were scarce. She piled a few lumps of her efforts onto a saucer for me and filled my cup with vodka. I pushed the food around on my plate. The quality of the food so far in Scotland hadn't been very good. I had a kernel of hope in this diner. The food would definitely be better if I could do the right thing with the space with proper equipment and cold and dry storage. But it seemed the old couple was leaning more toward alcohol than food—earmarking precious wall space for liquor shelves.

George was red faced and sweaty having had a couple of cups of the vodka already. He was singing the Scottish national anthem in his rumbling, loud, throaty voice. I coughed sympathetically. Jaime had asked him to sing, and he sat next to the man he seemed to admire so much clapping his bony, long hands together and laughing.

When the singing was over, it was back to business. Mrs. Morone and Marcia were busying themselves with feeding the children and cleaning the kitchen.

"I say we serve unlimited soda," declared the schoolteacher.

"Why sure, all you can drink," echoed the old Scotsman.

"We need to see if we can do a plate for the school kids—a burger, fries, soda for less than $5," he looked at me. "The guy across the street gets all of the school kids. We've gotta beat his price."

"Wow…less than that huh?" They stiffened in their seats. Doubt wasn't welcome at that table, but I persisted, determined to help them make sense. "We need to go backward and figure what our daily, then weekly income needs to be to meet expenses." It was like I was speaking Pig Latin…the words sounded vaguely familiar but making sense out of it took too much concentration. I kept going. "According to the plans that were taped to the window the permit is saying 18 seats," I cleared my throat about to go in deep. "Food cost wise the unlimited Coke won't hurt, but we can't afford to not turn tables while customers sip on free soda." I had said "we." Was that it? They eyed me strangely. I took a big slug of the vodka in my cup. I was losing the audience, "The good news is that your

300

rent is just, $1,250." The room grew quiet; I attempted to build a bridge, "That was my rent for my first place. That's definitely an advantage." What had I said, the old woman stared at me, as if I'd said the combination to the safe aloud. Then she turned her shocked expression to Jaime. He waved his hand at me, sort of a silencing air slap.

"Have you got the details of your 'pals' plan?" George fixed his eyes on Jaime. What I'd said didn't have any more significance than if I had sung my own anthem.

"Yes, yes. I almost forgot." Jaime sat up in his chair and pulled out a sketch of a card he'd designed. "We're calling it the 50 Pals Challenge." He was talking to the old woman, she stared at him, with the vodka sinking in and the fact she was a little socially out of touch made it hard for her to keep up. I was sure she'd have been giving him that same look had he been trying to explain Facebook or Google to her. George was still smiling, finishing the vodka in his cup. I sat at the far end of the table watching them.

"We're going to have about 30 people on staff," he said to her, writing 30 on a piece of paper. "Each of these kids has at least 50 friends."

"Why, sure, sure." George added, like a backup singer.

"They each get 50 of these cards offering 5% off of the order." Jaime drew and "x" and a "5 – 0" below the 30. He wrote "1500" underneath. The old woman's eyes grew wide and moistened. Her thin lips, drawn in with a smudge of pink lipstick, curled up into a smile. She brought her hands together and raised them over her head. She shook her clasped hands over her right ear and then her left. She had just won the checkers game, it looked like. The two old folks laughed, George slapping Jaime's back.

"He's quite smart, isn't he?" He said, pulling little Jaime close to him and kissing the top of his head. They were all counting money in their heads. As if a hand came in and snatched some of the bills from the old woman's stack, she confessed a little anxiety.

"That's a good plan," she volunteered, "I do like it. But we've got a lot to do before we're handing out those cards." She poured her cup full again. "We got our daughter Iris to help this weekend." She had pulled her hands down from above her head and was squeezing her fingers together. "It's just a lot harder than I thought it would be—the furnishings, the façade," she took a big sip from her cup. "I'm a bit anxious about it is all." The two men were silent. The happy euphoria of the vodka was coming to an end. I get it; I said to myself, I've been there. It is hard. But when I opened my mouth I went too far.

"Anyone can open a restaurant," the table had been quiet for a full 20 seconds, this was the edgewise I'd been waiting for to slip a bit of reason and humility into the conversation, "It's keeping it open. That's the hard part."

"Why, what…" the old woman cried.

"Whoa, now…" George rumbled.

Jaime turned in his chair so that his back was to me. I had spoken out of turn, and beyond my station. I sucked my lips back into my mouth. Perhaps the vodka had gotten a hold of me. I hadn't eaten now going on two days…. delirium, hysteria? I had counted on those granola bars, but they had been swept off the floor this morning. My heart was pounding loud thuds in my ears and I suddenly felt like I had put my head into the center of a foam pillow. I carefully stood up and used the back of the empty chairs to steady myself. I had to walk past the back of Jaime's chair to make it to my room.

I got up before everyone and pulled my plug adapter out of the Morone laptop so I could charge my phone. I surveyed my luggage. It still had the sticker declaring it "OVERSIZED" and "HEAVY". I had packed chef clothes and work boots. After a quiet bath, I put on clean clothes at last. I pulled out the binder and thumb drive I'd created for the diner. They'd hung a t-shirt they had made on my door at some point during their reveling. They drove my blasphemous words of doubt out of their thoughts with more vodka and sang and shouted well into the night. I lay awake on the coarse sheets Mrs. Morone had given me. She'd asked me before getting my plane ticket what color sheets I wanted. It's not the color that's important; I thanked her, just as long as they're cotton. These were a sandpaper like synthetic of bright hues of giant purple flowers. I looked at them. No wonder I can't sleep.

During our lost drive around town I noticed a small commercial strip and a bus stop at the top of the hill. There was a bank, a small grocery store, a taxi company, and across the street there was an ivy-covered wall to a boy's private school. It was a stiff walk of about half a mile. I was determined to learn this town and get about on my own. If I could convince them to pay me some money as I worked at this diner, perhaps I could score a room somewhere and get out of that house. I was going to get around by bus and gain some independence while I was here. I headed to the bank and converted the remainder of my $600. I had no idea how the bus worked in Kirkcaldy. The teller poured an odd assortment of change into my open hand.

"Do I have enough to take the bus?" I was hoping one of these ladies knew the fare.

"Whadya mean, sweetie?" she asked me, peeling colorful bills under the glass.

"I'm wondering if I have enough for bus fare."

"Darlin, you've got enough here for all of us to go." They all laughed soundly at me. And I joined them, we laughed until tears were in our eyes. I don't think I'd laughed at all that week.

"You'd better hurry," she pointed her chin toward the window. "Here he comes."

I took the bus to the High Street (destination determines fare) and found a crowded coffee shop. I walked the street surveying the competition and stopping in to glance menus and see who was eating out. I wandered into the library and didn't have to provide anything but the address on Black Street to get a card and free use of the computers.

I walked the hilly streets and hopped on a bus going somewhere, and then another bus going somewhere else and an entirely different bus coming back and looked out the window. The plywood of the American Diner was weathered and crooked in the façade. I stopped and got a $5 burger. School children were everywhere; some of them tipping tobacco into rolling papers and with the quick spin of thumb and forefinger had tightly rolled cigarettes between their lips. They used old flint lighters and pulled long, slow, smoke-loving drags from their filter-less, self-rolled smokes. I doubted any of these youngsters were going to call him Mr. Morone. And those Pal Challenge cards were going to stay in the pockets of jeans that were pulled off and left slack on the floor until next shift. I raised teenagers; I had survived the complicated pull and stretch for independence and needing mommy in my own children—the staying out all night without a call, the lying, the doing whatever she wanted that was always the opposite of what I'd asked. These teenagers were different. They were teenagers on steroids.

It was dark when I got back. I took the bus to Black Street and got off in front of the boy's school. I liked Scotland. Dogs rode the bus, calmly sitting down with their owners. The air was cold and crisp. If I turned my face just the right way, I could smell the sea. There were butcher shops and small stores with people cooking on ancient stoves. Everyone seemed to have a sense of humor. Even the old lady with a scowl would pause and listen to a dirty joke. The pubs were full of people in good spirits. I understood why Jaime, leaving the cold shoulder of sunny California, found Scots so easy to love.

The door was unlocked (it was then I realized I didn't have a key). Mrs. Morone and the children were sitting in front of a dark television that they couldn't get working.

"Is that you, Gillian?"

"Yes," I called to her. I had left that morning early and hadn't seen any of my hosts all day. I had been gone over 12 hours. I had meant to make it a work trip, measuring, surveying the space. But I'd only passed by on the bus, staring at the broken façade as the bus slowed down to turn left. I'd been to the bus depot and studied the map, memorizing what bus went where. I stared at the façade again going along High Street toward

Edinburgh on another bus entirely. "Why had he lied to me?" Mr. Morone was going to send me pictures of the chrome banded exterior with the big brightly lit sign. And they were months away from that in reality. How long was I going to be in Scotland not making any money, waiting for payoff in the form of two weeks in Turkey with an old couple that really didn't like me?

"Jaime and Marcia went out," Mrs. Morone stood in the doorway of my room. Her children had found something of mine to play with, body soap, and they were smearing it all over each other. She pulled the girls to her side and tucked them behind her pressing them into her puffy hips.

"Mr. Morone wanted me to ask you to look at the stove in this kitchen here." She started to walk back to the living room and stood in the doorway to the kitchen.

"Do you mean this stove here?"

"Yes, how do you think it will do in the diner?"

"It's a common house stove, by design they don't get very hot," I explained to her. I was standing in front of the stove clicking the knob toward light and watching a weak blue flame curl around a metal plate. "You won't get very good burgers from this."

"Yeah, but we can get it for $1,100."

"But…." There were dozens of reasons why this four-burner house stove was a bad idea. I didn't think anyone would listen to me. It was hopeless. How much of this would be me working with crazy people, on inadequate equipment, with ridiculous expectations from a partnership that had no idea of what needed to be done? I retreated to my room and shut the door. I quietly got undressed and headed to the bathroom. I sat in a tub of hot water. I could hear Mrs. Morone shout to me.

"Oh, and Gillian," she was talking over the girls as they crawled on top of her fighting over the useless remote. "Mr. Morone wants everyone up at 6. We're going to head over to the diner and help unload the truck." The diner package had finally made it through customs (eight days they hadn't counted on—meaning there was no need to rush across the pond). The girls were still struggling on top of her and her voice strained as one stood on her mother's breasts to stand taller than the other.

"We're going to head to High Street and put it together. All hands, ya know." She could barely contain her excitement.

I needed to leave tonight. I was not going to get up at 6 am and have anything more to do with this insanity. I got out of the tub. I was dressed and put on my socks and shoes and got into bed. I had put everything back into my suitcase except for the binder and thumb drive. I left those on the floor in the corner. There was no furniture in the room, only the mattress and the low bedframe I'd taken out of the box and put together as they cleaned up and said goodnight to the caterer. I pulled the covers over myself and waited. I didn't want conversation. And certainly didn't want a discussion with these strangers that would not listen and were convinced a stove from Sears would enable them to make burgers and hand cut fries, and omelets, and chili, and Dutch pancakes filled with apples, and tacos, and brownies, and lemon meringue pie.

I was shuddering under the covers and planning my escape. Staying awake, despite that I had been sleep deprived wasn't difficult. I knew they would not be able to open this restaurant without me. The years taught me a lot about people, about cooks. And about making that ordinary Joe into a cook. Who and how would they hire? I felt for them. They had no idea. How could I leave them now? What kind of person was I? But if I stayed.... how would I fight the feeling that came over me during The General Store days when I wanted to tumble out of the car as it sped along the highway?

My hair was finally growing back. The fatigue induced anemia that made my doctor think I was bleeding internally was over. This time, I could try harder. I could make them listen to me. It would take a few weeks, maybe a couple of disastrous services to get them to see things my way. Certainly, I could empathize. This was me not long ago. I could pull them through this. I could work that tiny kitchen by myself and give them a few months of solid cash flow. But hadn't I done that before? I flashed back to Evening Star and the nervous breakdown when I finally let that go. Getting labor costs down meant I worked the line every night and prepped all day. Still, I was subject to a weekly dressing down right after Sunday brunch and I was too exhausted to defend myself. Yet, if this was a success, how great would that be. I'd be on the ground floor of this incredible idea. But they were reluctant to share with me. Partnership was held out as a carrot. But there was no guarantee that they wouldn't leave me to single-handedly slave away while they grew fat with cash. I wasn't a quitter. But I couldn't get the sour expression of the old woman out of my head or that Jaime had turned his back to me. I wasn't a quitter. But I was a survivor. I didn't have to do this. I didn't have to wheedle my success out of the folly of others. Yes, I decided, sitting up and putting my feet quietly on the floor, I had to leave.

I made sure the front door was unlocked. The dead bolt sliding in the dark would certainly wake the house. I listened. The walls and doors were thin. I could hear the children talking and playing with dolls despite the hour. It was after ten and the side door off of the garage flew open. Jaime and Marcia stumbled in. I suspected they'd been to the Tavern at the end of Black Street. Hopefully they were drunk and Marcia in the room next to mine wouldn't hear me tip toe out. I lay there in that bed as still as I could, listening to the change in breathing that meant sleep. The furnace clicked on and churned a low hum, enough white noise I thought that I could sneak out and put my oversized luggage into the bushes. I didn't want anything to hold me up when it came time to make my escape. But with the suitcase in the bushes in the front under my window, I had committed to leaving tonight. It would be tough to explain at 6 am.

I got back into bed, waited and listened.

"Is someone there?" Mrs. Morone was awake. Her husband slept beside her the sweet, quiet unconscious brought on by alcohol. Should I answer or stay silent? If she keeps asking, she'll wake everyone up. I heard her get up and lock the door. She mumbled something about her husband's carelessness and the door.

"It's just me." I got up to answer, my head in the hallway.

"I keep hearing doors open."

"Yeah, I've got tummy troubles," bathroom excuses are always good conversation stoppers. "I might have gotten some dairy today."

"Oh...sorry to hear that. Goodnight."

I got back into bed and listened. She shushed the girls (who seemed to get less sleep than I was getting), but Marcia and Jaime were down, snoring blissfully. As if they hadn't a care. At the bus depot I read that a bus that stopped in front of the bank would take me to a transfer to Edinburgh, but it was scheduled at 5:30. That was cutting it too close. One of the Morone's would surely rise early to get the kids ready for a day at the diner. I had to make my way to that stop as soon as the house was asleep or dulled enough not to hear me head out the door. It was a little after 3 and I decided it was time. I stood up and pulled my watchman's cap over my head and tied my scarf around my neck.

I had been a stealthy tooth fairy when the girls were little. There was no Santa or Easter Bunny, but I made many late-night forays into their

313

rooms with a quarter or dollar bill to perpetuate the Tooth Fairy Myth. It was almost too easy to noiselessly turn the knob and lift the pillow. I had perfected the grab-the-tooth-place-the-money-with-one-hand trick, while the other hand held their little head and their pillow high enough. I pish poshed a mother who confided that she just tells them to leave the tooth on their dresser and she completes the mission by taping the bill to their headboard. I later learned this woman had a drinking problem and was usually stumbling around the dark room and occasionally forgot why she was in there. She even stretched out and fell asleep on the floor in the middle of her son's room next to dirty socks and Tonka trucks one night.

I quietly approached the door at the vestibule in the total darkness of the house. A naked bulb in the master bedroom provided the only light from under the door. I blinked the tears of strain from my eyes and opened them as wide as I could. There was enough sweat on my palms that the knob stuck to my hand and I could turn it with a simple rotation of my wrist. I gently closed it behind me. I was going to have to turn the deadbolt and the vestibule door just might be enough sound insulation. I heard a gentle hum as I gripped the deadbolt. Was someone awake? I paused and listened. I could hear the rumble and snort of Marcia and the blubber of air

314

pushing and pulling Jaime's lips and cheeks. It was the furnace, it disturbed the youngest girl and she breathed a low, "Momma." Her mother ignored her. I quickly snapped the deadbolt over and pulled the door slowly. I stepped out into the cold and pulled the door behind me. It clicked. I grabbed my bag out of the bushes and walked as fast as I could up the hill.

I was pulling a 75-pound bag behind me. My breath was coming hard and despite the 30-degree temperatures and light drizzle I was sweating. The skies were black. I was the only one in the street. I didn't remember the hill being so steep, but it was a sharp incline and I struggled to keep the heavy bag on its wheels. My heart was racing. I paused. I saw headlights coming toward me. "They were coming after me," I said to myself. "They're going to grab me and my bag and throw me into the back of that Escort." But the car whizzed by me. I talked myself into calm. Breathe. Breathe. I would never make it up that hill until I focused on pacing my steps and pulling the bag on my left so that my wild, unruly steps didn't kick it or get under the wheels and tip it over.

I was halfway up. I could see the ivy-covered wall of the boy's school in the distance. I put my head down and kept walking focusing on the right, left, right, left of my stride. I could see the traffic light at the top of the hill. I was just a few yards away now. There were headlights again. I pulled my bag away from the road and turned my collar up. If it was them, they certainly would know it was me. I couldn't hide. I practiced a determined, "NO, NO." Maybe a weapon. If I had a weapon, I could threaten them. I would tell them I left them all that they needed with that binder and thumb drive. They didn't need me. The car, with wipers flapping, sped by. The street was dark, and I was wearing all black and pulling a black bag. Maybe no one could see me. Maybe that was them, frantically searching for the American chef that was going to make them rich. But in the dark, I was invisible.

I made it to the bus stop. It was 3:30. I had two hours to wait in the darkness. I was in front of the small shop and the taxi company. Both were dark. I dialed the number on the taxi company window. There was no answer. I would have to wait for the bus. The streetlight over the bus stop would certainly give me away. I settled into the very back of the glass box, behind the bench. I'm sure I looked suspicious, scary even. My eyes were wild and my breathing sharp and fast. And I was cold and wet. I had to press my molars together to stop the chattering.

I waited there almost an hour when two older women drove up. They parked in front of the store and cranked open the rolling metal door halfway to reveal the storefront. One of them looked at me and whispered to the other. I'm sure they were terrified, but they continued with their morning routine of getting open. I wanted to get in there and get a cup of coffee, but I waited. In that store I could wait for the bus and be off the street before sunrise. They wouldn't think to look for me in there. I waited, even after the woman pushed the rolling metal door all the way up while the other flicked on the lights that lit the sign on the outside. They were open. I hesitated. I didn't want to scare the two old ladies and have them call the police. That would certainly undo everything I'd been through these passed six hours.

A road crew hopped off of a truck. Six of them piled into the store. A postman turned the corner and walked past me and went in. A young woman crossed the street from in front of the school and headed in. I slowly walked away from the bus stop. I left my heavy bag. The woman at the register looked at me. She was short and blonde gone gray. Her face was incredibly wrinkled, but she looked like she had decades left in her. Her brow was knotted just above her frameless glasses. I was a stranger;

she didn't have a smile or nod of recognition for me, but simply asked what I would like. I asked her for a cup of coffee, and I noticed something in the window that the road crew had been getting for their lunch boxes. There were rows and rows of perfectly baked Scottish meat pies. I ordered one of those and sat at the window with my coffee. I'm sure I looked like the poor little match girl, shaking off the chill with a cup of Americain and a meat pie that I held in both hands and devoured. I sat on a bar stool at the slab of wood in the window. The bus was here.

It wasn't the bus I was waiting for, but I got on it. Its last stop was a huge connection terminal. I had no idea where I was, I just knew I was out of Kirkcaldy and closer to Scotland's capital and airport. It was daylight now and pulling my oversized bag, I mingled with commuters and kids on their way to school. I waited another hour for a bus to Edinburgh. I thought of the Morones up early and getting ready to meet the truck. Would they find the binder and thumb drive? Would they heed my warnings? Or would they blindly follow their vision and brilliant ideas that they were convinced would make them the toast of Scotland? I imagined them shaking their fists at my disappearance and declaring with steely millennial resolve that they were going to do this without me.

The trip to Edinburgh was over an hour so the bus was a big touring kind with huge seats and luggage storage underneath. I settled into the chair and reclined the seat back and immediately fell asleep.

It was raining lightly in the city. I walked the streets that bustled like any street in New York. I checked in at a hotel right after spotting a nearby French restaurant. It was busy with customers, but I was too tired to eat. Later I would have dinner there—a filet mignon with a huge glass of wine. The wine was warm and soothing and made me giddy. I smiled at everyone. I even smiled at the couple whose child would not sit still. In fact, I giggled when he giggled and laughed when he embarrassed his parents by crawling under his chair. I went up to my room and took a long hot shower. When I settled into the cotton sheets, I sunk my head into the pillow. I giggled to myself over my escape. I laughed even harder at how they might have looked, opening the door to my room and finding me gone. Perhaps they tightened their belts and declared that this would not deter them. I was now laughing so hard, I was crying.

Chapter Ten

Rotate the Baking Sheet Halfway Through

I arrived in California having taken a one-way flight. Robin had helped her father put things back together after laying her mother to rest. Now he had fallen ill. And in six short months she was sitting in that room deciding what to put on his grave marker. We hadn't had a decent meal since I'd arrived, and all of her childhood haunts had disappeared or were owned by folks who just didn't understand. We were convinced that a restaurant that we built would be a raging success. Instead, Sue Ann's American Kitchen a 70's themed steak house complete with decorations that included wallpaper called "Woodstock", a vintage oven set in a brick wall surrounded by copper gelatin molds, light fixtures like the ones I grew up with, and 100% scratch cooking, a decent review from the local paper (which included a mention as one of the 10 best new restaurants—we placed five on the list) and at year's end my crab cakes made it on the same critic's "Best Thing I Ate This Year"; was a resolute failure. No one came. There were days where no one walked through our doors. The Chinese restaurant next door where a truck labeled "Frozen Meat" pulled in and delivered their supplies was killing us. I ran around pouring fresh, hot veal stock off of bones and cut well-marbled New York Strip from the loin; I could pause by the window and watch them nap on their patio after their rousing lunch business. Under the California sun they'd cinch aprons around their necks to give each other haircuts on their patio.

Before we opened, we spent hours decorating and looking for the right touches to add to the hundreds of feet of wall space. We shopped at a salvage yard for stove parts to paint and hang on the walls. The man who ran the yard was an aging hippie who had become an expert in junk over the years. He could look at whatever we held in our hands and tell us whether it was from Westinghouse or Western Holly stove and what year it was manufactured. He was curious to know what we were doing with all of the burner covers and knobs.

321

"A restaurant, huh." He dug his grubby nails into the days of growth on his jaw.

"It's a little nostalgia, fine dining, classic American." Robin added.

"Huh," he puzzled looking over at me the chef, "I can't imagine why you're doing that?"

"Uh…."

He didn't wait for me to explain.

"Can't understand why you're not doing something like soul food."

I was used to that kind of talk. I'd heard it before. White people and sometimes black assuming I had some connection and natural inclination to feature soul food in my restaurant. I'm the daughter of immigrants, a studied culinarian; soul food was not my genre and I could flap my gums all I wanted, no one was buying it. The image and notion of what I should be and should be cooking was irrefutable. I let it go.

One night I was cleaning paint brushes as Robin finished up with the two-tone ceiling trim—we had cans and cans of classic 1970s orange, avocado, and brown. I heard her talking to someone and figured I would be concerned, although it was late and the shopping center pretty much deserted, only if she screamed. I could hear that it was a man and he was helping himself to a tour. Robin was getting down from the ladder and would probably be answering his questions. We'd entertained a lot of looky-loos. I hadn't expected him in the doorway of the prep kitchen, shouting.

"Hey…you better get back here," he cried out loud enough for Robin to hear. "There's a black person in your kitchen." He sounded genuinely concerned. But what bothered me about the warning was that 1—it seemed so remote and unlikely that my white partner would be associating with a black person that I couldn't have any good reason to be in the building other than to be up to no good (never mind that I was wrapping an extension cord around my forearm and I was wearing paint stained clothes just like she was. 2—the way some people say black, it has two syllables and they hit the K really hard…buhll-lackkkk. I cringed. And this time I screamed, "ROBIN!"

We had a crowd opening day even though we were a couple of weeks from getting our liquor license. They were cleaning their plates. Many promised to be back once the wine was pouring. Our new neighbors had been regulars at the Old Italian place that preceded us in this room they had left greasy and caked with dust. Word on the street was that the owner had been coercing his young female staff into having sex with him. One was only 15, and when her father found out he came pretty close to killing the man. The matter went before a judge who ruled that he was forbidden from setting foot in the place and he landed on the sex offender registry. His wife did her best to run the operation, but she didn't have the interest or intestinal fortitude. After a couple of difficult years, she walked away.

I was peppered with questions when I touched tables. "How did you wind up here?"

"How long are you planning on doing this?"

"Why'd you pick this area?'

"What are you and Robin? Are you a couple?"

I didn't know how to answer. The years had made me suspect everyone and trust no one. I was cautious. Did this turn people off? We were pouring wine, and no one seemed to notice. Maybe we just needed to be patient. Usually a review, and a good one, brought the crowds. And with our product living up to the hype, our worries would be over, and folks would count on us for dinner when they didn't feel like cooking. Or they'd

324

take up the large center table for a birthday party. I wasn't used to this. To some folks I lied. I told them I was just driving through town and thought this building was perfect. I never let on that Robin and I were living together in her family home a few miles down the road. Still, we had a few encouraging busy days and nights. But more often the dining room was quiet, and we watched the sun go down and the sunset sensitive lights turn on and shine on the empty patio.

I started to let staff go. Jose, who confessed to coming in and trying to work drunk was the first. I would stand over him every day, exhorting him to follow the same instructions on the grill that I'd given him the day before. Stacey was next, she would wait until we'd open the doors for brunch before starting to whip the eggs for her hollandaise. Then as orders came in, she'd hand the bowl over to a booze-wobbly Jose who knew nothing about the burger burning on his grill let alone the mother sauce that I took so much pride in. I'd take the bowl from him and finish. The night the review came out the tickets stacked up and I watched Stacey collapse. She'd over toasted a burger bun and was using her tongs to scrape the black away. She needed three roasted chicken in the window, but she hadn't even started them.

"Stacey," I shouted over the sounds of fryer roiling and convection oven fan. "Are you doing drugs?" She just looked at me, inadvertently crushing the bun in her hands, not speaking.

It wasn't long before I was working the line on Saturday and Sunday brunch by myself and some nights during the week. We didn't do the numbers that made it a frenzied operation like at Colorado Kitchen. There was only the odd service that I'd get weeded. We'd lost a lot of staff, starting with the pastry chef with the incredible resume at only 19 years old. He had a portfolio of amazing cakes and sushi looking petit fours with berries masquerading as caviar. He frosted a strawberry cake that he made from a recipe I gave him…we'd used it to make cupcakes at The General Store that sold out in minutes. I struggled to get the knife through his interpretation. And when I tasted it, I wound up spitting it into a napkin. Pedro and I sat down for a talk. He was furious that I questioned his abilities. I fired him.

We were whittled down to a skeleton crew, barely able to meet payroll and not able pay ourselves.

Then the health inspector came with her bayonet thermometer and flashlight, she admonished us for hot-holding temperatures and a little

326

grime behind the stove wheels. For the Chinese place, she slapped a big sticker on the window and made them lock the doors. Would this be an opportunity to attract some of that loyal following that weren't the least bit curious about our burnt orange walls or the bright green chairs? With their favorite place shut down by the health department would they clutch their pearls or run a hand through their hair in disbelief and cross our threshold to be comforted by a slow roasted tri-tip bathed in our house made steak sauce. No.

They angrily yanked on the door. Buddha smiled at them from inside. They knocked furiously on the glass, the plastic-coated health department sign muffling the fury coming off of their knuckles. The next day we watched the Chinese restaurant folks forgo their nap and pull ice machines covered in black mold, soggy sofa beds, and chest freezers black with roach droppings into the parking lot. In a few days they were back up and running and the crowds resumed as if nothing had happened. Meanwhile, we hadn't been able to pay our rent, our taxes, or ourselves.

We puzzled why. We had created the perfect kitchen—an easily managed three-person line and a separate room for baking. Cakes were the star at Sue Ann's. On display in lighted boxes, were lovely frosted layers iced with bright blueberry buttercream or coated with toasted coconut. We'd thought of everything. Vintage televisions were stacked in the front of the dining room rolling tape of classic seventies shows. We piped hits we grew up listening to like "Please Come to Boston" and "Kung Fu Fighting," and even the ones our parents made part of our playlist like, Richard Harris crowing out "MacArthur Park."

Only the local restaurant critic noticed and wrote a huge review of the place with quarter-page sized pictures of Robin's beautiful layer cakes and my lobster pie. He gave us two stars out of four. Even so, that night and a few days after we were slammed. The review that followed in the next week's paper—even though he found a lot more to dislike—earned three stars. The chef was a white man, serving on white tablecloths who coincidentally had earned his culinary certificate at L'academie de Cuisine, my alma mater.

The critic or maybe the editor knew someone would notice the 2 vs 3-star disparity. So, he published a little paragraph explaining why Sue Ann's got the lower mark. None of it made sense to me. I scratched my head. But realizing it couldn't save us, I let it go. We were low on money and it seemed like we owed everyone...rent, payments for the POS,

328

purveyors. We'd do about a hundred dollars in sales a day. We had forecasted a modest $1,500.

Robin reached out to the local business community and signed Sue Ann's American Kitchen up as member of the City Chamber. She sat through meetings and they told her that new members are welcomed with a well-publicized ribbon cutting. In return, new members "put out a spread" and hosted a small gathering of the members posing for photo-ops that would appear in the Chamber's online newsletter.

They inadvertently planned the ceremony the day the review came out. We were short staffed and working like mad to have enough to serve a crowd that was suddenly in our dining room. It was about time for dinner service and the lunch crowds hadn't let up, but they sneered at the lobster pot pie the reviewer had gushed over, complained that we didn't have fountain soda or offered the crab cakes at lunch. They objected to our lack of beers like MGD and Bud Lite. Amid the chaos, the Chamber gathered outside and stretched a ribbon in front of our door. Robin ran interference and tried to call them off. Before long they were standing in the dining room. There was nowhere for them to sit and no canapes or crudité had been laid out for them.

"Where's our spread?" one of them shrieked. They stormed out taking their ribbon with them.

We followed the review with a tiny ad in the local paper, and an aggressive social media campaign. We mailed postcards and coupons to a five-mile radius of zip codes. When the local library sponsored a cooking contest and asked me to be one of the judges, I jumped at this publicity opportunity. I'd be joining some members of the library board and local Chamber. I was anxious to get to know my neighbors and make my presence known in the community that was now mine. I was introduced to a couple of the judges and we walked the stations, surveying the contestant's procedure and asking questions. I wanted to be part of this team, this effort to build a stronger community. I welcomed my role to use food and the discipline of making food to influence young minds. The Chairman of the Board saw me. I was the only one in a chef coat. She set her jaw and walked toward me like I was on fire and she was prepared to put me out.

"You're from Sue Ann's aren't you," she wasn't smiling. Still I nodded and held my hand out to her. She ignored it. "How's anyone supposed to know that you're open?" she snarled at me. She was an older

330

woman, a longtime resident and member of the community. She was royalty. She was a little angry old woman no taller than 4' 11". "You should be advertising," she wagged a finger in my face. "There isn't any way you're going to make it unless you do something. And be smart and quick about it." It was as if she heard I had been invited and was waiting for me so she could give me a piece of her mind. I'd seduced her husband, it seemed like.

"We actually have an ad in today's paper," I answered calmly, despite the fact that her cruelty had stunned me. I stifled the tremble in my voice. There was what seemed like an eternity of awkward silence before she turned her anger-twisted face from me, smiled at the judge beside me, and took his hand. The rest of the judges took her lead and walked away from me. I stood there alone. It was as if I had suddenly contracted Ebola virus.

There were several more encounters where I could sense the hostility; well, actually taste it. It was as if someone had slipped an aspirin into the candy bowl. And instead of a skittle, an old school Bayer tablet was slowly dissolving on my tongue. We had created a character of Sue Ann, a mid-western white girl from a rich family who married her ambitious high school sweetheart. We added Robin in a wig and shirt dress (just her back showing) to old photos of Hollywood elite. There she was serving Carroll O'Connor and Jean Stapleton her signature beef stew, another shot of her appearing cameo style in a movie still, then wearing an oven mitt high-fiving Kate Hepburn. I made a video telling our Facebook fans that Sue Ann had been one of my mentors. The socialite and accomplished home cook used her local television cooking show to feature solid and substantial American comfort food. What better tribute than a restaurant in her honor featuring the stove and gelatin molds that were part of her set? And now I felt it imperative that I do my best to hide behind her.

We had created such a real and identifiable character, who growing out of the shadow of her husband's business success, became a Hollywood party icon in her own right. When Hiram died suddenly (he choked on his morning toast which became the reason why we served biscuits at breakfast—toasters were banned) she picked herself up and carried on from cooking advice columnist to regular on Merv Griffin. She was someone to be admired. The character was so carefully constructed, and creatively substantiated that it wasn't unusual for a customer to claim that he had rented a house next to hers in Fullerton, or that someone spotted her at the Trader Joe's in Brea.

We punctuated our slow nights with a Sue Ann's birthday dinner. The kitchen cranked out over 50 pounds of pot roast and gravy for $6.95 a plate to commemorate the first recipe performed on her cooking show. It was one of our busiest nights as folks craned their necks whenever the door chimed open to see if the birthday girl was making an appearance.

For another event, Sue Ann's and my good-natured kitchen trash talk exploded into a full-on kitchen battle. Two menus, two chefs: a customer chooses the nameless four-course menu that catches his imagination and seduces his taste buds. The chef, whose anonymous menu was chosen by more customers, was the winner. Of course, I created both menus and we told everyone who asked to see her that Sue Ann, now pushing 80, had instructed the prep cooks and had gone home for the night. Or, jeez you just missed her; she had a champagne toast with the dining room just 10 minutes ago. No table wanted to deny that they'd been part of that. While many of our regulars were excited that two great chefs were putting up their best culinary efforts, there was a contingent in the dining room that wanted to give the win to the white woman. They strained to see anything familiar that might tip them off. Some recognized the use of peppermint in the chocolate dessert as a familiar garnish that I often used when a chocolate cake was on the menu. When peppermint appeared on the dessert course of one of the menus that night, it was enough to tip the scales in Sue Ann's favor. I laughed it off because I knew that I was Sue Ann. She was the accumulation of talent that was built, fostered, and egged on by the two chefs in my life who had the greatest influence on me (Susan Lindeborg and Ann Cashion.)

The packed nights of a cheap dinner and an opportunity to show up the black one dispelled all of the notions that we needed do more to get more people to know that we were open. They knew. They couldn't resist a $7 dinner or a chance to hand the black chef a defeat at the hands of the far superior old white lady who had shared her precious gifts with someone, by birth, unworthy. No one was behind us. Only our staff was in our corner. They had watched us build the place. We became a small crew with nothing but time on our hands to bond during the slow times and salve war wounds when it got busy.

We had a smattering of regulars, but even they weren't strong enough to turn the tide. Soon, however, there were no busy times. My numbers showed that we needed to do at least 80 customers a day. At most five or ten would come for lunch, and a "busy" dinner seated 30.

A town ordinance forbade the installation of a drive thru for restaurants or any business within the city limits. The McDonalds located in the shopping center directly across the four-lane road from us successfully lobbied for an exemption. It was the talk of the town that zoning had released the permit. In a few months the drive thru was open. Our sales plummeted. We once thought or hoped the angry man who slammed the menu down and shouted; "A steak dinner for $25?!" was in the minority. He headed out the door swearing to tell his neighbors, turning to give us one more piece of his mind, "That's highway robbery!" I was sure he wasn't going to tell the crowd that stood arms folded in his driveway that the price he was angry over was the cost of the 22-ounce T-bone steak for two.

We were on the verge of throwing in the towel. Robin invited a restaurant consultant to take a look. What had we missed when we made this place? Were we doing something wrong? He came in and ate lunch. He took Robin aside (the owner he assumed) and showed her what was left of the fried chicken waffle sandwich he had eaten. His plate was clean.

"It's way too soggy, greasy too." He told her.

"But you ate it all," she said, taking the plate in her hands and examining it for crumbs and lick marks. Just the sauce cup was left, but the contents, the Sriracha honey, was gone.

"Yeah…. I ate it." He explained, "I was being polite."

"You know," she told him quietly, "the chef made that sandwich. She beat Bobby Flay with that chicken." He backed off and half-heartedly admitted he was looking for an easy answer. He was looking to solve our problem quickly, only spending 25 minutes to order and demolish his lunch, looking around the colorful, concept-complete dining room while he devoured a 100% scratch waffle around what's been called the best fried chicken in the world.

He came back the next day to observe. Watching the quick delivery of food, the knowledgeable service, the clean and complete way food was prepared. He scratched his head, watching the Chinese restaurant next door fill to capacity before 7. He watched Oscar, the last cook on staff that worked beside me on our busier weekend nights.

"What do you think it is?' he asked quietly.

"I don't know." Oscar confessed. No one knew what it was, and we were all frustrated. I did have an image burned into my brain one Tuesday as we approached the dinner hour. An older couple parked in the space in front of our restaurant. I crossed my fingers and hoped they'd be coming in to try us out. They turned toward the big double doors of the Chinese place. But wait, the wife, with her cat glasses and up do, noticed the neon swirling steam of our sign. From outside she could see the Western Holly oven door so much like the one in her Mom's kitchen. She paused in front of our store. She started to smile. Her husband called to her. And when she didn't respond he got behind her and with his forearm in her back, pushed her away from our window and then in through the dark wooden doors of the Chinese place where she disappeared to eat their usual Tuesday night dinner of Sweet & Sour Chicken and Pork Fried Rice.

I also never forgot the old grumpy woman who came in with her daughter. She did not hide the fact that she'd been dragged here.

"Mom, this place was voted one of the 10 best new restaurants in Orange County," said the younger one, holding the menu open.

"Big deal," said the old woman, "There couldn't be that many restaurants opening every year." I wanted to say it out loud, but I retreated to the kitchen—over 100, over 100 in Orange County!

Plus, the words of a black family haunted me. It was Easter Sunday, probably our last busy brunch. They asked their server to get me. When the last plates had gone out, I went to their table. I had seen very few black people since I had arrived in Orange County. The black people I caught a glimpse of in a parking lot or at the 10 Items or fewer lane at the store too returned the stare. I stopped in my tracks to see where they were going, where they might be living so that I might see them again.

"We're glad to see you," said a woman about my age, her hair pulled back into a tight bun. "We've lived here for years, and I don't think we've seen a black-owned restaurant." I didn't correct her. She explained that Orange County wasn't like the rest of California or the country for that matter. The KKK thrived here. Her father nodded. He was probably pushing 80. "My father bought a house here in 1957. The town wouldn't let the purchase go through. He had to take it to court." Her father had single-handedly put an end to the town's ordinance against black families owning property.

338

A local realtor sat by himself during lunch. He kept to himself and ate without incident. It was his server that showed me his online review that appeared that night. He talked like he'd been to dinner...calling my amuse bouche "bland and unnecessary" ...huh? He critiqued my shared plate appetizer—the mini sandwich board of classic sandwiches. By his account, I was phoning in my Monte Cristo: a French toast style egg wash and flat top sear is what he claimed. No sir, definitely not. My Monte Cristo is the traditional jam and ham that is grilled, battered, deep fried and dusted with powdered sugar. He hadn't come to dinner, but his one-star review had a purpose. As a realtor he had an obligation. No black owned business would survive in his territory.

How did I not know the racist history of this town? I sat at the computer one night and found the article. Months before we opened and just blocks away, a black family came home to a cross burning on their lawn. They arrived home after the fire department had turned the nut on top of the hydrant to get the water flowing through the hose. The article read like a chapter written by Harper Lee. They had endured a series of terrorist acts that, before moving on to this street, they'd only read about or watched during some documentary or newsreel on recollections of the Jim

Crow South. One morning they found their tires had been slashed. Before the burning cross, they found NIGGER spray painted on their garage. Their children had been taunted, bullied. Rocks had been thrown through windows. So much hate. More hate than they could endure.

Some of the streets I had been driving on had been named for prominent Klan members. How could this be? The town had voted with their feet. My food and I weren't welcome. I'd much rather have failed on my merits....my food was terrible, the prices were too high, the building was filthy and did not pass department of health standards, we habitually food poisoned our customers. But to fail because of something I couldn't control and really made no difference in who I was, or what I was cooking, was devastating.

I was in Texas on a job interview when the auction house came to collect the furniture and equipment. I don't think I had the stomach to watch. In my mind, Sue Ann's was going to be the start of something big. I let go of the equipment and furniture I had in storage for the other restaurants I had planned for Orange County. But this was it. I was done.

Chapter Eleven

When a Pick Inserted Comes out Clean

I didn't want to own a restaurant anymore. In fact, I watched as other people signed leases, shopped for equipment, and thought of concepts with big smiles on their faces. They might as well be jumping out of an airplane. I stopped braking for "For Lease" signs. I'd sooner walk across the freeway at night.

I was on the job hunt. Years of experience, a published author, countless appearances on TV, proven leadership skills (every kitchen receiving critical acclaim)—how hard could this be? I had survived openings through demolition, permitting, kitchen design. I'd worked financials and established protocol. I'd maintained low food costs and labor costs. I took a barely secondary school educated band of rehabbers, ex-cons and formerly homeless and made a formidable culinary team out of them. Really, how hard could this be?

The first time I was asked this question, I have to admit, I didn't know how to answer. "How is being a woman going to work when you're trying to lead a kitchen."

"I've been leading kitchens for 15 years."

"You're a woman. How's that going to work?"

"Well, I've been a woman for a long time now."

"We've never had a woman in this position before. I'm not sure how that would work."

"I've worked for women. One of the toughest chef's I've worked for is about 5-foot-tall and a woman. Everyone is petrified of her."

"You gotta admit, you're going to have a hard time in there being a woman and all."

"I don't know why you're asking me this question. You obviously think you know the answer." I didn't say that. But today I wish I had. I spent about five awkward minutes pleading my case to a blank stare. Sometimes it was a blind side attack. The HR director, excited about my resume, would put my resume in front of the person who would be my boss. I think at this point I should tell you that I've removed all passive language from my resume and cover letter; there is no "I believe" or "I think". It is simply and emphatically "I" and "I am". Perhaps the confident and unapologetic language made these men believe they were interviewing another dude. And then in comes me without a penis.

"Ultimately, everyone I've seen or will see today can cook," he said after cleaning his plate from my demo. "I'm really looking for someone who I can sit down and have a beer with when the night's over with."

"I drink beer. I love beer. Oh, but, yeah, I get it. Your wife is going to come in and see that the new chef is a woman and suddenly start to wonder about your late-night beers at the bar with chef." No, I never said that either. But I was definitely beginning to see a pattern.

Then there was the response just seconds after getting my resume. An email would bounce off a satellite and into my inbox requesting a phone interview. As I sat at the appointed hour...oh, maybe I was supposed to call. Hmm, no answer. I guess I'll email a reconfirmation. Huh, nothing. Oh, well. Then I'd catch the job posting again, this time asking for a photograph to accompany the resume. So, phone interviews would be cancelled once someone clicked the link on my resume and found the videos from the Food Network shows.

"Wow, I never guessed after seeing that resume that we were dealing with a black woman." I imagined them saying as they watched me standing next to Guy Fieri.

I learned new terms like "cultural fit". I learned to read between the lines on job announcements "energetic" means they want someone young. "Hands-on" means they are trying to keep labor costs down so as executive chef, aside from handling all of your administrative tasks and working on cost cutting and menu updates and meeting with vendors and managing inventory, you're going to work the line every night.

A word I heard more and more was "articulate". When the HR coordinator called me, she told me of two jobs that were open. One required recipe development skill. The other was a bit bigger and she favored me for this one I would be part of a sales team developing and demonstrating. "Right in your wheelhouse," she said. I agreed. I waited for my plane ticket and hotel confirmation. Strangely, when I arrived I found I was interviewing for the recipe developer position. Nevertheless,

I was grateful for the opportunity. This company was huge and to have that logo on my chef coat would have been monumental. It was an all-day affair. I had 6 hours of meetings and then a one-hour allotment to cook one thing based on what was in their pantry. The position supporting the sales team had been filled. So here I was now, ideal job gone, just wanting my foot in the door.

The man who would be my boss, one of those chefs with letters after his name, and quite a few of them, came into the room. He was pensive and studied. And with a palette so sensitive, he could tell that I used a little more carrot than onion in my chicken stock during the tasting. I was in awe of him. I was talking about fear and overcoming personal obstacles when I attempted to weave a joke into the conversation.

"I was somewhat of a chicken when I started cooking. I mean there was a time I didn't even want a...."

"...spring form pan in your house. Yes, I've heard your work on NPR." Heard it? The dude had memorized it.

"I'm very upset," he confessed. "You're very articulate." There was that word. "You should be in that position we just filled." I left HQ without getting an offer, but with the promise that they would hang on to

345

my resume. The recorded evidence wasn't enough to bring me on to be considered for the speaking position. That stuff could be faked. The resume, pure hyperbole. I had to prove that I was fluent in Standard English and not just Ebonics (which I'm not very good and at times when hearing it I've needed a translator) by stepping into the room and speaking before a live audience.

If the corporate sous chef had been responsible for hiring me on this boat—he also called me articulate—I would not have gotten the job. It would have stung a little but not hurt in the long run. The six weeks of non-stop 14-hour days were more than I could stand. I was interviewed on a brand-new river cruise ship docked in New Orleans. I sat through a brief interview and then grabbed the market basket and seared a breast of duck to serve alongside a mushroom bread pudding.

I sauced a seared pork chop with a brandy spiked caramel and made my signature crab cakes. The pans were flat and the cook top outrageously hot. Thinking of the beautiful brightly lit, modern, and shiny kitchen helped me get on that plane; knowing that I would be away from everyone and everything I loved for a little over a month. My assignment on a boat cruising the Snake River, however, was the filthiest and oldest

346

boat in the fleet with equipment that didn't work, and decades of grime stomped into the floors. It was dark and depressing place to wake up to at sunrise and spend fourteen hours endlessly chopping, skinning, and slicing.

Although he had a speech impediment and confessed that he wasn't verbal until age 6, Chef Wheels, on the boat as part of my training, stepped in to handle the pre-shift meetings.

"Chef G told you kids about the sauce, a reduced veal stock." He looked at the young team of servers with serious as a heart attack expression, "Veal is a little baby cow, and the stock is the bones of this baby cow. You need to make sure your tables know that." He ignored the seat shifting uneasiness in the room. "Tonight, it is served on rayswooto. That is rice cooked in cream." He said as if he was angry, then turned around and went back into the kitchen. I took this opportunity to redirect.

"Kids, if anyone of you tells a table that we are serving them baby cow," I said quietly, "we are going to have a problem. And just so you know, there is no cream in the risotto."

When I got back into the kitchen, Chef Wheels was suggestively showing the assistant manager a zucchini. He didn't stop when I walked in. Actually, he raised the squash even closer to her face. When the laughter in the kitchen died down, including the young woman's nervous chuckle, Chef Wheels brought his knife through the bright green and in no time had reduced it to a perfect brunoise.

"I have to admit, G." he was busy with the zucchini while he spoke, "I didn't expect you to sound the way you did when you started speaking." I stared at his back. I was raised to help ease folks out of awkward, even if they created it themselves. My mother corrected us when we declared hate, "No...you dislike her." She'd convince me. "You can't hate her." I'd reluctantly agree. She'd smile and nod at the driver who insisted we stop by and take care of his lawn later in the day. He'd watched us trim the apple tree and rake the leaves and assumed we were staff. The thought never occurred to him that those black folks actually owned the well-kept house on the corner.

The kitchen was quiet. They were as curious as I to see where Wheels was headed with this. I had an inkling. I'd seen men like him before. They lived in white bread worlds surrounding themselves with white men all after the same thing—good grades, good school, good job. From infancy, through high school, college, the CIA.... he'd been playing, talking, drinking, working alongside men just like him. All he knew about black people was what he saw on TV. When a woman walked into the room she was whispered about, ogled, maybe shown a zucchini. I was determined to walk this white guy through this mine field.

"Yes, I don't have an accent or anything…raised in NY, lost it in Washington, DC…" I released the end of conversation dry chuckle. But he wasn't done.

"No, no…that's not what I'm trying to say." His knife was still. "It's just not what I expected."

"Yeah…I know. It's kinda deep, right." I'd never had to make a sharp left when trying to do this, usually the dry chuckle worked, or someone came in and interrupted. Pots and pans were still, everyone was breathing carefully. "All of those years doing college radio, if you don't find that lower register, it sounds—"

"No, no." that's not what I'm trying to say. His tone was sharp. He didn't want me interrupting anymore. Have at it then, was what I was thinking. Heads were down in the kitchen; I could tell most of the staff just wanted to disappear. "You actually speak properly, diction, vocabulary," he couldn't hide his wonder and amazement. "Not at all what I expected when I first saw you." Was this a compliment? "And on top of that you

349

even know what you're talking about. I'm impressed. Honestly, when I came in and they told me you were the executive chef.... well, I just wasn't expecting this." He was smiling at me.

I got busy with the special-order baked potatoes I'd put in the oven. In no time the servers were bounding in with their orders and we started the assembly-line like system of plating and serving dinner to 110 passengers on what some of the seasoned staff called a floating nursing home.

I was on that boat because I'd resigned from another job. My boss often told me that I was the most accomplished executive chef in the group. I had banked on his pre-offer vision that I would take on the role of corporate chef as the company expanded. I even weighed in on the menu of the new restaurant the group had just added. I was the only black woman in the Culinary Division. And I was grateful that despite being in the south, no one spoke of it. I was never called articulate. In fact, I was voted Best Chef in the city two years running. I delivered with a restaurant not known for its food, but for its outstanding service, and made it a restaurant known for its food. The numbers didn't lie. We were the company's top performer. We were the only store in the black. My efforts in the kitchen (and outside the kitchen on local television cooking segments) increased sales and decreased costs. When equipment failed or the roof leaked, or the old dish machine wet itself to a stop; I was confident that I could depend on my corporate to do the right thing. I was wrong.

I looked at the soot on pots and chef coats and determined that the stove's gas regulator was malfunctioning. When the director of facilities came to examine our poor equipment status, I explained to him that years of this soot might render the stove inefficient because of accumulation. He wrote my boss rejecting my request for new equipment, "Chef Gillian requested a new stove because she does not want to clean the old one." Tiles popped off of the plywood floor, it was too flexible. I suggested we pour an epoxy floor rather than continue to replace sections of tile only to have those pop off and reduce our health department scores. This, and the request for the installation of a used broiler, was laughed at. I had to show with photographic evidence that a new broiler placed above the stove would not restrict the ventilation.

But I had outgrown the executive chef role. My days were dull and unchallenging. The repetition and the days washing dishes by hand (staff quit and machine failure) made me feel like I was doing all of the dirty work. And management was doing nothing to help me get out of a dirty, wet chef coat. I called to find out why my new dish machine had yet to arrive, "Oh, sorry, chef," the service tech was calling up our account information on his laptop. "I have a note in the service agreement that says, 'no hurry.'" I lost it.

Nothing needed to change while I was there to keep my finger in the dyke. I was the most accomplished chef in the only profitable restaurant, but it didn't mean I deserved any common human decency. I wanted out of that kitchen.

"There is no corporate chef job," I was told during my annual review. "There never could be. We just don't see the company going that way." The lure of a shiny new kitchen on a well-staffed cruise ship, I snapped on it like a hungry grouper. The white man chef that replaced me got a new stove. He asked for a combi-oven—the revolutionary cooking tool that all you do is program and it will roast chickens, proof dough, and bake pies at the touch of a button—and it was delivered and installed, no questions asked. I was left bitter from rejection, failure, and empty promises.

But at the end of my 6-week tour on the cruise ship, I prayed for other options. I got off of that cruise ship intent on not returning. I concentrated on landing the job that represented my skills and experience. In fact, I came home in time for two very important interviews. One was with a local hotel; the food and beverage director had arranged it. He heard I was on the market. He took me aside and quietly advised, "They are going to ask you a lot of questions about corporate standards," he squeezed my forearm with a 'you got this' wink. I stunned the kitchen staff with my scratch layer cake. They were awed into silence when I got the huge whole grouper out of the market basket and reduced it to five neat filets. One of them volunteered, her mouth full of cake scraps, "The guy that was here yesterday wasn't very good." She wrinkled her nose, "and for some reason he didn't make enough food." I took a deep inhale, anxiety gone, and confidence boosted. My food was a big hit—a fine dining turn up of coastal favorites. But the guy in the suit who ran the hotel as hotel manager wasn't impressed.

"You have this restaurant on your resume," he looked at his fingernails, swinging his massive desk chair back and forth in a half circle.

He stopped the motion by planting his feet onto the floor and looked down at my resume on his desk, "Colorado Kitchen?"

"Yes, we were open for about 8 years." I loved talking about the Kitchen, my baby and the foundation for a lot of my success.

"We were—"

"Yeah, I lived in the area for about 6 years," he looked at me over his fingernails, "I've never heard of the place." Well, how do I answer that? Do I grab my cell phone and show him pictures…did I have any pictures? Does he really think I made it all up—all of it, all 20 years memorialized in that resume? He did.

When the big corporate chain called me I just about fell out of my chair. Global culinary research and development meant creative days in a kitchen and researching what new menu item might fly in Sydney or Jamaica. I was to meet in Dallas with the global director of culinary, he called me from London, and we spoke for over an hour. The interview in Dallas would include a food demo where I would prepare four shareable appetizers.

I practiced and thought about it. I did copious hours of research. My scotch eggs were a hit at Sue Ann's; something I'd admired at a pub when I was in Scotland, the barely done boiled egg, covered in pork sausage, breaded and fried was always a crowd pleaser. I cut planks of squid into strips like French fries and served those with tomato chutney. I wrapped a bouquet of enoki mushrooms with thinly sliced sirloin in a teriyaki glaze. I simmered chicken into a pot pie filling and folded it into a hand pie. I deboned a chicken leg, piped if full of crayfish mouse, batter fried it and served it with a creole sauce.

I was in an immaculate prep kitchen cooking after a breakfast interview that was relaxed and friendly. This was going well; unlike some tastings when I was ill-prepared or didn't really consider the difficult task of cooking in an unfamiliar kitchen. The fact is sometimes food that worked over here, does not work over there. I had a demo at a hotel in Minneapolis where the management was gaga over my resume and qualifications. They shopped for the ingredients I asked for and set me loose in front of a stove in the banquet kitchen. I was handed an old dull knife that had a missing rivet in the handle. The hole left by the lost fastener was filled with crumbs and debris (obviously from being years in the back of a drawer) and a cutting board as wobbly and bumpy as a kettle chip. The August tomatoes from the North Coast supplier were hard and white. They forgot to get my grits. The shrimp was frozen solid. And the chicken they handed me to use was green and slime covered. The rotten airline breast had been flattened to fit in a sandwich. I couldn't imagine how I could use it for my famous roasted chicken with thyme gravy. I suspected sabotage after I was advised to sear my two portions of tenderloin medium rare and medium. I was dinged in the presentation for not serving a consistent temperature. My shrimp and grits (made with polenta) didn't make any sense to the team who had never seen anything like that before.

The hotel group's corporate chef couldn't disguise his disappointment, "I was hoping you would come in here and just make us fried chicken." Is that what everyone wanted? It was a question I heard after many tastings—for large institutions, for fine dining, for caterers.

When I presented my shareable appetizers to the big corporate chain it was as if the crew I'd had a great breakfast with had been replaced by unhappy stand-ins. They hated everything. The hand pie was confusing (Is it an empanada? Just what are you trying to say here?) There wasn't enough sausage around the scotch eggs. The stuffed chicken leg—my attempt to offer a wing alternative as wing prices had skyrocketed under huge demand—was unnecessary. Price wasn't relevant. The assistant walked me to the front door of the huge headquarters building and left me in the parking lot. He assured me my ride to the airport would arrive any minute and he let the door close on my luggage. I began to understand that tastings and demos often disguised ulterior motives. The Dallas-based chain was negotiating with the current chef in the role I was trying to capture. He agreed on his salary increase and new contract right before my demo.

The man who handed me the wobbly cutting board in Minneapolis had been the interim chef, filling in on loan from one of the hotel corporate's properties in Ohio, and let it slip that it was a great job that he would love to have himself.

I was treated to a trip to a Louisiana town on the river to audition to be executive chef of a sprawling country club. There was a snack bar, fine dining, banquet facilities, and a huge job in a southern setting where I could make a name for myself and move up the ranks of this conglomerate of national clubs. It started in Dallas with a meeting with the corporate big wigs, and then the general manager and I drove to the facility that so desperately needed a chef. I would be cooking for the food and beverage director and club board of directors—the folks paying dearly to eat the food, golf with clients, and marry off their children on the premises. The general manager showed me the kitchen. I was devastated by the filth. The walk-in walls had rusted, and the aluminum was pock marked and warped where someone had tried to clean it with a harsh chemical. The floor of the walk-in cooler was two inches of degraded food with an anti-fatigue mat sinking into it. The walls of the kitchen were not covered with the standard stainless steel or the commonly found pebbled sheets of fiberglass reinforced plastic (FRP), but with white coated backer board—the type you'd unfold to tack onto the back of your IKEA bookcase. Pot handles and the edges of sheet trays had nicked and scratched the white off of the walls in a weird pattern that resembled marbling of a fine Kobe N.Y. Strip.

I hung in there although my skin was crawling. I disinfected a small section on a table and made a stuffed pork chop, a crab meat salad, and crawfish hand pies. The staff, accustomed to working in these conditions and probably grateful that there was no need to clean up after a shift (where would one begin?), busied about doing their standard preparation for lunch service. I was amazed no one had been poisoned. One of the cooks (they had warned me about bad attitudes and territorial behavior among the crew) asked if she could try one of my hand pies. I handed her one, dabbing it with the finely diced onion and ghost pepper salsa that I had made. She sunk her fractured and spaced out teeth into it. It barely glanced her taste buds before she began violently shaking her head and spit what she had allowed into her mouth into her hand.

"I had a doll that used to do that when I was a kid," I laughed. They didn't want a chef. They wanted to continue to recklessly cook the menu and fight amongst themselves to be in charge for the day or the week until they faced a confrontation with another power-greedy cook who forced them to back down. During my brief tour of the heart of the house I was shown the chef's office. There were stacks of binders, cooking magazines, old schedules all over the desk and overtaking the observation windows. Anything that came in the mail addressed to "chef" or anything they were reluctant to throw away was all over the chair and on the floor. The room had been made uninhabitable. Sort of a "don't even try to bring a chef in here" form of hoarding.

I brought my food into the dining room and presented it to the decision makers. They ate silently. Then one of the men in a blue button-down oxford and a tweed jacket put his fork down and spoke up.

"This is very good," he wiped his mouth on his cloth napkin and straightened up in his chair. I could tell this was going in a serious direction that my food had absolutely nothing to do with.

"What do you think of the kitchen?" he asked a question I didn't expect.

"Well," I hesitated. Had they never been back there? "There certainly is a lot of space." I deflected, "And the equipment seems to be holding up nicely."

"No, tell us what you really think." I looked at the serious faces around the room. They'd just forked out over a million to renovate the club dining rooms and outdoor spaces. They hadn't even thought about the kitchen.

"It's disgusting," I knew I didn't want this job. There was no way I was going back into that room. "I have never seen anything like it. The walk-in should just be demolished. There is no way any of that food is at the right temperature and the floor made me want to throw up." No one moved, so I kept going. "I don't know who you contracted to surface the walls, but the code is washable surface. That does not mean you can use IKEA bookcase painted cardboard. Frankly, you need to shut down and

360

not make food in there anymore. Someone is going to get sick. It needs to be gutted." They thanked me for my honesty. The food & beverage director sat me down in his office and offered me $20,000 less than what I told them I would accept as my base salary in my first interview. I knew now why they invited me there. They brought a credible and accomplished chef to tell the club board of directors that the kitchen was a shithole and more money needed to be spent.

There have also been the interviews and opportunities to cook for a job with the six-figure salary of my dreams. I now count three of those demos that I've done where I presented an outrageous selection of food. For the price of a plane ticket or a stay in a hotel (at the most $500), the restaurant or hotel had been treated to $5000 of work I would do if I were hired as a consultant. I'm sure now that some of those, "That was great. We'll call you," were thinly veiled attempts to get menu ideas.

Still, I accepted every opportunity to cook my way into a job. After hours of interviews where I talked technical skill, hard lessons from experience, awards and acclaim from every kitchen, and finally my determination and knack for building solid teams in back and front of the house—the invite to cook meant I was almost there. I just had one more thing to do to support all of those claims about myself. But the lack of sharp knives, the tub of artificial chicken stock, the difference in produce, flour, polenta—just about anything that a chef might stock in a pantry that is totally different from my own specifications can lead to disaster and a "Hey, I thought this one could cook. No way we can make this one an offer." All of that great stuff I said in four hours of interviews, that's immaterial now.

But then there are the demos where I've knocked it out of the park. The fates were with me and glorious good kitchen gods were on my shoulders. In those cases, I've been able to make a glorious sauce from the fake chicken stock.

"This is the best demo we've had"

"You nailed it. Everything you've prepared today could be on our menu." I'm beaming and I head home or to the airport confident that I've got this one. There were times I've received leading emails of thanks and congratulations after my performance. And then I never get the email or phone call I've been waiting on. The reasons are often flimsy (the other guy's food was more what we were thinking, you have a lot of independent experience and folks like that usually don't do well in our structure, we don't think you're the right fit.) I get it. Sometimes folks look at personality and imagine that they need someone just like them if they are going to work well together. Then there are the chefs that do a demo where they used ash, tweezers, see through rounds of radish standing straight up in a foam.... while impressive, they aren't me. Which is fine. But leading a kitchen takes much more than balancing a radish on a foam bubble.

I worked one of my in-between gigs at an airport steak house. I was a talented executive chef working incognito as an ordinary line cook. The chef had been affiliated with the restaurant group as far back as Chicago and moved to Virginia to open this place in the airport terminal. I heard wonderful things about Chef Nico and how talented he was. The food came from a corporate mandate so all I saw of Nico's talent was the occasional special...Hanger Steak with Pearl Onions was one. I watched Nico take cocktail onions from the bar and rinse the vinegar off of them before tossing them into a pan with butter, wine, and parsley. He poured that sour concoction over the steak which had not been cut amateurishly with the grain so that it resembled strips of red muscle fibers.

Nico's team-building skills were no better. Darrell and I told him the walk in—dark as a tomb—needed a new light bulb (all of those supplies like new mop heads and soap were under lock and key in a cage in his office.) "Yeah, yeah." He'd wave us off. "I've got it." Then we'd see him dressed in civilian clothes and heading out the door. There were also those times my phone rang just as I was getting up a little later than usual having worked the line on a busy night so busy that another hour was needed to clean the kitchen.

"Hey, can you come in early this morning, Sanos called out." I'd make my way over to the airport to relieve Nico who couldn't bear to work the line. I never saw him in anything but a spotlessly clean chef coat. We were going on week three with a dark walk in. Cooks, servers, bartenders had resorted to just throwing stuff anywhere. We tripped over oranges and crushed heads of celery under our feet.

I was not surprised when I came in for a late shift. Dishes were piled up because the daytime dishwasher was a no show. Kitchen staff was expected to wash on days like this. I got busy setting up the dish machine when I noticed dozens of soup bowls almost full of the house specialty, clam chowder. This soup is usually a hit. But there they were bowls of soup barely touched. I could tell some of the customers were trying to make it right by adding tons of crackers. Some of the bowls wore the five o'clock shadow of table grind. Others floated a blood in the water swirl of hot sauce. Still, the soup was inedible. I had to get to the bottom of this. I searched through the dirties to find the pot. There it was the big stainless-steel stock pot that the first cook of the day used to reheat the soup. I could smell it even before I rinsed the thin layer of soup from the bottom. There was the distinctive smell of burned down house coming from that pot; at the bottom, about an inch of carbon. The first cook in that morning had mercilessly scorched the soup, poured it into the service kettle, and served it all afternoon. No one cared to ask. No one cared to fix it. Just as no one cared to put a light bulb in the walk in.

Kitchens are complicated environments and I've heard first hand from the disappointed staffs who work for chefs who teach them nothing, give them nothing, and let them flounder on a busy Saturday night—they haven't organized prep to get through the night, the staff feels unsupported, or even the food takes too long to plate and the costs are out of whack.

I often left that restaurant at night shaking my head about Nico. He had no skills, but also no passion to ignite any desire to get better. And I'm sure before he was offered a job, he had very little to prove and everything on his resume was accepted without question. That same organization hired a sous chef. He was a big slob of a man that punctuated sentences with shit and fuck, but in an unnatural way as if he were attempting line cook talk. All of us in the back of the house could tell he'd never worked in a kitchen and his resume was a string of fibs. He didn't fold the cuffs of his chef coat, so his sleeves dragged through salad dressing. He also never thought to have a towel by his station, in his hand, or folded over his apron strings. He was constantly burning his himself and dropping pans of sauce or seared chicken breast—occasionally burning another cook. We'd watch him bumble his way through a recipe or say something like "We were always boiling some fucking stock when I worked at Red Lobster," chuckling to himself. He was always the only one laughing.

It's hard not to be discouraged, when I've gone 0 for 10 and the only difference is skin color and gender. While the winning chef excels at embracing the latest fadz, I'm most often the only candidate who has achieved the young chef ambitions: Food Network shows, published cookbook, critical acclaim, trainees becoming executive chefs after leaving my kitchens. If those in charge of staffing a kitchen have a picture in their head of who the chef will be, it never is a black woman. And I found even if I met the qualifications, there were certain restaurant groups that would instantly respond to my resume with a rejection letter. I was sure they'd seen my picture. My fears were supported by corporate websites with photo galleries featuring plenty of white men, a handful of white women, nobody of color. My suspicions led me to create a resume for Francis Clark (my male alter ego). Francis had never been on the Food Network, had never been photographed. We had the same career history, with plenty of accolades, but he'd carried out his stellar career in relative obscurity. Strangely, the very restaurant groups who had rejected my resume, emailed Francis to set up an interview. Uh oh. Now what. An HR director who had emailed me a rejection, called Francis three days later. Except, I answered the phone. I went from marking "chooses not to answer" on the EEOC part of the online application to checking "white" and "male". Maybe they'll look at my resume and realize they can't do without me.

I was really surprised when I sent a resume at nine one morning and the three partners toiling away to open an ocean front gastropub and biergarten emailed me to schedule an interview that same afternoon. They needed someone immediately as they were less than a month from opening day. I had sent them my full-on resume with links to videos that would expose my true race and gender. Those videos were my calling card. I figured they had to have seen them (why else would they pick my resume out of the pile and demand to see me NOW) and it would be no surprise when I walked in. But when I pushed open the door with a folder of extra copies of my resume and asked for Charles Winn, the man who had emailed me, I was met with an awkward reception. They confessed that they were hoping I was the health inspector. One of Charles' partners had started to laugh the minute I walked in without a badge or plastic department of health ID pinned to my sweater. Kiernan, the Scottish inspiration of the place explained why his heavy-set partner found the situation funny.

"Well, we read your name on your resume and we didn't know if you'd be a man or a woman." The fat guy laughed even harder now; there were tears in his eyes.

"Not that it matters," Charles interjected.

"No, No." the fat guy was holding his belly, "It don't matter at all."

I was mature and studied. I'd done this opening thing before so I knew exactly what they needed, and I told them what I would do first and how. They asked me for menu suggestions. I laid out a playful menu of gastropub favorites of sliders and wings, but also suggested we weave in items that were truly Scottish (I told them I had worked in Scotland and brought home quite a few ideas.) I suggested shareable things that promoted beer drinking and then a few stabs at fine dining—a really nice steak, a grilled whole lobster. How about the "best crab cakes on the planet?" They offered to show me around. I headed straight for the kitchen.

"Wow," said Charles, "None of the other candidates went straight to the kitchen."

"Really," I was genuinely surprised, "what is it they want to see more than the kitchen?"

"The bar."

Unfortunately, as much as they protested, the man vs woman thing *did* matter. And the laughter? They never in their wildest imagination expected a black woman. Of course, I didn't hear from them.

When I interviewed with the young ambitious squad from a Texas college town, I fell in love with their energy. They'd built a sprawling entertainment complex and were going to put a three-story restaurant smack dab in the middle between the surfing pool and the go-kart track.

This location was to be the flagship store. The executive chef who scored this job would lead the culinary division in establishing dozens of locations in college towns across the country. I was salivating. There was four hours of phone interviews with human resources, the head of marketing, and Andre the general manager, a man about my age who had moved his family from Northern California to this Texas town. Andre expressed a great appreciation for my work. He'd watched all of my TV appearances and listened to my work with NPR. He and his wife considered me a celebrity. And after we met, he had to endure a half hour of questioning from her about what I was like in person. Before I left, I handed him a signed copy of my book. He was overcome. I thought he was going to cry. While in Texas I sat at a table surrounded by nine men for whom I'd cooked. It was the first of three more hours of intense interviews. I had done this hundreds of times now.... for the media, in a book, and hours and hours of interviews.

The owner of the company appeared to like what I was saying. He invited me to join him on one of his excursions to Bolivia, Peru, and Argentina. He loved South America and considered himself an expert on the cuisine. Could we include some of those things in the southern inspired menu that was being bandied about? The menu and direction of the restaurant hadn't been decided. I figured an outdoorsy, fun-loving venue was going to require similar food. My offerings were playful, but grounded and familiar. They asked for wings. I prepared a standard honey-hot and crunchy, a recipe made famous and acclaimed in the first critic's review of Colorado Kitchen. My dessert, an updated American standard, apple pandowdy.

I got home to find an email from Andre, he thanked me for the book and congratulated me on my demo and ended with, "I can definitely see you succeeding in this role." I waited for my offer letter. It never came. Instead, weeks after I stopped hoping, I got a call from the recruiter. She called to let me know that they had decided to go in a different direction. What hadn't I answered correctly? I sat in a room full of folks nodding their heads and agreeing with me. I had brought the man I'd be working alongside to tears by presenting him a book. What could have gone wrong? She confided that they were about to make an offer to one of the two other candidates. The second candidate was a reserve in case the other turned them down. Wait...I didn't even make it to the top two? I couldn't imagine anyone sitting through a total of eight hours of interviews showing

371

themselves more capable. The recruiter gal agreed, I excelled in the interview portion of the selection criteria.

"Ultimately it came down to the culinary presentation that best matched what the owners had in mind."

"Basically, a lucky shot in the dark," I surmised. "You're going to discount my experience, and how I performed through intensive interview questions." (Can you detail specific benefits and drawbacks of your leadership style? Do you consider yourself a better chef or better businessman? Can you relate an actual outcome of a time you managed a team toward a specific goal?).

"Well, the other two candidates' food was more aligned with the vision."

There was no vision. They had confessed that they had no concept defined when I was first called in. All they knew so far was that they wanted late night bar food even when the kitchen had closed, and they were in the process of building a bakery and pizza oven. I reserved mentioning my plan for my heralded chili (my recipe had appeared in the New York Times food section) in a soup terrine behind the bar and bags of Fritos at the ready so that bartenders could dish out Frito Pie to hungry bar flies.

372

Maybe I should have let that one out during my interview. Would they have stolen it?

"Well…." I could tell she was at a loss. She had a script and I wasn't saying my lines. I pushed even further.

"Wanda," let's do this woman to woman I had nothing to lose now. "Do you think what really is happening here is that this group just doesn't want a black woman representing their brand?" They had an active social media campaign with photos of everyone and everything associated with the project. My black face under a white chef hat would surely stand out amid the almost exclusively white organization.

"No, that's not it at all," she answered weakly. She didn't sound insulted or outraged at my suggestion, surprised perhaps or maybe just irritated that I wasn't letting this go.

"I don't think my food was any less on target of a loosely conceived concept than those two white men you're tossing up there," I had worked myself into a lather, I guess. "It would be crazy to think that all of those white men in that room would consider me when they envisioned a white man for the role." I was ready to hang up now through her silence.

373

It was finally sinking in. Everything that I had done and everywhere I'd been had amounted to nothing. I was nobody.

Chapter Twelve

When it Turns an Amber Color, Add the Heavy Cream

"You'd be going backwards," she explained. I had applied to be an executive chef at a restaurant in New Orleans. "You just told me that you feel like you've outgrown that." The headhunter—who wasn't going to have to share a space with me and wonder if it would suddenly become filled with black people because I was now working there, or who now had to bite her tongue and not say something vulgar or racist—was a fan. She'd seen the videos and read the reviews.

"You're a corporate chef," she said, "Do that."

"Have you ever placed a woman," I had to ask. I had worked with a headhunter before who scratched his head when I didn't make it passed the first phone interview. He swore it was my cover letter. He advised me to tone it down. "I think you come off too…." He fumbled for the words, "like you're going to have a problem taking direction." Did it sound uppity; like I didn't know my place?

He rewrote paragraphs emphasizing that I did things "under the guidance of a management team" or "fulfilling the mandate of a knowledgeable ownership". Maybe I sounded too confident. Of course, this went against everything I'd ever heard about selling myself as a strong candidate. I wasn't a self-starter. I was a chess piece with no ability to think of the next steps. Were other candidates dumbing down their resumes the same way? Did getting the job mean that a woman needs to show up to the interview with clipped wings? And a black woman needs to attribute all of her success to her "owners?" I didn't have the heart to tell him what I thought was really going on. He created a package to present me to a group that when I looked them up on the internet there was nothing but plates of octopus, and men with hairy hands and 3-day growth standing with their arms folded in all of the pictures. The lone woman on the website was in charge of catering sales. He was always stunned when my CV with a girl's name on it wasn't picked from the pile of Steves, Josés, and Connors.

"I've never had a woman as a candidate," she confessed. She told me that she'd never thought about that. But all of the men that she's worked with found a perfect fit in a matter of a few weeks. She expected the same for me. There was a job in Florida with a well-known group that specialized in southern food. They were expanding and needed a competent opener, "You're perfect." She also sent her well-constructed presentation of me to a group in Washington, DC that had made a name for itself with a small dinner cruise operation. They needed someone to get in that commissary kitchen and start getting it to make sense.

She called me a few hours later to say that the Florida group had passed on me, but I was not to be discouraged. She was waiting on a return call, "I just want to know why they passed on your application so quickly. I'm curious. Maybe I missed something." I never heard from her again, but I took her advice. I was going to get that corporate chef job.

I typed corporate chef into the search box and sent my resume all over the country. I admit, some were long shots. And I was genuinely surprised when I made it out of thousands of applicants to get to the screening interview for some pretty high-profile chains. But they all ended there. The screening interview with an excited recruiter certain they had found the perfect candidate to pass on to the committee or director was as far as I got.

I lost count…100, definitely. I wasn't going to give up. But I admit I had moments of weakness and fear. Maybe, I'll never get that corporate chef job. I did send out a few resumes for executive chef. But even those I felt like I was knocking on the door of folks pretending not to be home.

"Wow, I must say," the one who got the job of sorting through the hundreds of applicants to narrow it down to 5 or 10 with that phone call and questions to make sure I fit the basic criteria. "You have a pretty impressive resume." I had been through hundreds of these interviews, so I never hesitate or wavered. My answers had been well-thought out, almost rehearsed.

"I'm going to pass this information on to the director of the department, you would be directly reporting to him," this is usually where my resume stalled. If I did get a phone call from this guy, he would sound uninterested and made sure he planted in my ear that he had a lot of resumes to look at. Sometimes I couldn't help but mirror in my own presentation of facts, descriptions, and philosophy his slow, sad tone.

I took the advice of Amy Cuddy, author of the book *Presence*. Cuddy is an American social psychologist, author and lecturer known for her research on stereotyping and discrimination, emotions, power, nonverbal behavior. Her research on "power posing" quickly became famous after a TED talk in 2012. I had been halfway through the book and was already using the power posing techniques; standing like wonder woman while the phone was ringing or in the parking lot before heading into the interview.

But then I got to the part where she talked about how white interviewers will appear uninterested, inattentive, and painfully unenthusiastic when interviewing people of color. The result was the job applicant responding in kind, mirroring the posture, and speech pattern and effectively interviewing poorly. I concentrated on fighting the subconscious response that resulted in my answering with a dull one word yes or no, my shoulders slacking—unimpressed with myself and wearing it. I fought it by being as upbeat and verbose as I was when the interviewer was thrilled to be listening to me. When it appeared that they were no longer listening to my answer I kept it up, throwing in a joke. One man seemed to be trying his best to put me to rest and slam closed the book between us. He looked distracted and, because he assumed, I had nothing interesting to say, I didn't.

"We're really working on building a chef-driven restaurant here," he explained tiredly as if I had never heard the term before. "Of course, with considerations to the concept." Was he stifling a yawn? He was preparing to end the conversation and show me the door. What did I have to lose by disagreeing with him? There was already an X next to my name.

"I am not a follower of that term 'chef driven.'" I countered. The term had always put images in my mind of a character that could barely pull himself from a mirror and it didn't matter what city, state, or building he was in he had to do HIS food. This chef grabbed on to a fad no matter how much people really didn't like it. He'd smear a lamb kidney with head cheese. Nobody really wants to eat nose to tail, but what did he care. Offal was in.

"It is a selfish and short-sighted chef that needs to do *his* food." I had his attention now. "A real chef does the food that needs to be done." His eyes lit up and he scrawled a note to himself on my resume. And I'm sure he began using the phrase himself, maybe when working on the menu with the new chef.

From out of nowhere came my dream job: corporate chef of a burgeoning restaurant group in New York City. I'd long considered New York to be the major leagues, a city full of smart people, running slick restaurants, with expert staff—line cooks with the skill and knowledge that would make them executive chefs anywhere else. I'd passed over countless job postings that required two and three years of New York experience. I would never be able to compete. I sent my resume almost as a joke to myself. When I got a phone call from the group looking to open two new concepts and to re-concept their two others, I felt like I'd won the lottery. Before I knew it, I was in New York cooking by myself in a kitchen still under construction. The space was small but the interior touches of exposed brick and neoclassic moldings in a milky blue slate were spot on for a place serving French-Canadian cuisine. I sauced French fries in new-fangled poutine and updated French classics like coq au vin with fried chicken and polenta. The two partners I met were young and starry eyed and talked of restaurants in their family and in the partnership that were thriving but, with changes in partnership, needed revamping.

I found an ambitious team that was grounded, funded, and looking for the missing piece in the form of the culinary creative. I accepted a so-so salary with a paragraph in my contract that promised an increase in my base as new restaurants came online and required my attention and as the new place we were building expanded, so would my income. There were plans to go beyond the 30-seat first floor with a live music rathskeller in the basement. A wall was going to be knocked down to the empty storefront next door. In a few months after opening the partners planned to expand the prep space and add another 20 seats and more room to pour cocktails. The owner and I drew plans on scrap paper of sinks and coolers. I tore my pants daily on sinks and table corners in the tight prep space. I was anxious for expansion.

I came to town in the winter a little intimidated by the city I'd left when I was younger and more fit. Subway stairs, alternate side of the street parking, cramped apartment living was something I was going to have to get used to. But I was excited about being able to prove myself in the city that represented a culinary milestone to me. I was also thrilled to be surrounded by a pace and forward thinking that is New York; a city running circles around the slow, sleepy, backward, and sometimes intolerant towns where I'd plied my trade.

I came into a kitchen I hadn't designed to do my demo. The equipment was an odd selection of old pieces (the stove was electric as gas wasn't available in that side of the building). The three-compartment sink took up most of the prep area with the wash sink unreachable behind a sandwich unit. I ran water but the pipes were not connected so when I drained the sink of soapy water, I was soaked to my socks. There was no walk in, but a selection of coolers that ran rough and breathed hot and heavy trying hard to cool to 40°. There was a reach-in freezer that groaned and clicked itself off, maintaining a temperature of 52° at best. The worktable in the back leaned into its bent leg. I was prepared to cook for five partners but only two (the two that I would work with for the months to come) were there. Nonetheless, we talked business and money. I liked them. They told me about the plans and projects on the horizon and of their connections to power brokers in the active online food media community.

Strangely, however when I researched the company and the stakeholders, it was as if they didn't exist. They had no internet presence at all. But they ignored mine, none of the ugliness was coming back to haunt me up here in New York. They had heard of my fried chicken, so I featured it in the coq au vin. But the electric equipment made it impossible. This was going to take some retooling.

In a matter of weeks, I had accepted the corporate chef position with this new group and was living in New York. I was told to report to the restaurant on my first day. Before I'd even started, I'd written the menu, compiled the recipe book and began studying for the New York Food Handler's exam. I was going to hit the ground running for the opening scheduled just a couple of weeks away. I called one of the partners to get a key. I had rented a temporary room around the corner and walked to meet him as he stained the newly installed wood floor. The building was cold, and lightbulbs hung loose. There'd been some improvements since I'd last been there, but not many. Gilded mirrors were on the brick wall, a long bench was built right under them. One of the other partners arrived and told me that we'd be doing a tasting for the leadership the following day at 6 pm. I would be auditioning as many of the menu items as I could. She tilted her head toward her partner as he dabbed a mop in the dark brown liquid.

"He wants to do a tasting every day until we open," She chuckled. I laughed also. We were weeks from opening—several weeks by the look of things. I was reluctant to fill the refrigerators full of food at this point. There was no shelving yet. And I hadn't even begun to find purveyors. Sure, one tasting for the partners was a great idea. But then I planned on finding suppliers, pots and pans, blenders—there weren't even plates. So, yes, I laughed. She had to be kidding.

A trip to the store, and a restaurant supply would be enough to rough through a few menu items. They agreed to meet me at 9am to head out in preparation for the tasting for ten important folks involved in the projects and restaurants to come. I was ready to take the city by storm but anxious. I had never cooked in this city that for me was as judgmental as the line in the song made famous by Sinatra. I didn't want to be the one who couldn't "make it" in New York. I went to my tiny room that night and stared at the ceiling. I jumped out of bed at 8am, and with a coffee in hand went to the space.

It was 9am so I let myself in. The newly stained floor was covered with paper. I could tell it had been nailed down but not sanded. I had done the floors at all of my restaurants—hardwood, vinyl tile, quarry tile. The swinging doors that led to the kitchen from the dining room snapped back hard and made it difficult to get in and out and near impossible if you were carrying something. The pass, where servers came to pick up plates, was a window about 3 feet by 3 feet aside a shelf under a warmer. I imagined how we would have to pass plates one by one to servers standing at that window. There was no way they'd be able to grab four at a time. Someone was going to have to stand there and man that window and play the role of plate passer. There were so many inefficiencies I lost count. The ten-burner electric stove was missing knobs and had to be shut off and on with the circuit breaker. Only half of the burners got hot. Two of those were hot enough to boil water. The hot line was long, almost fifteen feet, but barely wide enough at the stove for two people to pass by. Later, at work in the narrow space, I'd lose buttons edging through the line. And there was only one fryer. The emphasis on poutine was obviously an afterthought. Someone had made sure to install cameras. There were three alone in the tiny kitchen. One appeared to be always focused on me. I didn't want to see anymore, so I sat down on a bench and waited. And waited.

I was prepping menu items from zero. This meant lots of prep time. I needed to make sauces, salad dressings, desserts—basically I needed hours to set up mise en place to be able to efficiently prepare plates for 10 people. One of the partners finally arrived at 11. He wasn't in a hurry and having never cooked before didn't get why I was. We made our way through city traffic to the restaurant supply. On the way there were stories complete with name dropping and financial escapades—the kind that take a bank account from zero to sixty in 5 seconds. This guy owned companies all over and had family that had started a major international bank.

"They ask me every day if I need money," he thumbed through eBay on his phone with one hand on the steering wheel, "I say no, no…" he laughed. I watched his thumb stretching across the plus sized iPhone. It was smaller than my own and the nail was cut so short it made my fingers hurt. I could make out that on his eBay account he had 2,617 items in his shopping cart. This guy talked so much about his money and all he owned, I wondered why he would want to risk so much of it in a restaurant.

He looked to me like he'd never worked in food service before— not even as a busser. Opening a restaurant is serious business, and I had been there, done that. Because, for me, it made economic sense and was my sole source of income. I was a chef for goodness sake—classically trained with 20 plus years in a food service building. I fed my family and paid my bills with a restaurant. I imagined opening a dentist office, after having only been on the receiving end of dentistry. The act and ambition seemed similar to me. I could never open a dentist's office. I recalled my warning to the Scots years ago in the house on Black Street. There's nothing hard about opening a restaurant. But can you keep it open?

We left the supply store almost two hours later with over $1500 in pots, pans, measuring cups, ladles, strainers, mixing bowls, and whisks. The trip to the sprawling grocery store took just about as long and I panicked when I saw the checkout line. It was almost 3. I had just three hours to prep, cook, and serve 10 people. I calmed down with a trick I used to play on myself as I struggled to keep up at Colorado Kitchen. The two hours in between brunch and dinner service on Saturday always felt like two minutes. I would look up at the clock panting and sweating, my heart pounding out of my chest and my mind so distracted with "I'm never going to get it all done" that I would stare at the clock unable to move, my hands shaking and spilling precious sauce as I strained it.

"It's not five o'clock yet, relax." I'd whisper to myself, "It's not five o'clock yet." Even if it was 4:55, the mantra made me feel not so desperate. I had time.

As luck would have it, no one in that group was ever concerned about being anywhere on time. They gathered and sat around a table at close to 8. I had found 15 plates in the basement. I was going to have to wash (the water was still soaking my shoes) in between courses. I started with a poached pear salad with cider vinaigrette and moved on to a ham and gruyere layered between the puff pastry I had hunted for like a mad woman at the sprawling Asian-leaning store. The lone fryer wasn't yet connected yet, so I poured oil into one of the larger pots I'd found full of dust and debris in the basement. It heated inconsistently because the electric burners heated best when absolutely flat-bottomed cookware sat on them.

One of the partners requested that we add Hazelnut soup to the menu. I couldn't find any history or idea of this soup (other than brief mentions in the story of Rapunzel— a soup of parsnips thickened with hazelnut—and he shook his head....no, no that wasn't it). I peppered him with questions as he recalled a soup one of his grandfather's mistresses made when he brought her around his family.

"Are you sure its hazelnut," I asked, willing to give it a shot "was it cream based, a puree, tomato based. Are you sure it wasn't chestnut?" I was doing my best to stick to the French-Canadian theme. I had nixed the other partners request for cheesecake on the dessert menu and chicken wings done with a Thai marinade.

"No, definitely hazelnut...hazelnut, hazelnut."

There I was prepping for the tasting, the only filberts we could find at that supermarket were in the shell. I was able to extract about half a cup of them, broken and speckled with dark brown skin. My soup was ugly and thick, but it wasn't bad.

I fried bags and bags of fries in my makeshift deep fryer, pouring gravy on them and piling the tops with cheese. I cranked out house made pasta and coiled it around seared scallops with a sauce of shallots, lemon, butter and white wine. I tossed cubed squash with olive oil for ratatouille. I washed plates as quickly as I could and then served a French apple cake without the caramel and whipped cream I had planned in the menu (I had forgotten the heavy cream.) I had pulled it off. The partner came to me as

390

I stood by the tiny window at the pass, drinking his soup out of a paper coffee cup (there were no bowls or spoons.)

"You were right," he looked down at the brown speckled hot-cereal-thick liquid concoction in the cup, "its chestnut soup. She made us chestnut soup."

I had spent over $500 on groceries and they were all gone. I hadn't shopped for brie in the store or lobster in years. I wasn't used to retail prices. I hesitated to put more than two lobsters in the shopping cart at a whopping $18 a pound. The hazelnuts alone—all 4 pounds of them—came to $60. I hadn't thought to buy plastic wrap. My kitchens always had the giant rolls from the dry goods merchant. Things just hadn't occurred to me as I rushed to stock a bare kitchen in a mad dash through a grocery store. I wrapped the cheeses and sauces I had left in the plastic shopping bags. I was so glad it was over. It was a stress I hadn't had in a long time. I don't think I'd ever been thrown into a barely functioning kitchen with no small wares and an empty pantry after a whirlwind shopping spree and then cooked in less than three hours a selection of items from a theoretical menu for ten people; after scrounging for 6-inch plates in a dusty basement.

"That was great chef," one of the partners was pouring wine into plastic cups they'd bought. "Truly delicious." Times like these I can't help but feel like a domestic. It doesn't seem productive to me; it was just eating as if they were all at a fancy dinner I had been hired to cater. We didn't talk menu or plan. It wasn't at all like we were auditioning menu items. When I watch folks eat while I run around with inadequate supplies to make sure they have clean plates and silverware, I have a difficult time listening to their laughter and watching as they get drunk. Sure, I'm being compensated for my time, but I still have to shake off the bitterness to be polite. I largely view these tastings, unless they come with a conversation about concept and direction, to be a waste of time. It felt as if the two partners who had experienced my food a month ago during my demo were showing me off to the others, "We did good," they were saying, "she can cook."

My struggles in the poorly designed kitchen were immaterial because I'd pulled it off. But I wondered, with this dining room full of people and three or four servers bumbling around, how it would go. I went home that night, glad they were pleased, but also ready to forget about the stress of the day and look past how the experience made me feel like a servant. I decided to spend the day seeking out a produce company, studying for the food safety exam, and then later organizing the kitchen. I needed to walk the space and figure out storage and logistics. I had a terrible time doing that tasting; nothing was where I needed it to be. Organizing the kitchen into stations was going to make producing food in that small space just that much easier. These are the things I need to do to get a restaurant open. Tastings, as a way to thank, brag, or entertain friends, did nothing to get me closer to opening day.

I was in the library using the public Wi-Fi when my phone rang. I was sure it was one of the partners. I wasn't far away, but I hadn't planned on making it to the restaurant until later that afternoon. It was just after two. And I had three more chapters to read and four more study exams. If I wanted that Food Handler's license before opening day, I needed to get busy.

"Hi, chef," It was one of the partners, "We're thinking for tonight's tasting you'll make the charcuterie with the pate and we really want to taste the truffle fries."

"Uh….so another tasting tonight?"

"Yeah, didn't we…I guess we should have reminded you," she said, "We're gonna start at around 7. See you then."

Another tasting? I didn't have any groceries left. Were they serious about a tasting every day until we opened? I had laughed it off. I needed a hell of a lot more food than what I could get in a shopping cart. I didn't have much mise en place left. It was another day of stress. I'd been in town for two days. I had no idea where to buy groceries and I was running low on cash, having funded my own move up here.

It was another evening of me doing the impossible. I ran to a nearby supermarket with the little bit of cash I had left after paying for my room. I had a few poached pears left. I decided to make the ham & gruyere in puff pastry, I bought a few more scallops for the pasta I'd stored in the freezer, I caramelized onions for French onion soup, and I braised short ribs. I sliced potatoes for potatoes Anna.

When my guests poured in at 7, they were led in by the two partners that had hired me. And it appeared to be a family event. Marie Antoinette, as we started calling her a day or two after opening day, had planned this tasting for her mother and sisters. She appeared to resemble misguided French royalty more than a restaurant owner—preferring to be served than to help run food during busy times or play hostess when a line formed at the door. Louis XVI, Marie's doomed husband, was the name we gave the other operating partner. He often sat on the back patio smoking a cigar. He'd dial the restaurant from his cellphone to remind the servers to put money in his meter, so his Range Rover parked in front didn't get ticketed.

Here I was playing maid again. Marie and Louis were obviously concerned that their families might think this was an ill-advised move. But the mother and sisters oohed and aaahed over the mirrors and new light fixtures. Now they had food that they could show them. "We know what we're doing, mom." I get it. But this kind of thing should be reserved for opening day. I bit my tongue. It had taken me months to land what appeared to be everything I wanted—the thrill of new openings, creative control, and an opportunity to succeed in New York. I still held out hope that some smarts would kick in and they would give me a reason to believe that they knew what they were doing.

"Tomorrow we're going to have a tasting for *my* family," Louis XVI informed me. "You can do the same menu you did here tonight." He was a short man with big eyes and a nice smile. He was so easy going and relaxed about everything it was hard not to be charmed by him. Everything was under control and going exactly as planned. Me? I worried about training staff, if there was enough storage for dry goods, where were we going to put the mop, setting things up so that we passed the health inspection without question, and has anyone done anything about the POS machine or the liquor license?

Finally, with some advance notice I was able to shop early (now I was completely out of money) and start cooking as soon as I got up. I felt like a show pony, though, and not a serious professional who needed time to get this together. I had my own checklist and plan of action. Should I spring it on them after a tasting? Shouldn't we be sitting down with a list rather than eating?

The good news was that after the third tasting, there was no one left to cook for. The parents approved and I could finally get to the business of getting vendors, organizing the kitchen, compiling the recipe books, inventory spread sheets, getting faulty equipment fixed (everything was used and old). I settled into a routine of finding a bakery, a produce company, a dry goods purveyor, and meat and seafood companies in a dining room I shared with electricians, carpenters, and plumbers. I sat in

396

that room for days collecting account applications from salespeople and forwarding them to the partnership. I ordered shelves and looked into getting chemicals for the old dish machine acquired from a broken lease agreement that Louis XVI had bought. I had to ask him about the equipment—why a 15-foot hood, and where did all of these coolers come from (some of them without legs, another constantly tipping over because it only had three of the four.)

"This guy has all of this stuff," he said, running his hand over the dented metal surface of an old sandwich unit, admiring it. "I bought a lot from him. I have a lot in storage because after a while he was just leaving them in front of my house." To get the guy to stop, he had to pay for what he kept and finally called to report the broker for illegal dumping.

The 15-foot exhaust hood that dominated the cooking space was a find on eBay that he drove to Connecticut to retrieve. It hung out of the back of an open U-Haul as he raced down I-95. The old grease had turned to tar and made it near impossible to lift out the filters. It stretched from the stairs that led to the basement to a wall just five feet from the bathroom. It was huge. I might have gone with eight feet in favor of more space to build a larger window at the pass. The 10-burner stove, flat top, and combi-oven would have been perfect for a place with over 100 seats. Legally, the space could accommodate 30. I attributed the hi-capacity equipment to forward thinking. But the tiny window for servers to take plates to the dining room, though; there was so much I didn't get.

Louis XVI suggested I use Act Wholesale, "They've got everything you'll need," he assured me. It was the organic supplier the bakery next door was using for everything—well, flour and things to bake with. He had already gotten the account all lined up and they were waiting to hear from me. He also set up an account with a seafood company.

"And you should order soon," he handed me a catalog from Lobster Warehouse. "We're going to do a tasting for the folks that live in the apartments upstairs. And then we'll just leave the lights and door open." He was hoping that folks from the street would wander in and sit down and choose something from a limited menu; with just me in the kitchen that had just been swept of drywall dust and screws. There were no servers or dining room staff. I was the only hire. I didn't know how this was going to go. All I could do was tackle what was obviously in my in box. But I didn't know what else might get tossed in there while I slept. Louis was convinced that the food was so good that folks walking in off the street would sign the petition for the neighborhood approval for the liquor license and then make a reservation for Valentine's Day. I appreciated his confidence in me, but I also knew that the offer of free food makes people suspicious. And what if this Valentine's Day without servers, or napkins, drinking glasses, a cash register or anything a civilized dining room would have was a disaster? I had made it my business to always think of the worst thing that could happen and then go backwards to hunt down and kill the causes. Louis imagined only cotton candy falling from the sky. I admired his positivity and was simultaneously frightened of it.

"I want to be open by Valentine's Day," he said, "I ordered heart shaped lightbulbs for the ceiling fixtures." He was beaming. It was as if he imagined there would be idle strangers wandering the streets that night, and once they caught a glimpse of the restaurant he was making, they would hoist his little body up onto their shoulders and shout hoorah. I've always counted on cynicism and the wanton cruelty that fuels the offhand comment that spreads like wildfire. I'd been called the chef who mistreats her customers because I didn't smile while I worked. But cynicism can also manifest itself in the form of flagrant disregard. What if the doors were open and the smells of fabulous food wafted out into the street and potential customers nodded their heads as they paused by the tempered glass…? "Mmm, yes. Okay," and kept walking. There weren't enough chairs. Light fixtures dangled from loose wires waiting to be fully connected. We weren't ready to receive guests. In the rush to spring food onto people, it could hurt us in the end.

When I called Act I learned they were 100% organic, natural, and local, which meant they didn't have zucchini as it was out of season. The ratatouille Marie insisted be on this menu in winter was going to have to come from the store. And there were no tomatoes. They didn't break cases. So instead of being able to get three heads of celery or 10 pounds of lemons to make just enough mise en place for the 40 customers we might serve over the next day or so, I was stuck with enough produce for a week of busy nights. Plus, they didn't sell French fries. As much as Louis wanted to hand cut and fry our own potatoes (and even if I entertained the notion), we didn't have the room or a second fryer. And unless we cut, washed, blanched, and chilled case after case; we were going to be that French fry restaurant that never has fries. The only way out of this mess was to buy frozen fries. Act might have had everything that the bakery needed, but for a full-service restaurant, they didn't quite measure up.

"Have you ordered yet?" Louis was anxious. He wanted to open, and things needed to fall into place. And I seemed to be the only one that he could call and get results. The contractors had day jobs and would come by in between projects. The renovation was slow going. He was waiting for the heart shaped bulbs, but they weren't nearly as important as the food. "The lobster place was going to send me an email with the invoice," he was seriously worried that I wasn't getting ready for this one woman show of free food on Valentine's Day weekend.

"Yes," I answered blandly, "I ordered. In fact, they've all just left." I was surrounded by 800 pounds of product. I heaved cases into a cooler, stacked the things that could be left out like citrus and potatoes onto the wobbly bottom shelf of the prep table. I finagled cases of eggs and 50-pound sacks of flour through the snappy kitchen door, through the cramped space and into whatever nook or cranny would support the weight. This over stock of product would be an issue later as our opening day ticked passed February 14th. One of the contractors clicked off the electricity and everything in the prep room coolers rotted. I went home after meeting the partners and I guess they scrounged around in search of mise en place to snack on. There was pasta missing and bites out of meatballs. But I also got this phone call, "Chef, why did you order so much food, the lemons are spoiling," Marie was obviously calling after being instructed by Louis, I could hear him feeding her lines from her side of the phone.

"Remember," I never expected to be questioned by these two, "I ordered all of that stuff from Act like Louis asked me to do. He was certain we were going to open."

"But none of it is in the refrigerator," she was shocked, I was obviously an idiot.

"We don't have the space," I explained. Only three of the coolers were working and they were pretty full of product.

"These lemons…. they're all bad."

"Yeah, I've been trying to save as many as I can. Those are the ones that didn't fit in the reach in. They're organic so…"

"Wait, what are you saying, they spoil faster because they're organic?"

"Uh, yes, it's a natural product so there are no preservatives, or they haven't been waxed or treated with chemicals." Was I going to have to deal with this micromanaging for the long haul?

I set to work. I hadn't found a bread supplier, so I started the morning making baguette. While it proofed, I made the lobster bisque for one of the 13 varieties of poutine. I cranked pasta. There were five French apple cakes in the oven. I had a case of 144 apples, and this barely made a dent. I was working alongside plumbers and carpenters. These guys were fine if they got it done, and fine if they didn't. Like most contractors they didn't see anything to hurry about. It will get done when it gets done.

"We're going to have to turn off the water," the plumber was busy with a little sink on the line and a pot filler—a long necked faucet that came out of the wall to fill pots on the stove. He didn't wait for me to answer. I couldn't wash my hands or wash any of the utensils I was working with. Every minute or so I would instinctively turn a valve and the groaning and bongo drum like thumping reminded me. I did all I could that didn't require water. But now, I let it go. I was no longer the wide-eyed chef trying to impress by doing the impossible when I toiled away at Evening Star and

403

Mrs. Simpsons. The lessons of the Potomac River and all of the restaurants have taught me a simple phrase, "I can only do what I can do."

The phone was ringing. Louis had found on eBay an old-style phone, the classic from the 1920s known as the candlestick. I had to stand at the microphone holding the earpiece to my ear. A cordless that I could hold or place on speaker while I worked would have been much more efficient. But I stood there, hunched over into a cabinet that needed doors and still needed to be painted. It was one of the neighbors. They had no water. When I hung up after apologizing (the plumber had gone to get a part so I had no idea when the water would be on again.) there was the tenant everyone warned me about standing in the doorway. She had lived in the apartment on the third floor for 20 years. And she hated everybody.

Her gray hair was cut short and parted like a schoolboy's. She had on a big sweater and waited for me to walk over to her. But I could tell from the back of the building that she was seething. I let her yell at me and told her that I didn't have any water either. The phone rang much of the afternoon. Louis told me weeks ago how much the folks in the building loved him. Today, they would have torn the flesh from his bones.

I was surrounded by dirty dishes and did not have water to wash the plates that had finally arrived in dusty boxes. I was preparing to wrap all of the food and save it for another time. I wanted this day to be over. But the plumber, after getting a call from the angry landlord, rushed down the stairs and turned on the water.

Louis made it to the restaurant after I'd told Marie that the upstairs tenants were in no mood to come down here and eat.

"You're kidding me," he was sure that all he had to do was knock on doors and say, "Dinner's ready." It was then that I realized he'd never told them or sent them an invitation or email. He was going to ask them to stop what they're doing and come down to eat.

"They're not going to come down, Louis," I explained. I had been yelled at holding that silly phone to my ear and I stood there while the gray-haired old tenant gave me a piece of her mind over all of the construction incidents that inconvenienced her over the months. She didn't care that they had nothing to do with me. I was guilty by association. "They are pretty pissed, Louis." I reiterated. "They've gone all day without water."

"Nonsense," he had that big smile on. It was as if no one had ever been angry with him. He had no idea what it was like.

"I don't think it's a good idea," Marie chimed in. "Maybe we should do it another night."

"But tomorrow is Valentine's Day," Louis was determined to carry out his plan, "We'll have the tenants in here eating, and the door open....or maybe just the lights on, and people will come in off the street and make reservations for tomorrow." It all seemed so easy. How could it not work? I worried about the impression that the unfinished space the haphazard service would leave on anyone who ate in the place. What if they wanted water or coffee? We didn't even have the capacity to do that.

Louis headed upstairs. I imagined him knocking on doors. And maybe the people who yelled at me on the phone would have a different reaction to the person who shut off their water as he stood in front of them. Maybe they did love him, and he would smile and tell them a story or something soothing and like the pied piper he'd have a trail of tenants behind him. Or perhaps it would be more like a conga line and the old lady with the boy cut would be shaking it in the rear, holding on to her neighbors' hips as she kicked the air—full of so much excitement she couldn't contain it.

Louis had been gone for over an hour. It was now after 9. The chances of people strolling by catching a glimpse of people eating in that restaurant that hadn't opened yet were pretty slim. I was ready to call it a night.

"Louis didn't have any luck with the tenants upstairs," Marie confessed.

"Okay, so we're going to pack it in?"

"No," she smiled; relieved to tell me that my work all day wasn't going to go to waste, "He went to get his parents." I ignored the feeling of a punch to the gut and squinted to control my eye twitching. While I was going to go along with Louis' misguided publicity stunt, I unexpectedly became a maid again when the night turned into another meal for his family. They poured wine and enjoyed themselves. Louis and Marie didn't wait tables that night or pick up dirty plates (from the upstairs neighbors or new customers who were out for a stroll in front of the building.) No. They grabbed the plastic cups and a bottle of wine and slid into the bench beside the stand-in guests and had dinner, enjoying themselves as I ran around that tiny kitchen—the only one doing any heavy lifting. Sure, you pay your doctor to treat your diabetes, but you will surely die if you don't stop eating the jelly donuts. I was the doctor in this scenario for sure, and Marie and Louis had no interest in helping themselves, cramming their jaws full of jelly donuts.

Louis didn't take it too hard about Valentine's Day. We didn't open and the heart-shaped light bulbs arrived a few weeks later. He took me downstairs and showed me the basement. It had been completely cleared out and dusted. All of the old pots and pans were stacked in a corner.

"The partners want you to have all of the room you need," he said leading me back up the stairs and to the vacant space next door. "We're going to get to work on expansion as soon as we can."

"What's the hold up?" I was eager for the space, but also wanting my paycheck to reflect the work that came with expansion. Plus, I had outgrown the one-restaurant chef gig. Once I had staff trained and production from the kitchen was flowing, I was anxious to tackle another project. I knew in no time the little operation of that one restaurant would leave me yawning and looking for something else to do.

"We're waiting on the landlord to get us a lease." Louis had introduced me to the building owner; he had been at the first tasting. He was an approachable guy who believed that with my great food and Louis' imagination, the partnership was going places.

Louis also took this time to tell me how busy I was going to be, and that "no matter how much Alex or Mike asked," I really didn't have time to re-concept the other place in the partnership that was just around the corner. But it was too late. I walked by the spot shortly after I got into town and wrote a menu for a British pub inspired by the vintage London phone booth that sheltered the ATM outside the corner restaurant's front door. I had seen the small kitchen so I thought to bring some of the action into the dining room: a sausage and potato cart that wheeled around the tables dim sum style, and a roast in the dining room on Sunday nights, carved tableside and served with co-roasted root vegetables.

"I told her to hold on," he laughed dryly, his smile hanging on a little too long before sinking into a serious, wise expression, "Chef's going to be way too busy with this place." He spoke knowledgeably about the increased space and the combination of outside seating was going to make this place at least 100 seats and prep work was going to triple.

"Really, Louis," I didn't want to be shoved back into the simple chef role. My brain was expanding, the headhunter's words were in the lenses of my glasses, *"Don't go backwards, don't do that."* I shook my head. "That's why I'm here," I urged. Before the current project had even opened and ink had not yet been put to paper to draw up the expansion, Alex had hired a chef and re-opened the space around the corner after a few weeks of renovation. The menu was pastas and French food.

I spent the next two weeks interviewing servers and cooks. By the end of the month, I had a staff. I had one very experienced cook and three that required a little bit more training. There were few servers with any experience, but I've found that anyone willing to learn and was ambitious could get it. I had my work cut out for me. Not only did I have to establish dining room protocol, I had to make sure even the simplest things like sugar caddies and paper for the receipt printer was taken care of. Neither Marie nor Louis could concern themselves with any of the things that were needed to get off the ground.

There were times I felt like the only adult in the room. It was as if they had purchased the huge playset that came with a tiny kitchen and restaurant; the bright yellow plastic set also included a cash register with big buttons and a bell. I was the grown up; guiding, correcting, telling them things like they needed money in that register, forks and knives needed to

410

go like this, and dirty dishes went here. No, no George; you can't put chemicals near the iced tea. No, no Louis no one uses a paper napkin for their belly and a cloth one for their lap. Let's just do the one. No, no Marie. The health inspector isn't going to like your standing water of rotting apples and pears in a crock pot meant to make the building smell good. When Louis stood at the little plastic register and pushed enough buttons to open the drawer with a ding, I smiled and giggled right along with him. And I feigned surprise like any good parent when he fanned the pink and yellow dollar bills in his tiny hands and shouted, "Look, a million dollars!"

I looked around assessing what was done and what needed to be done and decided upon an opening day that made sense and told them— no, declared—that we were opening that day. Contractors and cleaning crew were called on and given a deadline. I doubted we would make it. I had placed orders and made the schedule in the midst of a blizzard. Marie and Louis were a bundle of nerves although they tried their best to hide it, but I could tell. I had been on that ride before. It's safer to be just about to open, with everyone around you a twitter with anticipation and hope. Opening day is terrifying, and the more you put it off and it remains remote and a happy thought, you never have to fail or let anyone down.

411

I waited out the blizzard at home and I was also resting a bit before what I knew would be weeks of 16-hour days. My phone was a buzz.

"Louis wants to know what you think about redoing the menu," it was Marie. I realized that Louis was probably too nervous to talk. I couldn't believe my ears.

"Wait, he wants to change the menu NOW?" my eye was twitching, and I reached up to yank a hair or two out of my eyebrow.

"Yeah, he thinks we should try like a Cajun, New Orleans thing."

"So, you know the menu is finished, recipes, and procedure and order guides are all done." I had to talk them out of this. "You're talking about an enormous undertaking at this point. We open next week."

"He thinks there's still time," Marie sounded like a cheerleader, and I was impressed that Louis could put a notion in her head and whether she bought it or not, she was going to sell it. "There's no one doing New Orleans food in the area. And Whalid thinks it will work." I was to hear a lot about Whalid. He was Louis' mentor. Handed the keys to a restaurant as the owner was deported after a post 9/11 crackdown, the young dishwasher took over and made the pizza place a huge success. He owned 15 restaurants and was full of advice. I never met Whalid but had to listen

412

to his wisdom daily. Was he a real person? I imagined that he was more like Fred Flintstone's Great Gazoo than a real person.

"There's no one doing this food either," I countered. There was no way out. There was an argument for every one of mine. I got her off the phone with the assurance that we'd do a special now and then, and that I would do a Cajun brunch menu when we got there. But we were opening with this menu, the die had been cast.

The morning of opening day everyone was dusting, folding napkins, and stuffing menus (these weren't getting done so I sat at the computer and formatted, and had it copied) into the menu holders I'd ordered. Once Louis gave me his credit card number, I got a lot done.

The kitchen staff had spent a week learning the menu and preparing mise en place. On the final day of training we served some of the more complicated dishes to the servers. The landlord wandered in, finally seeing positive activity in the building, and I took a minute to remind him about the lease for the expansion into next door.

"The lease," he looked at me matter of factly and helped himself to a gougere from the breadbasket on his table. I had decided on the French delicate cheese puff to be our bread service, "I gave that to Louis a couple of months ago. I'm waiting for him to sign it." Again, I found myself squinting away a twitch in my eye. He'd lied to me. I was back in Scotland looking at a building façade that wasn't finished, with broken windows and a bright neon sign that wasn't there. Why would he lie to me?

It was a difficult month bending cooks to the menu and the standards I had set for the quality of food and the plating. None of them had been tested in this way and told to remake or re-plate. I figured they'd been cooking without someone watching over them, putting close approximations on to plates which servers placed in front of customers who had lowered their standards after being subject to so much culinary negligence. I had to erase the "that'll do" from their cooking routines. It was exhausting work; I was the first one in; receiving deliveries and maneuvering in the tight spaces with boxes of apples and pears. I went high with shelves, so I stacked #10 cans, nuts, spices, vinegars with a ladder. I needed to be a constant presence in the building, watching, correcting, making sure corners weren't cut; instructing everyone from dish washer to host and everything in between. It meant 35 straight 16-hour days, going home just to sleep.

Some of the kitchen staff I'd hired back around Valentine's Day couldn't afford to hang on and wait for training and pay checks to begin. We opened a little short-handed and that was fine, later I'd add a baker and a daytime prep cook to take some of the load a few days a week. I'd add more staff as business increased. But giving staff, like the dish washer for example, two days off meant a few hours of my 16-hour day was spent washing dishes during dinner service. So far, we were open from 6 to 10; Louis was in the middle of getting the liquor license approved. There was no need to open as late as the bars in the neighborhood. We had nothing harder than fountain soda to offer them. We plodded along with a decent beginning. But those first days of restaurant full to capacity was mostly immediate and extended family of the partners, eating hundreds of dollars of food and not paying for it. We'd ring $1,200 on a moderately busy Thursday night, but collect less than half of it as Louis declared free food for his friends and relatives.

"How much would you charge to do a party," he asked one Saturday morning. I was alone in the quiet restaurant when he saw me through the front door camera. He had pulled up and parked in front less than an hour later.

"Well, that depends." We talked menu, number of people.

"It's for a guy retiring who works with my father in the City offices." We settled on a menu, but Louis was even more anxious to sell alcohol to the 85 people coming to celebrate the man's last day. "These folks drink a lot." His eyes glistened. We agreed to a bargain price of $45 per person with a cash bar. It was a Friday night party that would close the restaurant to regular customers. This price for 85 people (some of them were going to have to sit outdoors) I hoped would make up for a potentially busy night.

A small salad for everyone and a choice of entrée from a list of three, Marie would get the cake special ordered (I saw the receipt weeks later—that cake was $300). I had added a dish washer and a new cook to my roster. The cook was a woman who knew a lot more about life and human behavior than she did about cooking. Her willingness to learn was what got her hired. Often, while I pulled something out of the oven or mashed my knife flat into a garlic clove, showing her exactly how it should be done, she was lost in watching. The night of the party, I skimmed fat off of the braised short ribs while Patricia watched the dining room. Hurrying in as revelers arrived to decorate the room, Louis and his cousin bounded in toward the bar, struggling to carry cases of bourbon and gin past the tables and chairs.

"I hear they bought all of that liquor," Patricia sniffed unpleasantly, "because they think these folks are going to booze it up. I just want you to know chef, I'm leaving at 10." She pressed her lips together and folded her arms, inviting me to dare and ask.

"That's fine."

"Look at that," she whispered. "They're taking money." Patricia pointed at a manila envelope bulging in the bottom from a bump made of bills. We watched guests file in and before they sat, they handed Marie cash.

"I guess they are having the guests pay for the dinner." I reasoned.

"I don't think that money is for the restaurant," said Patricia, her eyesight was obviously better than mine. "They puttin' it an envelope with someone's name on it."

It was another night of food for almost 80 people and the money went to the retiree and not the cash register. The booze sales? They totaled about $300. This was just one more ill-advised scheme of win-win that Louis cooked up. With him in charge, I was certain the restaurant would never make any money. The Scotland prophecy would come true, and I'd be out of a job. I started to panic. I had to try and talk some sense into him.

It was a warm afternoon and it came so suddenly it took us by surprise. Furniture was hauled outside, and outdoor seating was now part of the equation. It boosted business because when spring comes to Brooklyn, it leads folks to seek the outdoor dining experience. I was surprised to see Dominque, our wine salesperson come in. She stopped by before we opened and was gearing up to sell us French wines as soon as our license would allow. All of us believed it would happen soon and she arranged a tasting so we could start a wine list for the place. Marie was anxious to participate so we arranged it so she could come by after her day job to sample a few bottles and decide what would work within the restaurants price point goals. Usually a wine rep brings bottles that she's picked out for many of her clients to sample. A two-ounce pour is usually enough to decide. On rare occasions, she'll leave me the full bottle, but the bottles for tasting are viewed as the wine rep's property.

This tacitly agreed upon arrangement was trampled on when Dominique brought five bottles for staff training. I stored them in a cabinet and told staff what they were there for. "Sometime after opening day we are going to use these wines to train you servers, okay." I asked them to make sure no one touched the wines. On opening night, I watched servers pouring wine to a few customers and to Marie and Louis' friends and family. "Where'd that wine come from?"

"Oh, it's theirs, we're doing BYOB."

I'd see another bottle being opened and poured, "Hey, where did that bottle come from?" I was given the same answer. It wasn't until the end of the night; did I notice that all of the bottles that Dominique had brought in for training were gone.

"Louis said it was okay." I was told. I fumed and clenched my fists. What was going on here? I had to explain everything to these two. They had no idea how any of this works.

Marie came to the tasting as I was polishing three glasses with a bar mop. She grabbed four more from behind the bar. She noticed us looking at her. "Oh," she rubbed a napkin around the rim and stem of a wine glass, "I invited a few friends." The seven bottles of wine that Dominique had brought for us to just sample and ponder were completely gone. Marie and her guests sipped and guzzled, filling their glasses and talking about men, dates, and wedding plans. There was no room to have a lucid discussion about what wines we'd choose and offer at the restaurant. And Mike, one of the partners of the group who had invited himself, could not contain his disappointment in the selection.

"What is the alcohol in this?" he snarled. "These aren't strong enough." This is the night I discovered his disappointment in the wine was no surprise. He preferred the kick of bourbon and drank it regularly. One afternoon I was alone in the building and Mike let himself in. He was wearing an expensive suit and his subdued jewelry and what it was worth was not lost on me. He had money. I could tell he was drunk. I did not want him to stay; I made some excuse and reason to leave to get him to leave with me. He got into his Mercedes SUV. I thought about it for a beat. He was drunk, he was always drunk. I'm certain he drove home from Brooklyn to Glen Cove drunk all of the time. Perhaps there would be a night that the NYPD intervened.

Dominique stood next to me admiring the patio. She was as almost as anxious as I was for the liquor license and the success of the place. She offered help. She knew a guy. We'd gotten the neighborhood council to sign off and now we needed the state. This could take another six months.

420

We were standing under the camera. A text came through on my phone. It was Louis, "We'll have the license by the end of next month." He wrote. "Tell Dominique I've got it taken care of." The cameras were recording us, so Louis could listen in on every conversation.

I imagined him sitting in his underwear with his computer screen the only light in the curtained room. How much of my day was he just sitting there listening to and watching? One morning it was a question texted to me as I washed pots and pans after prepping, "Who is that blonde woman in the kitchen today?" I didn't recall a blonde. Then I realized he meant the new prep cook I'd hired who had dyed her hair. She was Salvadoran, a country that doesn't produce many blondes so at first, I had no idea what he was talking about. The camera was his way of keeping tabs, of managing, of micromanaging. I confessed to Patricia that the cameras made me uncomfortable. "Do you have access to them?" she asked, looking right into the one over head in the prep kitchen, "If *you* can't see what's going on in the kitchen when you want because you don't have access," she shook her head and opened her purse in search of a cigarette, "then these cameras are here so they can watch *you*."

This started my campaign to disable the cameras in the kitchen. I clouded lenses with spray oil, I loosened plugs, and I stuck blue tape over the aperture. Days or weeks would go by and plugs were tightened, tape would be removed, focus adjusted. Then I'd start all over again.

Despite the chaos, the good reviews piling in, I was hoping that losing my nose to the grindstone would lead to level ground. Perhaps we could stumble through this awkward phase of a management team that didn't know how a restaurant operated to a thriving business despite them. After all, I was in the day to day; they were remote and giving me plenty of leash. I started to enjoy my time alone in the building. I got a lot done and I could set up the kitchen in the quiet of the place without being interrupted. I had stopped answering the phone. They could call back when front of the house staff arrived.

The phone was ringing one morning while I reduced the bordelaise. I had my paté in the hot water bath, and I had the meringue for dacquoise cooling in the closed oven. I was expecting it to ring eight or nine times—that's when the caller usually gave up. But on ring number three, someone answered it. It was Brendan, the high school graduate that I'd hired to be a server. He was dressed for work in black dress slacks and a button-down shirt and was pulling the chairs off of the tables. He'd come in early before usually for a quiet place indoors to eat his takeout. I asked him what he was doing. It was only a little after 1pm.

"Today is the grand opening, Chef." He grabbed a stack of napkins. "We open at 4 today. Louis wants us here early today so we can get ready."

"You're kidding." We'd been open a month already.

"Grand opening..." he felt he needed to explain the very concept to me. "They've invited the media and folks. It's going to be crazy." I took a look around now. The door swung open and another server came in and then another. I didn't have kitchen staff scheduled to arrive until 4. What the hell? I checked the dining room again. There were no balloons, no decorations of any kind. Was there going to be free food, samples? I hadn't been part of the planning.

A well-dressed man walked in, dark blue suit with wide lapels and a colorful tie that matched his pocket square. The phone rang; it was Louis instructing Brendan that the new arrival (he watched him enter from the cameras), his good friend Stephan, was to be shown the building. Stephan came by and congratulated me on the grand opening. How does this guy know, and no one told me? And why?

"So, Chef," Stephan was one of those well-dressed men with a slightly out-there hair cut who, sharply in tune with his own sexuality, could charm a man or a woman. It wasn't working on me. "What will you make me to eat?" He was waiting for Louis and he would be waiting for hours. This was not a good time for Stephan to request a snack. I could barely contain my irritation. I had to get the kitchen ready to open by myself. Kitchen staff clocked in at 4 and used those two hours to set up their stations—chop parsley, gather mise en place, shape burgers, make polenta, heat up sauces—I was on my own. I didn't have time to make friends with Stephan.

The restaurant filled up at 4, but all of the faces were familiar. I recognized Marie's mother and Louis' uncle. Cousins were back who hadn't been since opening day. It was another night of family dining for free. There was sparkling wine and cocktails. After we had served dessert to the last table, I straightened my back and untied my apron. The busy night had cost us a lot of inventory. It was going to be a busy prep day tomorrow. I hadn't prepared by increasing counts at ordering or by bringing more staff in for the day.

Why hadn't they told me? I was glad it was over, but I had to give myself a pep talk to fall asleep. "I can do this", I chanted my head into the pillow. I hadn't given up hope. I had the muscle, so I thought, to steer this in the right direction. A direction that made sense, made great food, and made money. I had quit Evening Star before I could—although physically and emotionally exhausted—turn it around. And now it was a forceful restaurant group. What might I be doing now if I'd stuck it out?

But I wondered if the new restaurants that were part of the plan, would operate the same way—with me in the dark. I kept my mouth shut. I was a good sport. I could take it. It took me months to find this job, and it wasn't it the one I wanted? I had to keep my eyes on the prize. The prize at the end was a thriving restaurant group in the capitol of the world.

I had a lot of years still left in me for heavy lifting. It was me that hoisted the cases of potatoes and fries one by one down to the new old walk-in. I lifted over 200 pounds down the stairs every day for two months (I finally got the key to unlock the trap door so deliveries could go straight to the basement.) The old walk-in box was put together by a guy who gave

Louis a "deal". The panels didn't fit, and the half-foot gaps were covered by strips of stainless steel secured by self-tapping screws and liquid nails. Hot air seeped into the holes. Cold air flowed out through the gaps.

Brendan came in early again the next day. He started pulling chairs down from the tables at 3.

"What's going on today?"

"We open at 4 now, Chef." He was eating a sandwich and yanking chairs down with one hand. He chuckled, "They didn't tell you?"

"No." And here I was running around again to get everything done by myself just like in the old days at my first chef job. I recalled those owner-greedy days of labor cuts when I cut staff down to such slim levels that I spent all day prepping and then went well into the night cooking the line. Exhausted at night's end, I called to order produce at home; sitting for the first time that day at the edge of my bed. I couldn't help but melt into the bedspread. Sometimes I couldn't keep my eyes open.

"5 pounds of HVs, 1 case of I-80s…. zzzzzzz."

"Uh…. Chef…Chef?"

When they finally got around to it Marie Antoinette and Louis XVI informed me that the new hours were 4 to midnight. There were longer

426

days for me and my staff as we stood in a kitchen with stacks of cold pans—the dining room empty—waiting for midnight to come. We didn't have the alcohol to support a happy hour or the late night drinking the neighborhood was known for.

I recalled my conversation with Dominique with the promise of a liquor license by month's end. Winter was over and we were headed into summer with no promised cocktail menu. Did Louis get it wrong? He rushed in with the neighborhood approval and a keg. He had the old taps he'd yanked out of storage installed and lines run down to the walk-in cooler. Later we all learned that the neighborhood sign off was a small step one. Steps two, three, four and five were in the hands of the state. These steps could take as long as a year. Every day there was more evidence that filled my heart with dread. He talked a good game, but Louis had no idea what he was doing.

"Hey Chef," he said as he pulled away from the parking spot in front of the restaurant. We were off to see a new space he wanted to re-concept. He wasn't done fancying himself a make-over artist, he'd been tapped by wealthy entrepreneurs to take over the lease on this spot or that

427

location after wife or daughter had become bored with it. "Don't let Marie bother you about staff hours."

"Yeah." I didn't know what else to say, "We are open twice as long."

"I know," he brushed it off with a pout and a quick shake of his head, "Besides, you need to staff up so you can focus on the new places." We drove to a small spot in Manhattan where he wanted to feature my fried chicken. Of course, I'd be a partner, he told me, adding that he had already met with the attorneys and I would have papers to sign first thing Monday. But in my no-liquor-license and free-party fueled moment of doubt, I had accepted an invitation to interview for a position at a posh Manhattan restaurant managed by the one of the most prestigious restaurant groups in the nation.

"I'm done with Mike and Alex," he confessed in hushed tones, as if Mike was in the back seat or there was a camera in his car. "I want us to build on this partnership." He used his thumb and index finger of his child-sized right hand to include me and him in this invisible cone of restaurant making. As a partner I could really stop being subservient and exert some control. I canceled my interview (it's better to rule in hell than to serve in heaven, I reasoned.) The calls from folks in the business wanting to partner with Louis XVI had nothing to do with his restaurant expertise, I realized that these Moroccans who wanted to expand into Brooklyn, or the baker next door wanting to do something bigger all thought Louis had a sack full of doubloons in his purse.

And then there was the long, narrow underground bar that his friend and famous mixologist, Oscar, wanted to transform with the food I was doing. The space was narrow and dark in the basement of a retail space. The hat store above, always empty, was a suspected money laundering operation for the Russian mob.

"The rent is $50,000. And it doesn't need much work." He pushed the heavy door open and led me through a dark foyer, passed a large lit up bar, and through ox-blood curtains. The kitchen was a tiny room just big enough for one person behind the stove.

"No way, Louis," I said, talk of partnership made me bold, "We'll never make enough to cover that rent." I opened my eyes as wide as I could stretch them to see in the lightless space. There was room for 15 people to sit at the bar but no more than 30 seats in the small dining room.

"I'm thinking a cigar bar," he had two in the pocket of his wool vest. I imagined the dark place filled with smoke and old men. "They just closed the two uptown that I used to go to."

"Nobody smokes cigars, Louis." I still could not catch my breath. He may as well have been blowing the smoke from his Cubans right into my nose. "$50,000 a month?" Saying it out loud made me weak kneed. I could sense the fragility of my new partner. He was usually the one in his circle who had the bright ideas. I'd need the testosterone levels of an alpha male to break through the way Whalid had. I proceeded delicately.

"There's a reason why cigar bars close," I said gently. That was a sentence that could cut to the quick. I needed to lessen the blow with innocent enthusiasm. Now wasn't the time to do what a man might do and blow my own horn; heralding in bombastic speak my restaurant successes. I walked quickly around the space, channeling Julie Andrews on a hill in Austria about to sing. "Doesn't this place look like the inside of a railcar?" If I could get him excited about the notion, I could turn off this cigar bar light bulb. "And we could do the food with the Canadian theme Oscar likes so much—but with the feel of the Trans Canada Railway…. sort of a low brow Orient Express." I talked about fancy food like roasted tenderloin carved tableside. And then poutine with roasted duck and black cherries or a foie gras studded gravy. "And then…we could…" I found a little area behind the curtain that led to a courtyard. "We could enclose this space and make this the secret cigar area." Louis was all in. I went back to the office and worked on a menu and a design of the kitchen. Louis worked at turning the inside of that windowless tube of a space into a railcar. CCTVs showed passing scenery. Doors slid on hanging hinges cattle-car style. But when I looked at the numbers, there was no way even filled to capacity every night could the new concept survive with an annual rent of more than half a million Louis was telling me.

"Are you sure you want to do this," I interrupted him as he listed the other concepts we were about to tackle—a Spanish restaurant in a vacant space a friend was hanging on to, the pop-up hosting luncheonette on the street across from the park (I later found out that the luncheonette wasn't a pop-up space at all, but really a thriving restaurant well into a 10 year lease.).

"I forgot to tell you," he confessed. "I got it wrong." Apparently, it was Oscar's Bolivian accent that led him to the wrong number; the rent was $15,000 not 50. That was a relief, but still too high not to get this right

431

the first time. It was a battle, but I pressed the inclusion of two fryers, a freezer, and a purveyor who'd deliver product (Oscar had been going to the supermarket).

"We're going to be doing volume." I explained that going to the grocery store was going to cost us money in our goal to sell a minimum $2000 in food and beverage a day. Where would we store the inventory? I talked Louis into a six-foot extension on the end of the kitchen into the dining room for storage and dishwashing and a freezer upstairs.

Monday came and went and there were no partnership papers. Instead I was introduced to a new partner, an art student turned restaurant manager Suzy Quan. Her father was a Chinese billionaire who was extending his reach beyond the furniture industry into foodservice in the United States. She told me she wanted to do a tasting for the menu for the new space. "She loves your menu," Louis stood behind her, giving me an encouraging thumbs up behind Suzy's distracted look. Her phone rang and she spun away and barked Mandarin rapidly into her cellphone. I hated tastings. It was no longer a secret. And with this crew, it was never easy or productive. But Louis assured me that Suzy was all business. She was running a small chain of authentic Chinese dumpling stores, cracking the

432

whip and firing slackers. I got ready to sample the six or seven Louis counted off making a tight little fist and then popping stubby fingers out to mark each diner.

"Suzy, Oscar, Marie, Jonathan...let's just say eight." He gave me a "don't worry" wink. I didn't believe for a minute that everything was going to be fine. There was something about Suzy and Oscar that worried me. They were distracted. Never sitting still to listen to my pitch or answer a direct question. Had they read the menu? Did they know how the Trans Canada concept was going to come alive on the plates? It meant a totally different way, a different direction, but it was the way Louis had gotten behind. He was looking at buying server carts and fancy plate covers. He didn't like the tables that were scattered around the place. They were dark brown Formica tops, the edges cleaned up with a black band. Louis sneered at the fake wood.

"We need to cover these tables," he ran his hand over one. "What are those things? They come in white, don't they?" It was so obvious it was impossible for me to guess. "What are they called, table drapes?"

"Do you mean tablecloths?" I wondered now if Louis had had a traumatic brain injury or if he had been raised in the wilderness in a remote cabin.

The day of the tasting I got in early. The old freezer had finally given up and was whirring and sputtering cries of help as I emptied as much as I could out of it. There were bags of fries and trays of pasta that had gone limp. The open freezer was filling the room with the sweet, putrid smell of death. I taped the door shut with blue painter's tape. I slapped a date/item label from the kitchen at eye level. 'DO NOT USE', I wrote in black Sharpie.

I got back to cooking for my eight guests; I folded puff pastry over a mushroom and chopped beef filling. I roasted a wedge of tenderloin to medium rare. Pair of duck breasts was resting as I reduced a black cherry jam in brandy. I whisked hunks of foie gras into chicken gravy. I snipped the bone out of a chicken leg and this time piped in a lobster mousse. The door swung open and it was Louis, Marie, and Oscar. They got the dining room ready as Suzy opened the door for one young Chinese girl after another.

I looked up and counted 25 sitting around seven tables they'd pushed together. I just watched. Suzy spoke in Mandarin to one of the girls who bounded out of the building and returned with paper plates and plastic forks. I didn't have enough food. Not even close. I knew how this was going to go and all of the ways it was going to fail. The eight plates would go out—each item delicately sauced and plated just so. They would land on the table and be passed around and each person would take a swipe. The sauce would be lost as they grabbed a second plate and made a Sunday picnic plate of four or five courses. The flavor and effect of the individual item as the crew who confessed that they hadn't eaten expecting a feast, made a mess of what each menu item represented. Suzy was combining tasting with server training. I hadn't seen anything like this. And Oscar with his Bolivian accent played translator. Chausson, the meat filled little pastries, became "croissant" in the dining room and in this fork-diving game of telephone was called a "crust" by the time the Guatemalan bar back got a hold of it.

Suzy was not impressed. She approached me with a notebook full of ideas to make this work. The Trans-Canadian thing was lost on her.

"We just want you to do fried chicken." She implored, "We want your fried chicken at all of the locations." Louis stood behind her again, nodding vigorously.

"My fried chicken," I echoed. My fried chicken fears were coming to life again. It would eclipse everything like in my nightmares. Even a lobster filled crispy chicken leg did not hit the mark. French fries laced with medium rare strips of duck breast and drunken black cherries were no match for it.

"Yes, like your fried chicken that you're doing here."

"I'm not doing my fried chicken here," I was going to stop this right now. "I adapted a fried chicken recipe for the menu here." Louis and Suzy looked at me like I had kicked them in the shin. Their mouths sagged open and they said it almost completely in unison.

"Wait…. this isn't YOU'RE fried chicken on this menu?" I had explained before that the stove just didn't get hot enough. And I explained it again. The fried chicken with the coq au vin was marinated and then slow roasted before being dredged in seasoned flour and then deep fried. Everyone loved it, but it wasn't the chicken everybody begged me to make and wanted to call their own, build restaurants around, and cash in on.

436

Suzy wasn't satisfied with any of the menus I attempted after that. I wasn't living up to the hype. She'd eat out and have meatballs, "We need meatballs on the menu." She'd pass a food truck selling grilled cheese and in a couple of hours she was talking tomato soup and cheese sandwiches. She wanted popcorn at the bar. "How do we make it," her eyes were full of wonder, "What type of machine?"

She was convinced that she needed an eager young culinary school grad to come in and cook. Without my fried chicken, I was nobody to her. I walked the finished space with its industrial rail car like touches and scenery speeding by on TVs around the room. The kitchen had been slapped together with a dish machine that soaked the floor and shelves that tipped away from the walls. The fryers wouldn't stay lit and the bargain stove Louis installed worked fine up top, but the oven below could not be regulated and burnt everything in seconds. He tucked a steamer in a spot I'd reserved for a worktable. It was large enough for a food manufacturing facility and dominated the small cooking space. "Chef, use this oven." He pointed to the small pizza oven on top of the 8-foot-tall steamer (useless as it was not connected to electricity or water supply). Louis had gotten both the little pizza oven and the steamer from his storage unit. His contribution to the partnership was his old useless equipment. Was he putting a value on these, buying his way into partnerships with junk?

"It's a pizza oven," I opened the little door. It was hot as blazes, but the opening was only three inches high.

Louis smiled; he'd gotten it practically for free. "See, it works!"

Suzy was proud of how things turned out. She'd never seen a kitchen so full of new shiny stainless steel and shelves that reflected so much light. A working dish machine was a huge achievement. If only the plumber could get it to drain and not flood the floor. She sopped a dirty mop around in it. And then remembered there was one more thing that was going to make this all come together better than planned.

"We have a backup freezer upstairs," she clapped her hands cheering the progress that filled her with hope that this place would be a cash cow. "It took six men to get it up here." I followed her up the metal steps off of the courtyard to a partially covered deck. There it was, a reach-in freezer, up on the second-floor courtyard, tall and lonely under a sheet of corrugated plastic. It was taped shut with blue painter's tape and someone had slapped a kitchen label on it. Written in black marker over the factory print date/item were the words "DO NOT USE."

After exactly 29 days I was taken off of the project. Louis said that Suzy and Oscar did not think my food was working. They wanted to work with someone more imaginative. I was tossed out of the rail car one day before my pay would have increased to include the expansion with the new place. I was kicking myself now for canceling that interview.

I settled back in to the first location. The food was getting great reviews and my team was meeting expectations. With the Trans Canada distraction taken out of my inbox, I was back to my original team full time. I was surprised they'd stayed considering the overtime issue. Louis had increased the hours but refused to pay them overtime. My objections were met with a reaction that was not the usual carefree, I-got-plenty-of-money Louis XVI. He was echoing Marie Antoinette with things like "there was too much staff" and "why are there so many people working today?"

I trimmed hours. I scheduled myself for a lonely day of prepping and setting up the line. I pushed staff back to coming in just an hour before service; dish washers an hour after. I pulled our sales numbers from the computer when we had reached the three-month mark. I figured this was a great time to get Louis and Co. together to look at our progress. I was hoping also to get some answers. What was he prepared to do and how much did he have left in him? The liquor license was weeks away I was told. Sales were on the steady incline. June was looking like the month where we would hit our stride and meet lofty goals like $6000 in food sales a week. That's when Louis sort of broke the news to us.

"We're having the fire suppression checked by the Fire Marshall tomorrow," he explained; reminding me to keep the stove cold until after the inspection. "Turns out the state won't look at your liquor license application until all of your permits have closed," he said with a nervous chuckle. I had asked about the fire suppression the day before we opened. Louis laughed and dismissed the question with a wave of his hand. We didn't need it to work to open. So long as we did the inspection within the year. We'd gone months without the protection of the system in the event of a fire. Louis, put it off. But now here he was finally calling for the inspection. And now, passing as we did on the second try, the liquor license application would finally be looked at. We were at square one. How did we go into this not knowing? We sat around the table with Louis' looking at the chair legs. I announced the sales figures and commented on the trend. We were in a positive position. I asked if sales tax had been paid. The column was printed in red ink and it was accumulating to a hefty sum.

Louis did not answer this with the conviction I expected. "Uh...yeah. Yes. Taken care of." He offered. But the number that I circled was the amount of food we'd given away. Eight percent of our sales had been taken out of the pile. Eight percent of sales had been erased as free food for Louis' and Marie's friends and family. Considering we had cleared just under $50,000 for the three months, it was a considerable sum.

Here I was fighting the labor hours battle, so his mom and sister got a free dinner, complete with a precious dacquoise (it took 2 days to make) for dessert. And me, I had been taking only one day off and working 16-hour days. On my day off, Louis counted how many staff were in the kitchen from the cameras and called the restaurant to send one of them home. Yet, he'd hold staff over on a slow Sunday night to feed his visiting uncle. The kitchen staff would stand around wiping dust or old grease from whatever surface they could reach, stirring sauces with ladles to keep them from separating. The three left in the kitchen for two or three extra hours to serve Louis' uncle added up: about $130 in labor for his uncle to eat for free or not show.

But it was the weird corrective emails that clued me in. Marie would reprimand me for not telling her of a new hire that replaced an employee. Suddenly, Louis had nothing to say to me except that he had not enjoyed his pasta he'd ordered late on a Sunday after I'd left. In fact, they were both appearing as if they waited in the car, watching me stride out the door on the camera feed. Then there they were in the restaurant, not having to face me. That's when I knew. It was a matter of time.

It started with the vendors. Only bread and produce would deliver. No one else was getting paid. Louis owed thousands of dollars. The utility company would come in, big men wielding giant wrenches. "We're here to shut off the powa." They'd wander around the dining room, admiring a gilded mirror or a carnation in a vase. "Can I call my boss?" Reaching for my cellphone, my hands shaking. I had $800 of meat and cheese in that cooler and the way things were going, I wasn't sure I'd get a delivery to replace what went bad. Staff couldn't cash their checks and were humiliated at the bank or the check cashing center.

"I can't cash this!" the cashier would shout loud enough for the entire line to hear on a Friday night. "Your boss owes us for three bounced checks." It could be any day now. This was the shaky startup. So often I found myself with this demographic. As I hit my head on that Lexan ceiling, unable to advance to the higher positions in food, I settled for the job with the shaky restaurant; sometimes desperate themselves to fill the spot. Louis had hired a chef before me, I learned later on. He had stormed out. I was a pleasant surprise; walking in from nowhere and anxious to see his vision through. But someone told Marie and Louis that it would be easy and that reaching $1.3 million in sales their first year was a possibility. The comedy of errors that followed—no liquor license, hours that ensured high labor costs, and magnanimity with his friends and family we could ill afford. My paycheck was too much for them to bear and they were going to try and make it work without me.

I'd been here before. I was shown the door at a restaurant or two that could no longer afford a chef. I had created the critically acclaimed food, trained the staff, organized and built a space that worked for food making efficiency and for food safety. But I cashed the highest paycheck. I felt for Louis. I owned a restaurant too. I owned a restaurant that failed. But when I asked him about cash flow and if the restaurant was struggling to meet expenses, I suggested a conversation and maybe together we could work on it. He reminded me that it was not meeting financial goals—as if it was something I had done. So, the failure to meet $1.3 million in first year sales was on me? But he assured me it wasn't the cash that had let him down. It was me. His rubbery pasta one night was proof that I didn't know what I was doing. My staff training had fallen short and he questioned my ability to lead the team now and in the future.

It took a little over a month for him to get up the nerve to end it. I was coaching staff through the second week of a fall menu change, and it was one of my line cooks that noticed him, "Wow, Louis and Marie are here." They haven't come in going on a month or so. When they left, I thought I had lucked into one more week in the space that he and his contractors certainly built, but that I had brought to life. But they called and told the manager to have me head to the partner restaurant around the corner, the tiny place Alex had made over. Ahead of me was a slow walk in the dark to my own execution. They wanted me to face the guillotine alone. It would be easier to do without my staff, who would probably react as if the Nanny who'd taught them to sing was tossed out of the house. I quietly went around the room and collected my pens, my knives; I scooped tarts out of tart pans and tossed them into the sink to wash. I was stalling. I didn't want to go. Not like this. My hands were shaking as I rubbed a stainless-steel pad around my pans and placed them on a towel to dry. How did it turn so ugly in a few months? When the reviews were coming in, I

444

was carried around the room on their shoulders. Now I was a nothing, a nobody—worse, a cancer that had to be removed. I was just going to walk out of the building and go home. I didn't want to look at anyone or face anyone. But as I stood over the sink, I noticed it was Louis standing behind me, tired of waiting in the restaurant down the street; his own stomach, I'm sure, in knots.

"So...yeah," I couldn't look at him, I was disgusted and sad enough to start sobbing. But strangely full of anger and hate, "I wasn't going to walk down the street to get fired." He wasn't looking at me.

"How long are you going to be?"

"Well, I am on the schedule until 9." I had a few more pans to wash. He was looking at the collection of them in the sink, "But I can leave after I finish this; half an hour maybe." I expected him to walk away at this point; it wasn't as hard as he thought it would be. I was not making it hard. Should I? "What do you want to do about my expenses and last check?" He promised a check for me in the morning. But I knew there wouldn't be one. My staff was waiting for me with tear stained faces. I told them to make sure to not burn the puff pastry for vol au vent, and to freeze the extra burgers, don't over reduce the lobster bisque, and to make plenty of gravy.

445

I paused on the steps, "Don't cry. Work hard." I walked out of the door into the rain.

Chapter Thirteen

Allow to Come to Room Temperature Before Unmolding

I loved my husband. Slowly, Hakim chipped away at that. He was a mean drunk, an aggressive alter-ego to his mild-mannered more sober self. He'd start arguments over a blouse I bought or come at me if I had a tiny bit of good news. I remember racing home to tell him that I had sold my first house at the start of my short-lived career in real estate. He had already called the office looking for me. He knew. The house was dark, and he was sitting in the room drunk and angry. He was waiting for me, waiting to destroy me. He insulted me and called me names until he passed out. Hakim had grown to hate everything about me, my ambition, my enthusiasm, my ability to let things go and sell real estate while working

447

as an independent marketing consultant. He hated that I didn't have to drown something that was on fire inside me the way he did. I felt his hate years later in the courtroom, and the few times I had to cut his visits with the girls short and throw him out of my house.

I hated him for a flash too. When I'd see the hurt in Magalee's eyes when he didn't send her the pictures he promised. Or the contempt he showed Sian because she would rather make the lima beans dance with each other than eat them. I hated him when he dug his heels in and refused to pay the few dollars of child support the courts asked of him. He had broken my heart. Before I got too busy raising my two babies into women, (Magalee graduated from Oberlin having become a big woman on campus. She spent a few years teaching English around the world before landing a job with a global tech company. Sian studied Sociology at College of Charleston and was sewing, bridal retailing her way to a career in fashion) working two jobs to make sure the rent was paid, and then finally working 90-hours a week so that I could keep that higher paying chef's job; I had plenty of time to feel the pain. It was a constant pressure in my chest. Taking a full breath, letting my chest rise up as I filled my lungs with air would almost always result in a sobbing exhale. I learned to round my shoulders and bring my chin down to my collar bone. I could bring my ribs in and dull the pain.

I had been all in. I was a good wife. I listened, I ironed, I gardened, I cooked, I kept the house clean. I was his cheerleader and his instigator. I'd like to think I made a warm and loving place for him to come home to. I encouraged him to follow crazy dreams and I was there to help him sweep up a mess or talk sense into him when he entertained a foolish notion. For him to grow to hate me, despite everything; was something that made me angry and then terribly sad. I don't think anything is more painful. And now, I can do nothing but appreciate the resilience of the human heart and soul. I can go days without giving Hakim a thought. Our lives had shifted into place, and there was money, and babysitters, and new apartments—the girls and I put it back together and realized carrying on without him wouldn't be so hard after all. But when I do think of him, I can't help but ask, "Why do you hate me?"

Hate seemed to consume Marie Antoinette and Louis XVI. They avoided me during my last days and then as the door closed behind me; Louis clapped his tiny hands together and declared things were finally going to be done right. I couldn't help but peak and I found their new

449

menu—they added four soups and five salads and misspelled just about everything. Less than a month later, a young cook who I'd taught to poach eggs and whisk a perfect hollandaise called to tell me they had closed the place down. There were no deliveries coming in and soon all of the mise en place that I'd prepared that week was gone and there was no product coming in to replace it.

The news didn't make it sting any less; it took years for me to not feel my ex-husband's misguided anger. And knowing that behind the hate was their own fear, self-loathing, and insecurity didn't make it sit any better either. I had been the subject of hate before. When my career took off and I'd reached a level where people recognized my work and food critics counted me as someone to follow, haters came out of the woodwork and I wondered how I'd failed them. What expectation was I failing to live up to? Were the claims that I didn't smile enough just cover for some other notion?

I've wondered if I was being held to a secret standard that my detractors weren't even able to put a finger on. Few black women had reached such culinary status in the nation's capital at the turn of this century. I hadn't thought much about it. There was work to be done; at first, very little, and then suddenly more than I could handle. I had it easy in other jobs. Aside from teaching, I hadn't had hard work until I ran a restaurant.

I sold real estate for a year, and the hardest part of that was figuring how to break into the busy enclave of agents that were actually making money. I joined forces with a middle-aged Polish countess. We schemed and plotted and, while I never made it, she eventually did. We left town together on a July 4th weekend when the city was slow but full of tourists and headed to a coastal town on the Eastern Shore. We came up with a fool-proof plan sitting on docks and in the salons of boats we didn't own. The team of Potocka-Clark was going to focus on FSBOs (For Sale by Owners—people intent on selling their own home to keep the commission). We would create a handbook that looked like pure generosity on our part but was actually 200 pages of to do lists and things you didn't know needed to be done—holy crap this is a lot of work to close a sale on a home. The sellers would come crawling to us and begging for help and we'd get the listing. We were so excited about our scheme that we jumped into the car in a hurry to get back to a civilization and a computer.

The back wheels of my minivan blew gravel onto the manicured grass of the curbside. But we didn't get very far. The only road out of town was closed for the July 4th parade. Shoot, well how long can it go on? After sitting in the car for a full five minutes we decided to get out and watch with the rest of the town—about 250 people. The other 100 were marching by in a high school band, twirling around as part of the town's dance troupe, on horseback, slowly steering the fire truck with an actual Dalmatian in the passenger seat. We took our cue from the crowd— applauding, cheering, and then watching them fold up their lawn chairs; we started to head for the side street where we'd parked. But with chairs folded the crowd of locals who'd lived there all of their lives stopped and grew silent. There was more to this parade.

No one was in the street. The bands, baton twirlers, and flag bearers had made it through. I could hear the sputter and whine of an old engine. Emerging from the edge of the slight hill in the road was a model T, it was black and shiny with a canvas roof. It was as if Henry Ford himself had rubbed the hood ornament with the thick fabric on his elbow just five minutes ago. Then came an Edsel, low to the ground and dull green. The top was down and the black people inside were dressed in

452

vintage clothes—her in a flapper's bonnet, and he wore an argyle vest and clipped a pipe between his teeth. One after another, vintage cars loaded with black people came up the hill, and the white folks in tank tops and polyester shorts on the sidewalk watched them silently. No one breathed or cheered or clapped. If I thought about clapping, there was no way I could have. I was paralyzed. Because in that moment, I realized that I was the only black person in that town that minute who wasn't riding in the street right now.

Then came a 1930 Cadillac with its huge lights reflecting the sun and its spare tire chained to the side and covered in a canvas that matched the roof. There was a woman with a mink wrap on her shoulders and her long silver-gloved arm stretched out of the window. A bracelet with huge pearls and silver beads hung from her wrist. The feather in her hat was so long it stretched from her head out of the window and its tip bent slightly against the top of the canvas roof of the old car. The woman in the feather hat locked her steely brown eyes to mine. She wasn't smiling. None of them were. None of those black people in those cars that they nursed and polished and created costumes of an almost forgotten life were smiling. There we were, the flapper seated beside her dandy and me, staring at each other. I didn't know what to do or how to react. But her eyes boring into me told me everything. She raised her chin just slightly still keeping her eyes on mine, and then slowly lowered it. That nod was the only move she made. Her arm, even the feather was perfectly still. I stood there staring at that woman, the car, and then the back of that car for what seemed like forever.

"Are you okay?" Potocka, had watched the whole thing.

"Yeah," my voice cracked a bit and I held her arm to steady myself, "I'm fine." We drove a bit in silence, while I absorbed the meaning of that parade. There was a lot to it but also there was something that I forget, and at that age I forgot all of the time. Nowadays, the space I occupy won't let me. I forget that for some people, for a lot of people skin color has considerable significance. While I go days without thinking about it, there are those who see me and that's all they see.

Hard distinctions of race and the rules that come with it are hard to give up. Like a "this is how it's always been" comfort zone of racial bias. That parade was how that town did July 4th for decades—segregated and diminishing. And for me carrying on as a chef, I rustled many a comfort zone. Perhaps the only acceptable black woman in a kitchen wore the light blue cotton dress and apron of a domestic. This woman would make the grilled cheese if you wanted her to and smiled the minute you came into view. She wasn't concerned about her business' bottom line, so she let you sit anywhere, pay anything and do anything you wanted in her dining room. I do not fit into that domestic outline. I did not inherit recipes, and I did not graduate to my own restaurant after having worked years in white women's kitchens. In the years that followed my infamous days as a very visible chef, I came to understand that I didn't live up to the notions of domesticity perhaps conjured up by primal memory. I was not raised by my grandparents. I grew up with a very present father. I didn't fall back on a cooking career because it was my only option. This was something a lot of folks of all ethnicities who eat out find hard to believe. My generation of black women was raised to go to medical school or law school. Our parents sought out the best educations and pushed us like Tiger Moms.

It's more common or accepted to find the college educated white man who, tripping, stumbling to the beat of a different drummer, finds his way and himself in the kitchen...a black woman who chooses chef coat and hounds tooth rather than a stethoscope is an anomaly. But how are they to know unless I tell them? And how can I appear anything but resentful if I shrugged off the labels of a domestic. A domestic is not a chef—I'm not allowed to wear that, cook that, or charge that. And I definitely can't say what I just said. It's a role that if I accept it makes everyone a lot more comfortable. I can dissolve into the woman that used to work at your grandmother's house. I attribute some of the negative opinions of me to that I never lived down to these expectations. A black woman safely tucked into an expected role is a lot easier to deal with and a solid linchpin of a comfort zone. Anything less than a smile, the no carry-out policy, restrictions on substitutions, no I'm not making grilled cheese for your kid— is me not breaking to the will of customers who perceive themselves to be my benefactor.

No, you cannot leave your children in my care. I am neither side kick nor confidant. It may be essential to your comfort when you cross my threshold to believe that I can wave you from behind the crowd and sit you at a roughhewn table because I was expecting you. I call you "honey chile" and tie the napkin for you. I can see your pain and help you with it. Unfortunately, I was too busy refining my craft, building a career, generating publicity, laying floor tiles to study up on this and I never signed up to do this mammy thing.

But it is these images of mammy and the servile smiling black woman that I've spent my career battling. The Lexan ceiling, locking black women out of the higher positions in food service, does nothing but preserve a food service management and leadership comfort zone. The lack of diversity in kitchens and workplaces around the world has created an underappreciated workforce who has never enjoyed the comfort zone that makes for steady hands with that tweezer and the temerity to present plates that lack generosity—a dot of sauce or to a dinner covered with ash and steamed in a pig belly. The "let me come in your mouth" of modern nose to tail are an unabashed and the most profound expression of privilege and cultural appropriation—example: soul food's pig feet become the white chef's trotters.

During my decades in Washington, DC, I received more than my share of media attention. With several kitchens under my watch listed as among the best in the city, countless numbers of food network appearances, a regular spot on National Public Radio, and a published cookbook; I enjoyed a great deal of favorable press.

457

The flip side of that is the negative stuff that almost always follows. Like many black women in the public eye, I was often spied through a different lens than my white male and even white female counterparts. The biggest complaint was that I worked my 16-hour day in front of a stove and didn't smile while I did it. The restaurant, which I owned with my front of the house chief, Robin Smith had only 14 tables. So, after turning away larger parties on too many Friday nights, we enacted a strict seating policy (not uncommon in busy restaurants.) We also were slammed beyond our capacity for Sunday brunch and had hour long wait times. This made folks quite angry and they peppered the message boards with complaints about my bad mood and crowded store.

Articles compared me to Joan Crawford as she was depicted in *Mommy Dearest.* Food Section cover stories went on for pages about my sour expression and unwelcoming pout while I used my knee to close the oven, spun around in the barely hip wide space to sauce the mashed potatoes (which were running low and I paused only to mumble a prayer that they'd last the night), then quickly turned around to flip the fish in the pan with my left hand, tossing green beans into a pan of buttered water with my right. No one marveled at my ability to perform nightly for a dining room that was one of the first to be truly integrated, bringing Manassas and Bethesda to what upper income black folks called the Gold Coast. There was no understudy; the chef and owner cooked every meal, made your soup. I was there every night to receive the lauds and the pot shots; one night even that insanely angry, "What kind of chef runs out of meatloaf!?"

"No one else is called out for not smiling." I exclaimed in my defense.

"But you've got an open kitchen," came the quick answer.

"But I have servers who smile and greet, I'm in charge of the food," I'd explain. The food is how I show my love is a personal philosophy I never imagined I'd have to explain. No one believed me when I said that the face is one of concentration. Is the expression more palatable on white skin? A black face where the teeth aren't showing in the grin of a simpleton is a threat.

Food writers pish poshed my explanations and gave inflamed voice to the haters that suffered my non-smiling face to enjoy the critically acclaimed dining experience. One writer followed a particularly damaging article (readers called me to apologize for the irresponsibility of the piece), grabbing social media high fives as he congratulated himself for holding a mirror to me so that I could see my internal damage evident in a 20-year career of cooking without smiling. This article follows me still— "Is this true?" "We can't possibly hire you?" "Can you explain this?"

While I was defending my right not to smile, working into my sixth year as owner and chef of Colorado Kitchen; men chefs were building war chests—smiling, not smiling. I'm sure no one noticed. Reading about how much money was thrown at some of these men and about the deals from developers, I recalled taking the last $120 from my checking account (all the money I had in the world) to fill the Colorado Kitchen cash register for opening day.

And now reading about some of these same male chefs had been brought down by the #MeToo movement and had reached the end of their empires, I wondered how food writers found the time to write about my facial expression and never delved into the real issues in the food industry. I wasn't smiling, but I also wasn't celebrating a Monday night in a strip club or a cigar smoke filled room with paid escorts the way some of the men in the industry did. I wasn't hiring a hostess or a server because of the size of her breasts. And I wasn't pressuring anyone who worked for me for sexual favors. The women chefs in town were well aware of the club of male chefs known to carry on. We had our own group that met Mondays at Chef Susan Lindeborg's Southeast Washington townhouse. Women chefs and cooks each brought a dish to this star-studded potluck. There was no male stripper—just commiserating, wine drinking, networking. We started calling these gatherings Maven Mondays. But this clique of male chefs was quietly notorious. They gathered by invitation only. I knew of chefs who—preferring the unfaltering company of their wives on that rare night off—declined.

What food journalists missed while focusing on my demeanor was the inequities in the industry. Women staff restaurant kitchens at a rate of 54% but are only represented by 16% of the leadership (according to the Bureau of Labor Statistics). While there are several men who lead kitchens and restaurants without making women staff (and male) feel like prey, there is a group that needs to be exposed and rooted out. "Holding a mirror" to a chef who cooks with a pout may have made for an easy target; but it also gave voice and legitimacy to a racist notion—a black woman chef that doesn't smile while she's working is news. The quality of her cooking is immaterial. She must yield—not charge as much for lobster because of her

461

address, make grilled cheese sandwiches on demand, let us sit wherever we want, and just not be so busy on Sunday.

You would think that someone behind the typewriter would say, "Wait, wait. Why do we want her to smile at us again?" Nope. How brave a question that would be to challenge the smile demanders—Is she out of context; not exemplifying a subservient attitude while engaged in what has become a white male space? Would a smile make me more like Aunt Jemima, one of our culture's oldest controlling images created to sustain the image of the black woman as a domestic. If I smiled more, perhaps, I would fit this ideal—an authority in the kitchen, but still subservient. There would be comfort in this smiling evidence that I knew my "place."

This journalism did not challenge us. It did not make us question our thinking or the status quo. This journalism ignored what was really damaging. My smile did no harm or good to the industry. It is quite unlike a skirt chasing, heavy-drinking, breast-grabbing, ass-slapping restaurant leadership that squelches and deters talent—as sex objects are rarely mentored—while soaking up millions in funding that might have launched dozens of sustainable careers.

Unfortunately, toxic masculinity in the kitchen often attacks the young and untried. I'm an old burnt up cook, I'm safe from harm. Much of what I've endured was the, "Is your boss here?" as I stood in the kitchen of my own restaurant. But I watched a young cook I worked with years ago accept our boss's invitation to join him at a fancy restaurant, "It will be a learning experience to eat there," he persuaded. The next morning while she shredded carrots for a salad, she fought back tears, her face reddened when I asked her about her evening. He'd asked her to wear something nice. She obliged, her blonde curls bouncing on bare shoulders. He led her through the kitchen where she was whistled at and ogled. The chef congratulated our boss on his "accessory". They exchanged creepy chortles surveying the young woman in her dress as she stood there an awkward, excluded object. The chef led our boss out of the kitchen; he was going to be seated with a group in a private room. He glanced back at the young cook, her ankles buckling a bit because of the heels she'd taken out of the box just for tonight. "You can take a cab home, right?" He said as the chef led him out of the kitchen.

It is a business that drives us hard and renders many of us unable to contain the intensity—to quiet our night without alcohol, to shut the door on the volume and rude directness we use on our teams, or to channel the hyper-stimulation of a busy night into tender lovemaking with a receptive partner. The highs and lows of this business are more volatile in combination with toxic masculinity. But, alas, no, I confess, I do not smile while I cook. The dining public is just going to have to be okay with that.

There have been countless times in my career where I felt like I was on the outside looking in; craving a cushy something of an easy chair, piles of down and cotton sheets that meant an end to my days of fighting stereotypes and false expectations. It reminds me of the days in gym class when the gym teachers, probably for their own amusement, dove headfirst into Title IX and pitted boys against girls in a "friendly" game of dodgeball. It happened more times than I care to remember. Of course, the girls always lost. The boys thought nothing of using their quickness and better upper body strength to hand us defeat in the most humiliating ways. It didn't help that many of the girls had no interest in winning. They wanted to carve a heart into a tree with Chuck Newsome, not beat him at dodge ball. As I grew up and started dating boys myself, I admit I was a late bloomer; I eventually got how important it was to let the guy win, especially if you wanted to date him. There were only a couple of us who did not want to go down easy.

But there was a day where the stars aligned, and a few lucky shots landed on our side. Before being hit and tossed out by a zinger to the back of the head, Ginny was able to knock two guys out by hitting Brett as he loaded up to get me and the ball bounced off of him and glanced Michael. It was a lucky shot, but it brought the sides even. It was two against two, and I held my breath thinking Randy Shapiro and I had a chance to win this, but also knowing the boys were going to dial in now and fight us as if we were men. Randy and I stood there ready to be killed.

There were plenty of bright red balls at our feet, but we didn't dare reach down to retrieve one. That would be all of the target Chuck or Evan Daniels needed. They were the best at the game. They had powerful wiry arms and their slight boyish bodies were thin, malleable, hard-to-strike targets. They pranced on their tip toes in and out of gym, so this fast action evasive ballet was second nature to them. The gym was quiet as everyone waited to see who would get it first and where—a shot to the face for me, or a hard ricochet off the top of Randy's head. Anything above the neck was the ultimate in humiliation and a huge part of the boys' game. My heart was racing as I waited; even though, I played every day with my two older brothers—football, baseball, soccer.

I would come up to bat, the only girl on the pick-up baseball team and the boys in the field who didn't know me on the playground would come in, waving their teammates to follow their lead. My brothers would giggle to themselves. Mark, the louder of the two, would say something like "Yeah, she just follows us everywhere guys," he'd shrug, "come in." And then he'd watch me bash the first pitch over everyone's head. I would give anything right now to have my brother beside me for this dodgeball firing squad. My hands were perspiring and my throat so dry I could have coughed up sand. And then it was coming right at me. The bright red ball got bigger and bigger as it left Chuck's jai lai cesta looking arm. It was headed straight for my face. But I jumped. I leapt into the air with just enough height to wrap the red-hot dodge ball in my arms. The look on Chuck's face cut through my out of body confusion. He was out. The gym was still silent, and Chuck stared at me as I held the ball I had caught, his mouth open in disbelief. Randy broke the silence, "She caught it." The girls who had been clacking gum, filing their nails, and talking about boys were suddenly riveted to the action on the gym floor and, despite themselves and their thoughts of prom dates, started cheering. But it all came quickly to an end. I still held the ball and, standing motionless, watched Chuck's face contort from surprise to anger. It came out of nowhere and smacked me so hard on the side of my cheek that I was dizzy. Evan, avenging his teammate's dodgeball death threw me out with a rifle shot to the face.

These dodgeball games and other experiences of childhood that we recall in weepy moments reliving awkward phases, bullying, and growing pains are the tragedies of youth that build our character. I, and the women chefs and black women in the workforce, suffered the dodgeball game daily—well beyond the gym at school, but every day at work. You have everything stacked against you, and you're expected to not just lose but to go down in humiliating defeat. Then there is that one time you catch one.

As much as it scared me, I learned that day, that I've got to catch, not dodge. There can be no hiding or faking. The industry demands authenticity and a real presentation of self. Any black woman who has reached boss status, has taken a few shots to the face, but she's also learned to catch one. That is a black woman's journey through the dominance of white maleness in this industry of giving. Survive the game of dodgeball and then get some rest in the bed of nails reserved for the black woman chef who dares to do what everyone else is doing in their role as chef.

There is no one more powerful a leader in any kitchen or food service establishment, or one more proven and tested, than this woman—this woman who hasn't been allowed to stand still enough to acquire a comfort zone. Being relegated to the new place—the shaky startup, the poorly run organization that no sane person wants to work for—the times I've landed jobs outside of ownership, have made me battle savvy. I've gotten to know myself pretty well.

Moreover, I know why I rub some people the wrong way. Chef Ann Cashion pegged it years ago when I garnished an asparagus soufflé with roasted almond slivers and roasted garlic slivers (toasted just enough to look exactly alike.) She smirked, watching me fan my slivers next to the bright green soufflé on top of the roasted garlic sauce, "I see what you're doing there," she said. You never knew which one you were going to get next. I was urging the eater to get out of his comfort zone.

I've never had one. Awkward uncertainty was a way of life for me as an excruciatingly shy child to an early-maturing pre-pubescent wearing a 36D in 6th grade. I was without a comfort zone for most of my formative years. I learned to live with it and to find the comfort zone of the moment. Once you let go, you're open to things you never imagined. I urge folks to try it. Step out. Maybe at one time I was jealous and pushed. Now I entice, because I know on the other side is growth, happiness. There's this feeling good and accomplished that comes from flying without a net. A lot of folks dive in, others resist and resent—they have to have it just the way their mother made it, or they have to get carry-out because they have never felt comfortable eating in a restaurant.

With only one arm free so he could hang on to his liquid security blanket, Hakim couldn't stand the tight shoes and itchy sweater of letting go of his addiction to become a complete person, a supportive husband, or dependable father. Louis XVI was so sunk into the down comforter of his every day—believing he had it all under control. This could only be preserved with the rejection of the contributions of more knowledgeable authorities. Louis found comfort in his heightened and unwarranted opinion of himself. It was his own arrogance that stroked his neck and rocked him until he drifted off to sleep. To hang on to this was everything, even if it cost him his business.

I accepted another period of joblessness. I did not crumple into despair this time. My first swim in the Potomac and the years after, beating this piñata of a life and career of mine, have made me see the value of myself—my somebodiness. I sought a comfort zone in the cheers and lauds, the elusive understanding and appreciation of my audience. When it was gone, when the restaurants left me and I was nobody, I had nothing and no one to cook for; the glimmer and hope for that fuzzy slipper, that giant dog bed was gone. I was chasing a comfort zone I linked to my very survival. I needed the constant reassurance that they loved me, my food was everything and more, the food writers would notice, and I'd need that camera-ready clean chef coat on a hanger. Now it was hopeless. I'd never get there again. I had to get through this, to learn to exist again without one. But with the demands to smile, the pressure to live a false identity, the insistence that I participate in a make-believe agenda (the let's play restaurant of inexperienced owners) made the "comfort zone" more a rusty Brillo™ pad. I realized that I was chasing a comfort zone that had been inside me the whole time. I've quit cooking for the comfort zone. Instead, I've grabbed the water-soaked limb of a tree, shook the river water out of my hair and knew; I didn't need one.

470

Made in the USA
Middletown, DE
09 June 2020

97322144R00283